STUDIES IN GAME THEORY
AND MATHEMATICAL ECONOMICS

General Editor: Andrew Schotter (New York University)

Advisory Editorial Board:

Volumes in this Series:

ABOUT THE SERIES

Game theory, since its creation in 1944 by John von Neumann and Oskar Morgenstern, has been applied to a wide variety of social phenomena by scholars in economics, political science, sociology, philosophy and even biology. This series attempts to bring to the academic community a set of books dedicated to the belief that game theory can be a major tool in applied science. It publishes original monographs, textbooks and conference volumes which present work that is both of high technical quality and pertinent to the world we live in today.

1

AUCTIONS, BIDDING, AND CONTRACTING:
Uses and Theory

Edited by
Richard Engelbrecht-Wiggans
Martin Shubik
Robert M. Stark

AℲ

NEW YORK UNIVERSITY PRESS
NEW YORK
1983

Library of Congress Cataloging in Publication Data
Main entry under title:

Auctions, bidding, and contracting.

(Studies in game theory and mathematical economics)
Bibliography: p.
1. Contracts, Letting of—Mathematical models—
Addresses, essays, lectures.   2. Auctions—Mathematical
models—Addresses, essays, lectures.   3. Industrial
procurement—Mathematical models—Addresses, essays,
lectures.   4. Government purchasing—Mathematical
models—Addresses, essays, lectures.   I. Engelbrecht
–Wiggans, Richard, 1952–   .   II. Shubik, Martin.
III. Stark, Robert M., 1930–   .   IV. Series.
HD2365.A92 1983   658.7'23   83-3938
ISBN 0-8147-7827-5

The medallion on the cover of this series was designed by the
French contemporary artist Georges Mathieu as one of
a set of medals struck in Paris by the Musée de la Monnaie in 1971. Eighteen
medals were created by Mathieu to "commemorate 18 stages in the
development of western consciousness." The Edict of Milan in 313
was the first, Game Theory, 1944, was number seventeen.

Manufactured in the United States of America

*Clothbound editions of New York University Press books are Smythe-sewn and
printed on permanent and durable acid-free paper.*

AUCTIONS, BIDDING, AND CONTRACTING: USES AND THEORY

This volume is based primarily upon selections of work associated with two conferences. The first, held by The Project Center for Competitive and Conflict Systems Research of the Cowles Foundation, met at Seven Springs, New York from December 6 to 8, 1979. The second, an ORSA/TIMS Special Interest Conference organized by the University of Delaware Operations Research Program took place at Williamsburg, Virginia from April 14 to 16, 1980.

ACKNOWLEDGMENTS

The editors wish to acknowledge the generous help of the Office of Naval Research and the unflagging assistance of Glena Ames, Karen Eisenman and Linda Abelli-Smith. The foresight of Professor Morgenstern led to the previous publication of a book in this series devoted to the study of bidding. His urging that this topic is of both practical and theoretical importance has encouraged us to continue these investigations.

CONTENTS

Contents

Contents

INTRODUCTION

This book has its genesis in the papers and proceedings of two occasions: the first, a conference organized by the Project Center for Competitive and Conflict Systems Research at the Cowles Foundation at Yale, sponsored by the Office of Naval Research on December 6–8, 1979 and the second, organized by the University of Delaware Operations Research Program as an ORSA/TIMS Special Interest Conference in Williamsburg, Virginia on April 14–16, 1980.

Bidding, procurement, and estimation have been occupations since antiquity, while procurement and taxation may have been the earliest economic acts of government. It is surprising that among the abundant and sophisticated exchanges of ideas between the military and academic communities concerning conflict studies, little deals with contracting, bidding, estimation, and procurement.

The two proceedings were designed as intensive working conferences. There was an exchange of information on the state of the art, and, although some remarks were on retrospective summaries, the stress was on current and prospective work of importance to bidding and procurement. In particular, several basic questions were asked. What are the interesting and fertile questions to the practitioner and to the theorist? What are the applications? If new resources were available how could they be productively allocated?

Twenty-five years ago, in spite of the importance of the bidding estimation and procurement processes, there was very little research literature. Stark's bibliography in 1971[1] identified about 100 references; more than half dated between 1966 and 1971. The earliest references to theoretical work, aside from Boehm-Bawerk's celebrated horse-market auction,[2] are by D. Emblen[3] in 1944 and by L. Friedman in *Operations Research* in 1956.[4] An updated bibliography by Stark and Rothkopf in *Operations Research* in 1979 identifies about 500 references.[5] The volume of analytical and empirical literature on competitive bidding, auctions, estimation, procurement, and incentive systems design related to contracting is growing rapidly. It indicates that the time is ripe for the development of both theory and applications.

[1] Stark (1971).
[2] Boehm-Bawerk (1923).
[3] Emblen (1944).
[4] Friedman (1956).
[5] Stark and Rothkopf (1979).

Introduction

In 1975 the first conference on bidding and auctioning was initiated by Professor Oskar Morgenstern at the Center for Applied Economics at New York University with the sponsorship of the Office of Naval Research. The editing of the papers and proceedings of this conference resulted in the publication of a book in 1976 entitled *Bidding and Auctioning for Procurement and Allocation*.[6] This volume is in some sense a continuation of that effort.

The material is divided into five major sections:
1. Overview of auctions, bidding, and contracting.
2. Issues in the theory of auctions.
3. Recent developments in the theory and applications of competitive bidding.
4. Experimental and empirical bidding.
5. Methods and problems in procurement, estimation, and bidding.

REFERENCES

Amihud, Y. (1976), ed. *Bidding and Auctioning for Procurement and Allocation.* New York: New York University Press.

Boehm-Bawerk, E. von (1923). *Positive Theory of Capital* (translated from German; original 1891). New York: G. E. Steckert.

Emblen, D. (1944). "Competitive Bidding for Corporate Securities," Ph.D Dissertation, Columbia University.

Friedman, L. (1956). "A Competitive Bidding Strategy," *Operations Research,* Vol. 4, pp. 104–12.

Stark, R. M. (1971). "Competitive Bidding: A Comprehensive Bibliography," *Operations Research,* Vol. 19, pp. 484–90.

Stark, R. M. and M. Rothkopf (1979). "Competitive Bidding: A Comprehensive Bibliography," *Operations Research,* Vol. 27, pp. 364–90.

[6] Amihud (1976).

AUCTIONS, BIDDING, AND CONTRACTING:
Uses and Theory

PART ONE

OVERVIEW ON AUCTIONS, BIDDING, AND CONTRACTING

0227
0262

1

ON AUCTIONS, BIDDING, AND CONTRACTING*
Martin Shubik

1. INTRODUCTION

For many individuals the auction has held a fas-
cination as a form of gambling and an exciting way to
buy items such as art, antiques, or used goods and
furnishings from estates. Still others recall small
auction houses in the market towns of rural America
or in places such as 42nd Street in New York, or Atlantic City, or at circuses and fairs where a group
of relatively small-time pitchmen practiced their art
of extracting top dollar from the crowd for junk

---

*This work relates to Department of the Navy Contract
N00014-77-C-0518 issued by the Office of Naval Research under Contract Authority NR 047-006.

jewelry, watches of dubious provenance, and other as-
sorted trinkets. In certain rural areas cattle auctions, tobacco auctions, and other commodity auctions,
as well as land and estate auctions, were, and in
some instances still are, events of economic significance.

All of the auctions described above utilize a
means to dispose of or sell goods which are the same
as or nearly the same as the English auction. Bids
are, in essence, open or "noisy" (although the pros
may devote some energy to concealing their provenance).
The ambiance in a Southby's or a Parke-Bernet auction
may be different from that on the boardwalk in Atlantic
City or Coney Island, but, whether the accent is Eton-
ian or pure Brooklyn, the coaxing of the bids from
the crowd is, in essence, the same. (In the United
States in 1980 an aspiring auctioneer could take a
course on how to conduct an auction for $300.)[1]

Related to, but different from, the English auction is the sealed bid. It is well known that the
Dutch auction, used for selling tulip bulbs, is mathematically equivalent to the auction by sealed bid as
the two are currently modeled. In the Dutch auction
the participants watch the price on a price clock
gradually decrease. The auction ends when someone

---

[1]Wall Street Journal (1980).

presses a button and stops the clock. In an auction
based on sealed bids, bidders must submit independent
closed bids on or before an appointed time to a specific agency or institution. The bids are then opened
and compared and the item, or job is awarded according to some previously specified convention. In general, especially if the bid or offer involves nothing
more than a single amount of money, the rule frequently
is that an item for sale is awarded to the highest
bidder (with some tie-breaking rule specified) or the
contract or job is awarded to the bidder who names
the lowest price for delivery.

In ancient times it appears that auctions were
used to dispose of booty.[2] In modern times, governments have turned to sealed bids both as a means of
disposal and for procurement. Oil leases are sold by
sealed bid; surplus stores are sold by sealed bid,
as are other items. Far outweighing the use of sealed
bids to dispose of surplus stores, is the use by governments of sealed bids for procurement. Municipalities
may request bids for the construction of roads, schools,
libraries, hospitals, and other public buildings as
well as repairs and maintenance. The central government may solicit bids for armaments systems, missiles,
radar, bombers, fighters, tanks, submarines, aircraft

---

[2]Talamanca (1954).

carriers, and so forth. Major corporations may vie
with each other in buying or supplying cargo ships,
large turbines, transformers, and other custom-built
"big ticket" capital goods, including complete "turnkey systems" for which the customer may expect a
complete complex system to be installed and operational prior to taking delivery.

Related to, but somewhat different from, both
the auction and sealed bid is the double-auction
market used on the New York Stock Exchange. In essence, both potential buyers and sellers submit bids
which are more or less secret or anonymous to other
bidders and offerors. The markets are cleared almost
continuously. Other financial instruments, such as
Treasury notes, are sold by sealed bid.

In the United States a considerable amount of
corporate business is accomplished by contracts worked
out in bilateral negotiation between the two parties
involved. Both the length and complexity of such arrangements may be considerable.

The type and complexity of disposal and procurement may vary anywhere from the immediate disposal of
10,000 pairs of surplus standard socks to the elicit-
ing of bids for a new class of helicopters which must
be designed according to specification, may be modified several times while being built, and will take

several years to design and build, or a nuclear power
plant which may take five or six years of paperwork
and five or six years to build.

When the item is highly complex and may cost
anywhere between several hundred million and several
billion dollars, there are few firms that are even in
a position to submit a bid on the job. The cost of
the estimation and the design engineering in the preparation of a meaningful bid may be millions of dollars. Thus, it may be necessary to have bids for bids,
with the first round resulting in the reward of funds
to do the estimation and engineering work necessary
to prepare a bid for the main contract.

How does one go about estimating the costs to produce a new and complex untested system which may take
years to produce, is subject to changes, costs enormous
sums of money, may be produced by large conglomerate
firms with highly complicated overhead costs and whose
cost audits must meet GAO standards and public political inquiry? The design of mechanisms to encourage
rational economic behavior to the mutual benefit of
industry and society presents a challenge which calls
for collaboration between practitioners in government
and industry and between practitioners and the academic
communities.

The problems require a great amount of economic

insight, but the subtleties and difficulties do not
lie with economics alone. Engineering, accounting,
and law are of considerable importance. Furthermore,
a precise scientific judgment and a complete understanding is required of the bureaucratic and societal
constraints which may limit the design and use of
various mechanisms.

The economic functions in any society involve
production and distribution for consumption and investment. The general questions and problems concerning who should get what, and why they should get it,
belong to a broad domain of ethics, politics, and socio-
economic considerations. The narrower questions of
how to design a system to deliver or distribute the
goods and services of the society to its members,
given that the goals are known, involves economics,
law, and the politico-economic design of institutions
and other mechanisms to bring about the desired distribution.

In a separate publication the number of different
ways used by a society to distribute resources has
been discussed.[3] In particular, it was suggested that
among the methods available are fiat, force, chance,
custom, fraud, deceit, the competitive market, auctions, sealed bids, voting, bargaining, and contract.

---

[3]Shubik (1970).

The concern here is with auctions, bidding, and contracting because they, among the alternatives available, appear to be most relevant to considerable
economic activity associated with procurement and
disposal of assets at all levels of government as
well as to certain public economic mechanisms dealing
with commodities and certain other special items.

Economic theory, especially that part which deals
with the description and analysis of production and
distribution by means of a competitive price system,
implicitly assumes some form of nonspecified myster-
ious entity called a "competitive market" where price
is determined by the forces of competition. There
are at least two approaches we may adopt in trying
to bring some precision to the concept of "competitive market." We may actually specify some form of
trading mechanism complete with institutional details,
or we may alternatively try to axiomatize the properties of a competitive market mechanism. Dubey, Mas-
Colell, and Shubik have adopted the latter approach.[4]
A truly competitive market should be an anonymous,
aggregating device which takes in bids and offers
from all indiscriminately and produces prices and
trades. It has been shown that, for a broad class
of market mechanisms, if it is assumed that traders

---

[4] Dubey, Mas-Colell, and Shubik (1980).

are so numerous as to be of insignificant power in
the market place, the competitive price will emerge
from independent optimizing behavior, more or less,
independent of the details of any specific market
mechanism.[5] Unfortunately, when we deal with procurement processes or the disposal of estates the condition on competitors rarely, if ever, holds.

In military procurement there is, in essence,
one federal government which wants to buy a new weapons system from one of the three or four firms capable of supplying it. It may want a ship such as a
nuclear aircraft carrier for which there are only
one, two or three shipyards which can build it.
Furthermore, in the course of construction (which may
take anywhere from one or two to ten years) many modifications may be called for.

The total number of items in a class may require
that one item be built as a prototype, and then, depending upon size, complexity, and expense, from two
or three more up to several hundred or thousands may
be ordered. At one end of this range are items such
as nuclear aircraft carriers, at the other end, tanks.

When the government is on one side of the market
and only two or three domestic bidders or contractors
are available (and foreign contracts cannot be enter-

---

[5]Dubey, Mas-Colell, and Shubik (1980).

tained), then the realities of both the bureaucratic
or organizational structure and the constraints of the
political environment must be taken into account.

2.   THEORY, PRACTICE, AND INCENTIVES

     In the past 20 years, partly under the stimulus
of the development of the noncooperative equilibrium
solution of game theory, operations research personnel,
economic theorists, and others have started to inves-
tigate bidding, auctioning, and contracting processes,
in particular, and the design of incentive systems,
in general. Approaching the problem of complex procurement from a completely different viewpoint, engineering has come to characterize the complexity of estimation.

     Quantitative differences frequently lead to fun-
damentally qualitative differences in the design and
use of incentive mechanisms. Casual analogies can
mislead even a highly skilled theorist into believing
that the scope of his models is far broader than is
actually the case. It may be that the optimal-bidding
mechanism for oil leases should be fundamentally different from the bidding mechanism used for ship construction. In the first instance, a single sealed
bid may be all that is required for fairness and

efficiency; in the second instance, a fixed-fee plus
overrun cost-sharing formula may be far more efficient.

Mathematical models applied to management are
rarely, if ever, logically wrong when they are built
by competent practitioners. The three major reasons
for their failure to be of use is that they are in-
tractible mathematically; they are formulated in such
a way as to make their data requirements virtually
impossible to fulfill; or they ignore some of the critical relevant features of the phenomenon they purport
to be modeling. In particular, time, costs, the complexity involved in making an estimate, and needs for
modification are all factors which may be critical
in differentiating between economic activity in bidding for oil leases, as contrasted with bidding for
weapons contracts.

The literature pertaining to the letting of major
contracts has been concentrated on bidding and auctions, on contracting and incentive-system design, and
on cost estimation. The first pertains to the economics of information, the second to bargaining theory,
industrial organization, law, bureaucratic studies, and
game theory, and the last primarily to engineering.

Table 1 presents some of the fundamental distinc-
tions in process and goals which may determine what
type of buying or selling mechanism should be used.

TABLE 1

	Auction	Sealed Bid	Contract	Competitive Market
numbers of buyers/ sellers	1/many or many/1	1/few to many or few to many/1	1 among few with 1 among few	many/many
bid preparation costs	low	moderate to high	moderate to high	low
bid preparation time	short	moderate to long	moderate to long	short
delivery time of items	instant	short to very long	medium to very long	short
estimation & evaluation problems	few, well defined & can be handled fast	may be critical time consuming & hard to define & handle	may be critical time consuming & hard to define & handle	few
production & distribution	second-hand goods, commodities	major liquidations, special manufacturing	special production items-- turnkey systems	mass markets mass production
importance of modifications & learning	none	little to high	little to high	none
socio-political constraints on process	sometimes, but usually no	frequently highly important	frequently highly important	essentially minor
special importance of information	experts vs. amateurs	corrections, trust, information & expertise	corrections, trust, information & expertise	generally not important

We see that military procurement are obtained by means
of sealed bids and contracts. Many oil leases are
let by the sealed bid. The selling of art and antiques,
surplus equipment, or the contents of buildings being
given up by liquidating firms are conveniently handled
by auctions at the location.

Numbers. The auction and sealed bid tend to be used
when there is one buyer (usually of services or a manufacturing contract) or seller against many on the
other side of the market. When, as in an auction,
there are several sellers, they come up sequentially
against all of the buyers. Contracting is essentially
one on one, but prior to contracting the process may
have involved a search and matching among a few firms
or institutions on either side of the market.

Bid Preparation Costs. In auctions, in general, the
professionals have inspected the items on which they
are bidding. The bidders tend to be experienced professionals who can estimate accurately the resale potential of most of the items being offered. Little
explicit planning needs to be done prior to an auction.
However, when bidders are bidding on an oil lease,
preliminary geological work may be time consuming
and expensive. When they are bidding for a construction contract for a nonstandard item, the bidders'

preparation costs can be so significant that they
may be deterred from even considering making a bid
without some form of funding or sharing the bid preparation costs. The risk-sharing aspects of bid
preparation can be modified virtually continuously
by contracting.

Bid Preparation Time. An expert buying an already
extant item from a professional needs little more
than basic inspection and validation. A bid or contract which calls for a systems design calls for considerable preliminary expenditure of time and an understanding concerning the nature of future work which
may have to be done after the bid is accepted and
the contract awarded, even if no modifications are
contemplated.

Delivery Time of Items. When a painting is sold at
auction, the title changes hands quickly and decisive-
ly. When oil lands are leased the conditions are
specified and operating control passes quickly to
the winning bidder. When a bid is let for a nuclear
plant or a major ship both sides have entered into a
marriage.

Estimation and Evaluation Problems. At an auction,
bid preparation and estimation or evaluation are almost the same. It may be necessary to authenticate

a painting, check the condition of an antique, or
run a piece of second-hand machinery. In contrast,
bid preparation, estimating, and evaluating go hand
in hand when new systems are projected. And the time
and uncertainty may be critical. An example is provided by the Sidney Opera House in Australia where
final costs came in at more than ten times the original estimate.

Production and Distribution. Auctions appear to be
best suited for the distribution of existing goods.
They provide an excellent device for quick liquidation. In the broadest of economic theory, they are
not necessarily efficient, but when transactions costs
are considered, the case for efficiency may be made
because the goods can be transferred quickly and
cheaply.

For most manufacturing one of the advantages of
the auction is no longer important. That is the speed
at which goods can be moved. Production timing and
decisions, rather than distribution timing, becomes
dominant.

Importance of Modifications and Learning. The concepts of modification and learning must be associated
with production and some form of contractual relationship over time. When new weapons, ships, or aircraft
are being constructed, the production experience with

the prototype, or the lead ship, for example, may be
considerably different from the follow-on or major
production run that takes place subsequently. Learning and feasibility testing are clearly important
as progress is made on a new manufacture. The hidden
uncertainties abound even when the goals are given
and stay fixed, for economic conditions will not remain unchanged for a period of five or ten years.
If the contracting agency wishes to reserve its rights
to modify or cancel a program, it must assume the
appropriate financial responsibilities for the cost
of extra uncertainty to the manufacturer. In this
process, the "moral hazard" problem may be difficult
to sort out from change in economic conditions, unsatisfactory work, bad estimating, or error in specifications. In other words, it may be difficult to
sort out that which is attributable to bad luck,
bad planning, bad management, change in circumstances,
poor work, poor estimation, or genuine dishonesty.
Almost all of these problems require a hand-tailored
treatment, that is, a contractual arrangement designed
to deal with the specifics.

Sociopolitical Constraints on Process. When a private art dealer buys a painting at an auction the
transaction is, in essence, purely economic. It is
unlikely that the dealer worries about the welfare

or the continued prosperity and competence of any particular auctioneer. At most, his legal concerns involve protection against fraud, correct transfer of
title, and proper accounting that will stand up under
audit. When two or three billion dollars is spent
on a modern aircraft carrier, the government contracting agency must take into account numerous special
problems which exist as part of sociopolitical and
national reality. In particular, when there are only
two or three shipyards in the country capable of building a specific ship, how can a method be devised which
both promotes competition yet preserves competitors?
How can national security needs for long-run capacity
be reconciled with a competitive-bidding mechanism
or an alternative public security as meeting the appropriate levels of fairness and economic efficiency?

A good public system designed to award contracts
not only needs to be "cheatproof" and efficient to a
high degree; it also needs to be ridicule proof.
The public is not in a position to spend much time
understanding the intricacies of inventory theory,
PERT charts, or estimation procedures. When it is
told that the navy has a 40-year supply of oyster
forks, or that a contract has been let to the higher
of two bidders, material has been supplied for comment
that cannot necessarily be properly satisfied by

offering detailed scientific evidence. The possibility
that good inventory theory under highly fluctuating
circumstances might result in a decentralized system
overbuying and that statements such as "40-years over-
supply" depend delicately on the index of normal consumption selected are economic facts that may not be
heard by a public already overburdened with undigested
scientific and economic information.

When the possibility must be faced that it may
be economically wiser to award a contract to the higher
of two bidders because the expected final cost may be
lower, it becomes critical that a scheme be devised
that makes this point transparently in a manner that
is publicly understandable, economically efficient,
legally defensible, and sociopolitically acceptable.
When simple bids are compared with cost plus fixed-
fee formulae or with two-parameter bidding schemes
or with other mechanisms, the comparison should be
based upon all features, not merely on considerations
of economic efficiency, ignoring transactions costs,
estimation problems, and many special sociopolitical
and defense constraints which characterize major defense procurement processes.

Special Importance of Information. The term "information" refers to several qualitatively different
phenomena. At its simplest, we may have a concept

of a set of messages without semantic content such as
that described by Shannon.[6] In terms of game theory,
it is possible to study solutions to games in extensive form which differ only in information sets and
see how the solution changes.[7] Thus, in a limited
way, it is possible to discuss the value of information.

Another type of information (or lack of it) concerns individuals' knowledge of the true costs and
value of various items to others.[8] Problems arising
from moral hazard beset the insurance business because
they may issue policies to individuals who find it
profitable to conceal features which make them poorer
risks than others. In contrast, the contractor,
especially if it happens to be a large complex corporation, can include front-end loading and assign joint
costs which cannot be as well known to its customer
as it is to itself.

A totally different use of the term "information"
comes in such phrases as a "well-informed individual."
What is usually meant is not merely an individual who
is aware of various bits of information but who can

---

[6] Shannon (1949).

[7] von Neumann and Morgenstern (1944).

[8] Harsanyi (1967).

interpret them competently. Frequently it is not
what the numbers are, but what they mean that counts.
The role of the expert in estimation and evaluation
is clearly of considerable importance in contracting
for the construction of new systems. Yet, not only
is the understanding of what constitutes an expert
not in the proper domain of economic analysis, the
characterization of what constitutes an expert and
how expertise influences decision systems is still
not well formulated.

Closely tied in with problems concerning information is the nature of communication, cooperation,
trust, and reputation. From one point of view it
makes perfectly good sense that a middle-grade officer who has spent much of his career in procurement
should join a contracting firm upon retirement. His
understanding and his circle of acquaintances on both
sides of the fence could be of great value to all
concerned. Yet from another point of view, the conditions have been set up to promote less than arms'
length dealings. The specific conditions of communication, long-term acquaintanceship, and trust, all
of which should favor efficiency and facilitate work,
are at the same time factors militating against competition.

In auctions, short of outright fraud, personal

acquaintanceship is of little importance. In bidding
and contracting, where the parties must work together
for up to ten years, it may be of considerable value.

3.   APPROACHES TO THE STUDY OF AUCTIONS, BIDDING,
     AND CONTRACTING

The diversity of purpose and problems in procurement can be seen by the many schemes used, approaches
adopted, and proposals considered both in the United
States and elsewhere.

In some countries major military procurement is
regarded as meriting the maintenance of a nationalized
manufacturing system. Even with nationalized shipyards,
many of the problems of economic efficiency and incentive still remain. For many small countries, economic
and technological realities dominate military desires
or security claims. Advanced expensive equipment must
be procured abroad. Hence, ships or planes or tanks
are procured in a process that is highly politically
determined. The means of procuring military equipment vary from buying it from nationalized industry,
a partially nationalized company, a private, but non-
foreign, industry, or from foreign as well as domestic
companies.

Some years ago the popular political phrase

"military-industrial complex" was used to suggest
that the military and industrialists of the United
States were in collusion. At the level of the design
of a contract this appears to be contrary to experience, yet this suggestion draws attention to a different institutional structure which may fit Japan
better than the United States. The high level of
coordination between an implicitly structured Zaibatsu
industrial organization and the government gives Japan
(to paraphrase Admiral Mahan) an armaments "industry-
in-being" of considerable size and flexibility. Although the institutional environment in the United
States is primarily private, the means that the government has available to procure supplies are many.
This can be seen from the language of contracting.
Thus, there is sole source contracting by which the
original contractor remains the solitary supplier.
(The French tend to favor this approach.)[9] In essence,
the contract is awarded on the first round of bidding.

There may be buy-out or split-award contracting
for further work. Legal requirements, GAO considerations, and simplicity make publicly advertised calls
for a sealed bid with a fixed price seem attractive,
but there are difficulties in using this bid when
the risk-sharing features of new systems design are
considered. Cost plus fixed-percentage profit, or
cost plus fixed-fee contracts offer simplicity, risk

---

[9]Ponssard (1980).

sharing, but poor incentives. Some years ago, when
the moon was the target, industry in the United States
in its belief that outer space and the inner city
could both be analyzed and contracted for in the same
way, used phrases such as "total package deal" and
"turnkey system delivery."

With the growing realization of the specifics
of the complexity of procurement involving construction of new items over a considerable span of time,
the need for multiple evaluation factor bids has been
recognized. As with every scheme where a relatively
simple procedure is utilized to control a complicated
process, the project-specific pros and cons must be
weighed. It is relatively easy to produce a general
impossibility theorem to show that no simple rule
will be universally optimal for the multifaceted needs
of large-scale procurement. The difficult problem
is to be able to characterize optimal rules for specific, but important, classes of problems. A blend
of empirical observation, technical understanding,
modeling ability, sociopolitical understanding, and
mathematical insight is required. For example, all
of these factors indicate that the auction is a highly
efficient procedure for selling many commodities but
is not good for procurement of large systems.

There are both important applied and theoretical

problems which merit consideration at this time.
Work has been proceeding in parallel in several different modes.

Bidding and Auctioning Theory. As recently as five
years ago Oskar Morgenstern observed that, in spite
of the antiquity of bidding and auctions, little had
been done in the development of the theory of these
important allocation mechanisms.[10] Stark and Rothkopf
noted that scarcely 50 articles had been written by
1965 that covered both theory and application.[11]
Two hundred had been published by 1975 and over 500
since then. An important pioneering work was that
of Vickrey.[12] Engelbrecht-Wiggans recently has provided a detailed, critical review of the current
theory.[13] In spite of the considerable growth in
investigation, there are many fundamental questions
still unanswered, such as the effect of capacity constraints on bidding or the circumstances under which
the sealed bid clearly is the most efficient price
formation mechanism.

---

[10]Morgenstern (1976).

[11]Stark and Rothkopf (1979).

[12]Vickrey (1961).

[13]Engelbrecht-Wiggans (1980).

Information, Economics and Incentive System Design.
Investigations have been made on bidding and auctioning. Studies have been made on the strategic importance of information in the game theoretic analysis
of competition.[14] Also, partly as a result of concern
with the modern theories of finance and industrial
organization and with agency problems, information
economics has begun to manifest a swift growth related
to, but apart from investigation of bidding and auctions. There also has been a considerable growth in
interest in economic theory in the formulation of
economic mechanisms as games in strategic or extensive
form which can be studied for their noncooperative
equilibria.[15] (The specifics of incentives in contracting have been considered by Holmstrom.)[16]

Consideration of how information can be obtained
poses many problems. A sampling of a few of them
includes how do we characterize experts and amateurs;
what price should one pay for information whose worth
cannot be ascertained until it has been obtained?
Related to the last question is how can one determine
the veracity of information in order to make a cost

---

[14]Harsanyi (1967).

[15]Hurwicz (1973); Shubik (1973).

[16]Holmstrom (1977).

estimate? All other factors being equal, what are
the conditions which will supply the best incentives
to an organization to produce accurate cost and time
estimates for future jobs in a world loaded with complicated bureaucratic structures, tax considerations,
accounting conventions with considerable leeway and
institutions with multiple goals and hidden agenda?
The theorist may not be in a position to produce
formal models of sufficient depth to calculate answers.
But the identification and the clarification of questions is frequently valuable for both the theorist
and practitioner.

Game Theory, Programming, and the New Industrial Organization. Procurement is an ongoing activity. A satisfactory characterization of procurement, auctions or
markets and economic activity, in general, calls for
dynamics. In the past thirty years the mathematical
techniques of game theory and of programming have
begun to provide the tools for the description of
process. The extensive form of the game provides
a means for modeling detail, and programming methods
provide ways for actually calculating suggested solutions to processes or games in extensive form provided
that we have a decent concept of what should constitute a solution. The formal study of games in extensive form tells us that no generally acceptable

solution theories exist.

At first glance the conclusion that there does
not appear to be a universally acceptable solution
might distress those individuals seeking the help
of formal methods to solve problems of practical importance. Yet, in actuality, the potential for development is by no means bleak. Variations of the
noncooperative equilibrium solution of game theory
appear to be reasonable in some situations, but, in
general, this is not an a priori proposition but depends upon the nature of specific structure.

In general, if a solution predicts too broadly,
by adding more detail concerning the description of
the environment, the domain of the solution may be
cut down. In particular, the noncooperative equilibrium may, under certain circumstances, be reasonable
as a solution, but an ad hoc knowledge of the problem
at hand is required before this conclusion can be
drawn. This observation can be restated by saying
that it is of considerable help to know your business
in detail especially if you wish to use analytical
methods to aid in policy formation. The recent work
in the theory of industrial organization has begun
to emphasized this theme. If we are to understand
an industry, theory must be combined with institutional
detail. Table 1 has been presented in keeping with
this observation. Bidding for oil leases, antiques,

or shipbuilding contracts at one level of theorizing
may have some features in common, but at a more operational level the bidding procedures differ considerably and to portray the differences requires an understanding of time lags, contractual relationships,
goals, and special constraints which characterize the
specific problem at hand. A challenge to the theorist
and practitioner is to characterize in detail the special features of important activities such as the procurement of major defense contracts, the auctioning
of oil leases, or of Treasury issues so that the development of theory and specific application can be
mutually beneficial. As yet, this has scarcely been
done.

Engineering, Costing, Accounting, and Law. The economist cannot afford to work in an institutional vacuum.
Much of his data and many of his "economic facts" are
determined by others. In particular, when large projects are being considered which will be executed by
large organizations, the detailed understanding of the
relevance of the biases introduced by engineering
cost estimating procedures, accounting conventions,
and tax law definitions is critical as has been noted
in the work of Stark on project estimation.[17]

---

[17] Stark (1976).

REFERENCES

Dubey, P., A. Mas-Colell, and M. Shubik (1980). "Ef-
  ficiency Properties of Strategic Market Games: An
  Axiomatic Approach," Journal of Economic Theory,
  Vol. 22, No. 2, pp. 339-62.

Engelbrecht-Wiggans, R. (1980). "Auctions and Bidding
  Models: A Survey," Management Science, Vol. 26,
  No. 2, pp. 119-42.

Harsanyi, J. (1967). "Games with Incomplete Information Played by 'Bayesian' Players, Part I: The
  Basic Model," Management Science, Vol. 14, No. 3,
  pp. 159-82.

Holmstrom, B. (1977). "On Incentives and Control
  in Organizations," unpublished Ph.D Thesis, Stanford University.

Hurwicz, L. (1973). "The Design of Mechanisms for
  Resource Allocating," American Economic Review,
  Vol. 63, No. 2, pp. 1-30.

Morgenstern, O. (1976). Forward, in Y. Amihud (ed.),
  Bidding and Auctioning for Procurement and Allocation. New York: New York University Press.

Ponssard, J. (1980). "Military Procurement in France:
  Regulation and Incentive Contracts," Ecole Polytechnique Research Paper.

Shannon, C. E. (1949). The Mathematical Theory of
  Communication. Urbana, Ill.: University of Illinois
  Press.

Shubik, M. (1970). "On Different Methods for Allocating Resources," Kyklos, Vol. XXIII, No. 2, pp.
  332-37.

Shubik, M. (1973). "Commodity Money, Oligopoly, Credit and Bankruptcy in a General Equilibrium Model," Western Economic Journal, Vol. XI, No. 1, pp. 24-38.

Stark, R. (1976). "An Estimating Technology for Unbalancing Unit Bid Proposals," in Y. Amihud (ed.), Bidding and Auctioning for Procurement and Allocation. New York: New York University Press, pp. 21-34.

Stark, R. and M. H. Rothkopf (1979). "Competitive Bidding: A Comprehensive Bibliography," Operations Research, Vol. 27, pp. 364-90.

Talamanca, M. (1954). "Contributi Allo Studio delle Vendite all'asta nel Mondo Classico," Serie VIII, Vol. VI, Fascicolo 2. Rome: Accademia Nazionale dei Lincei.

Vickrey, W. (1961). "Counterspeculation, Auctions, and Competitive Sealed Tenders," Journal of Finance, Vol. 16, pp. 8-37.

von Neumann, J. and O. Morgenstern (1944). Theory of Games and Economic Behavior. Princeton, N.J.: Princeton University Press.

Wall Street Journal, October 10, 1980, p. 1.

0412
0430
0277

2

AUCTIONS, BIDDING, AND MARKETS: AN HISTORICAL SKETCH*
Martin Shubik

MARKETS, TAXATION, AND PROCUREMENT

A fundamental question in any society is how does
one allocate and produce goods and resources? There
appear to be around a dozen methods. They include markets, and under this category there are competitive
markets, oligopolistic competition, auctions, and
sealed bids. There is barter, there is bilateral bargaining and contracting, and there is allocation by
voting. Also, there is allocation by a fiat or legi-
timized power, and this particular form of allocation
can be broken down into two categories. There is
direct allocation and allocation by a bureaucratic
system. The mere fact that the emperor commands something to be done does not necessarily imply that it

*This work related to Department of the Navy Contract
N00014-77-C-0518 issued by the Office of Naval Research
under Contract Authority NR 047-006.

is going to be done if it requires implementation through
a large bureaucracy.

There is also allocation by nonlegitimized force,
fraud, and deceit. Other important forms of allocation are by chance and by gift. A slightly different
categorization of these different forms of allocation
is given in the work of Polanyi, Arensburg, and Pearson
on ancient markets and markets in ancient empires.[1]

The development of anonymous mass markets and the
economy, as we know it today, appears to be extremely
recent. The mass competitive market which is frequently
eulogized by many practicing economists is a phenomenon
that essentially was formed in the mid-seventeenth
century. Trade and technology was increased in the
early 1700s and by the mid-1700s the growth was exploding
along with population and communication, over much of
the world. It is probably no coincidence that this was
the period in which Adam Smith and others developed
their theories, and economics became a recognized pro-
fession.

A glance at the history of the Babylonian, Egyptian, or the Chinese civilizations indicates that one
of the first economic acts appears to have been the
imposition of taxes to pay for government and war.
Because taxation was levied in kind, there had to be

---

[1]Polanyi, Arensburg, and Pearson (1957).

inventorying. And probably soon after a procedure
to take inventory was established, accounting and
auditing principles had to be agreed upon. Thus,
before the people in these empires utilized money,
they had formed a system of taxation, inventorying,
auditing, procurement by force, and disbursement by
fiat.

About the earliest records available on prices
(not markets but prices) are Egyptian and Babylonian
records.[2] It appears that the Egyptians and Babylon-
ians imposed fixed prices on basic commodities backed
up with a centralized inventory policy over most of
the goods necessary for the survival of the population
at the time. Flexible pricing and what one might wish
to call the competitive mechanism appears to have
evolved only after international trade became extensive. An illustration of the importance of transaction costs in trade is given by the delivery price
of Egyptian wheat in Rome which was roughly ten times
the price of Egyptian wheat in Egypt. The price differential was due to transactions costs.

Concerning international trade, the various empires, such as the Persian empire, the Babylonian
empire, and the Egyptian, appeared to have countenanced
port towns which were not part of their empires.

---

[2]Janssen (1975).

For example, the Phoenicians operated a set of international trade depots where the hinterland countries
probably could have but did not wish to take control
of the ports of entry. These centers were regarded
by all traders as havens. The traders knew that if
the ports could be reached, they could unload cargo,
obtain warehousing entrepôt, and transshipment facilities. A game theoretic justification of such an arrangement is clear. A surrounding empire might wish
to minimize the fears of a trader concerning the dangers
of trade with it. It may have been better for all to
trade through neutral territory than a national port.
To this very day there are transshipment areas which
have virtually these features. However, the control
of prices requires government and enforceable law,
and international trade made such control much more
difficult.

Possibly even more central to governments is
procurement and taxation. From the Romans through
to the French kings of the late Middle Ages a pattern
can be discerned. The early monarchs' procurement
and taxation problems were market free and uncompli-
cated. One of the money raising techniques of newly
elected Roman emperors was to declare many of the
richest citizens, and merchants as traitors to the
realm, have them executed or banished, and confiscate

all their goods. It was an extremely simple procurement procedure and apparently worked fairly well.

   This particular procedure was delivered its death
blow in England and Holland. These were two countries
in which absolute monarchy ended relatively early,
and the royal funding game changed. With the waning
of the divine right of kings it became necessary to
borrow from the citizens. A completely new fiscal
situation arose, which was the need for a public debt.
Before that time, public debt was a curiosum; a king
did not need a public debt; one executed a few bankers,
closed monastaries, confiscated goods, or took other
appropriate acts. But with William the old monarchy
was over. A public debt was needed especially to
finance wars. Along with the public debt came institutions, such as the Bank of England, that managed
the public debt and, together with the Bank of England,
came the South Sea Company and the East India Company.
The South Sea Company flotation was devised as a means
of getting rid of the public debt by exchanging debt
paper for a relatively recently invented piece of
paper, equity paper, or an early form of common stock.
This was a period of both a great financial revolution
and an industrial revolution. Which caused which, is
hard to assess, they were most likely parallel parts
of an evolving process. Both were needed for the

new economy. In the late seventeenth century and
early in the eighteenth century financial institutions
were developed to modernize and solidify the economies
of England and Holland. In addition, the demand by
citizens for legal and political rights radically
changed the methods of funding and procurement.

AUCTIONS AND BIDDING

(Part of this material in this section is based
upon an unpublished 1961 translation of a work in
Italian on the history of auctions by Talamanca and
the research assistance of C. Dougherty.)[3]
Among the earliest of mechanisms used by governments to dispose of surplus property was the auction.
(The sealed bid used for procurement appears to be of
considerably later origin.) Auctions, as a method
of selling, have only appeared in the comparatively
civilized societies after the necessary conditions
for their existence were fulfilled: an adequate concentration of the population to provide sufficient
numbers of buyers and sellers, and a coinage so that
the values of bids could be determined quickly. Thus,
before the seventeenth century there were few regularly
scheduled auctions sales. This method of selling

---

[3]Talamanca (1954).

appears to have found little favor in the Orient where bargaining has been traditional and little importance was attached to the time to make a sale. Consequently, the use of the auction has followed the economic development in the West.

The earliest reference to a regular organized auction market is probably Herodotus' description of the annual Babylonian marriage market. This was unique in that bidding often started at a negative price.

> Of their [Babylonian] customs, whereof I shall now proceed to give an account, the following, which I understand belongs to them in common with the Illyrian tribe of the Eneti, is the wisest in my judgment. Once a year in each village the maidens of age to marry were collected all together into one place, while the men stood round them in a circle. Then a herald called up the damsels one by one, and offered them for sale. He began with the most beautiful. When she was sold for no small sum of money, he offered for sale the one who came next to her in beauty. All of them were sold to be wives. The richest of the Babylonians who wished to wed bid against each other for the loveliest maidens, while the humbler wife-seekers who were indifferent about beauty, took the more homely damsels with marriage-portions. For the custom was that when the herald had gone through the whole number of the beautiful damsels, he should then call up the ugliest--a cripple if there chanced to be one--

and offer her to the men, asking who
would agree to take her with the smallest marriage-portion. And the man who
offered to take the smallest sum had her
assigned to him. The marriage-portions
were furnished by the money paid for the
beautiful damsels, and thus the fairer
maidens portioned out the uglier. No
one was allowed to give his daughter in
marriage to the man of his choice, nor
might any one carry away the damsel whom
he had purchased without finding bail
really and truly to make her his wife;
if, however, it turned out that they did
not agree, the money might be paid back.
All who liked might come even from dis-
tant villages and bid for the women.
This was the best of their customs, but
it has now fallen into disuse.

Auctions also were held to dispose of mine con-
cessions in ancient Greece and were conducted regularly in Roman times mostly to sell shared and confiscated property, and it is from Latin words that
the words "auction," "subasta," and "encan" are derived. "Auction" comes from "auctio," an increase;
"encan" comes from incanto," "I cry"; "subasta" is
a shortened form of "sub hasta" meaning "under spear."
Roman soldiers would auction off surplus spoils of
war on the battlefield by driving a spear into the
ground and selling off the booty gathered round it
to the highest bidders. This led to slave auctions
being held under the sign of a spear in the forum

and so the word was perpetuated. Often the slaves
thus sold were captives from a Roman military victory
and the money obtained was used to help pay for the
campaign. Antonius Matthaeus, in his work De Auction-
ibus quotes Damhonderos who believed that "subhastatio"
was a corruption of "ab hastario": Hastarium was the
name of a place used as a market. However, Matthaeus
does not agree with him.

> Either he [Pompey] will be ruling his own
> Quirites, by pronouncing judgment, when,
> on high, he shall be seated on the ivory
> chair, conspicuous with its carvings; or
> he shall be adjusting the revenues of the
> people by the erected spear, and he will
> not allow the resources of the great city
> to be diminished.

Ovid, in 10 A.D. mentions the practice of selling the rights to the state revenues to the highest
bidder, relieving the government of collecting them.

One of Cicero's court cases, c. 80 B.C., concerned
the hasty auction of property left as a surety by his
client who had not expected it to be sold. It was customary for debtors' property to be confiscated and
auctioned. Sulla extended the practice to enemies of
his regime, thereby eliminating all opposition and
gaining enormous amounts of money for his treasury
at the same time.

The status of auctioneers at the time is indicated
by Juvenal who, in his third satire, classes them with

various unsavoury types. He is more charitable in
his seventh satire:

> Whatever hope we have, whatever induce-
>   ment to study,
> Rests on Caesar alone, the Muses' only
>   respector
> In these sorrowful days, when poets of
>   high reputation
> In order to make a few cents, think of a
>   bakeshop
> Here in Rome, or perhaps try crying the
>   sales at an auction.
> None too great a disgrace, after all; any
>   one of the Muses
> Starving, could hardly be blamed for leaving
>   Helicon's fountains
> In hot haste for a job in the auction rooms
>   of the city,
> More or less content with Machaera's trade
>   and his profits,
> Bawling "Going! Gone!" over wine casks,
>   bookcases, tripods,
> Copies of plays, for example the 'Thebes'
>   of 'Tereus' of Faustus,
> Paccius' masterpiece, the one about Minyas'
>   daughter
> Changed to a bat. A better career, to be
>   sure, than appearing
> In some police court case, claiming you
>   saw what you did not.
> Leave all that to our new-made knights,
>   the ex-slaves from Asia,
> Cappadocia, Gaul, with the chalk marks
>   still on their ankles!

After the murder of the Emperor Pertinax in 193
A.D., the Praetorians, who were in command, auctioned
off the empire between two contenders which was won

by Didius Juliannus who offered the largest bribe.
(He remained in power for two months until overthrown
and executed by Septimus Severus.)

Use of auctions in early times is excellently
described in the translation of the summary of Talamanca's work.[4]

> The intent of the work is to point out
> some of the most notable aspects of auc-
> tion sales during classical antiquity.
> The first part of the study discusses the
> modalities of such sales in Ptolemiac
> Egypt, referring to the sale of real es-
> tate held (for whatever reason) by the
> fiscal authorities, to public works, to
> the lease of estates belonging to the
> crown, or to the judicial sale of the goods
> of insolvent debtors. The study of the
> two first points is particularly detailed,
> as the major portion of the documentation
> refers to them.
>
> The second part is divided into two chap-
> ters concerning auction sales (auctiones)
> in Roman law. The first chapter deals with
> auctiones in private law and attempts to
> establish their origin and dogmatic con-
> figuration during the classical period. In
> the second chapter which is dedicated to
> public auctiones, the venditio sub corona
> and the sectio bonorum, which represent the
> most ancient forms of auctio known in Rome,
> are studied. Here an attempt is made to
> delineate the regime of fiscal alienations
> during the period of the Principality,

---

[4]Talamanca (1954).

taking into account the administrative accounts of Greco-Roman Egypt, which results
from paleographical documents and from the
constitutions of the IIIrd and IVth centuries B.C., which have been conserved in
the Justinian Code.

The main object in this research is above
all to bring to light the form of the fiscal sales, the cases in which the problem
was solved by purchases a fisco and of the
effects of the payment of the prices obtained upon the transfer of the property
involved.

In the period of time between the end of the
Roman empire and the eighteenth century few auctions
were held. In the Middle Ages self-sufficiency was
the rule and the great mass of the population had
little money to spend. The feudal peasants owed part
of their time and crops to their lords and otherwise
only grew and made what they needed. Any necessities
that they could not fabricate for themselves they
were able to buy at the annual fairs or could buy
from others by barter. The small size of the population and the small quantity of circulating coinage
made it virtually impossible to hold auctions. In
Antiquex, Histoires et Singularitez de Paris, Ville
Capitale du Royaume de France, published in 1550,
Gilles Corrozet writes:

Au mois d'aoust audit temps (1550) furent
vendures publiquement en la Megisserie

> plusiers images, tables, autolz, peintures
> et autres ornements d'eglise qu'on avoit
> apportez at sauvez des eglises d'Angleterre.

This is possibly the earliest mention of a public sale
of works of art, but it is not certain that they were
sold by auction.

In an act of 1556 in France, the office of Huissier-
Priseur was created to deal with and appraise and sell
property left by death or taken in execution. In the
Charter of London, granted by Charles I, only one auction was to be held for the whole of London. In 1649,
the belongings of Cardinal Mazarin were sold and the
notice said, "tous les meubles estant dans la maison
audit cardinal seront vendus au plus offrant." Then,
in 1676, Matthias Nicholl was appointed vender master
in New York; he gave ₤2000 security, which indicates
the importance attached to the post at the time.

Auctions were held more frequently beginning
in the seventeenth century. There were four distinct
types--auctions using the hammer, the hourglass, or
the candle, and Dutch auctions. The latter originated
in Holland and were not much used. The hammer auctions were of the type normally used today. The hourglass and candle auctions allowed the bidders only a
limited time for bidding and were very similar except
that the candle auctions afforded greater opportunity
to use skill. An account of one is given by Pepys in

his diary for November 6th, 1660:

> To our office, where we meet all, for the
> sale of two ships by an ince of candle
> (the first time that ever I saw any of
> this kind), where I observed how they do
> invite one another, and at last how they
> all do cry, and we have much to do to
> tell who did cry last. The ships were
> the Indian, sold for £1300, and the Half-
> moon, sold for £830. After dinner we met
> and sold the Weymouth, Success and Fellow-
> ship hulks; where pleasant to see how
> backward men are at first to bid, and yet
> when the candle is going out, how they
> bawl and dispute afterwards who bid the
> most first. And here I observed one man
> cunninger than the rest, that was sure to
> bid the last man, and to carry it; and
> enquiring the reason, he told me that,
> just as the flame goes out, the smoke
> descends, which is a thing I never ob-
> served before, and by that he do know
> the instant when to bid last.

The earliest auction catalogue extant is that for a
sale of books for Ebenezer Pemberton at Boston in
1717. Auctioneers soon obtained a bad reputation
for dishonest practices and in 1799 the Select Society of Auctioneers was formed in England for the
purpose of training them and making the occupation
respectable. This body still exists today but only
in token form.

In 1844, Garraways in London was operating in
a specially designed building, and auctions for

various kinds of goods could be held there by appoint-
ment. Tattersall's was also in London then, and it
was auctioning horses of all kinds. Nowadays it holds
its auctions in Newmarket and specializes in race-
horses.

In 1852, the Hotel Drouot opened in Paris amid
general acclaim, replacing the Hotel Bullion as the
auction centre in Paris. The 'Temple du Bric-a-Brac'
still retains its position and deals in paintings,
furniture, collections and large quantities of junk.
The prices obtained are influenced by the time of day,
and profits have been made by buying at 2 p.m., when
the auctions start and selling at 4 p.m., when more
people attend. Auctions in France follow the same
pattern as elsewhere but the post of auctioneer is
difficult to obtain since it must be bought or inher-
ited, there being a fixed number of them. The auctioneer is known as the comisseur-priseur. The 'Revue
de Paris' of 1934 notes that 'On nait comisseur-
priseur prestigieux comme on nait rotisseur' and that
a sale by a master-auctioneer may realize up to 30%
more than one held by 'un collegue apathique, dis-
trait, a la digestion laborieuse,...' Le crieur is
the assistant of the commisseur-priseur:

> Si l'on compare le jeu aerien des en-
> cheres au coup de raquette du jeu de
> tennis, le crieur apparait comme le

> partenaire qui ramasse les balles phone-
> tiques chiffrees, les renvoie d'un revers,
> leur fait un sort si elles sont bonnes,
> les neglige quand elles sont "out"....

The French utilized the inch of candle method for auctioning real estate. The object is to allow the bidding to be unhurried. The auction is not closed until three candles lit successively after the last bid have gone out. If in that time more bids are made, the auction is not closed until two candles have gone out after the final bid. An alternative timing mechanism has been sought, but none more satisfactory has been found. Anyone may bid during the next eight days after this initial auction, but such a bid must be at least 1/6 higher than the one reached previously.

In 1886, the Auctioneers' and Estate Agents Institute of the United Kingdom was founded and this organized the auctioneers in that country and improved their reputation.

It is possible that auctions predate the reference given by Herodotus, however, it appears unlikely that auctions predate coinage. Even though auctions may have started in other locals than Babylon, Greece, and Rome, it is surprising that the earliest known reference in the Far East is to the sale of the belongings of deceased monks in the seventh century A.D.[5]

---

[5] Yang (1950).

We must place in a separate class of auctions where
goods have to be sold, either by order of law or
through necessity, to the highest bidder at no matter
what price. These are apart from the economic framework since time, or, in the case of government auctions,
justice, are the primary factors and profit is of
secondary importance. Examples of these types are
auctions of the belongings of deceased or bankrupt
persons and the sales of surplus government equipment
which by law have to take place by auction to hinder
collusion and ensure equal chance for all to buy.

CURRENT AUCTIONING AND BIDDING

Cassady offers a useful description of the conditions for efficient auction markets together with
observations on the types of commodities sold and
the structure of the trade in the United States.[6]
He indicates that in the 1960s in the United States
there were between 20,000 and 35,000 auctioneers;
about 1900 wholesale auction houses sold around $3.4
billion and around 1600 retail firms earned over $220
million in commissions. The items sold at auction
are, for the most part, tobacco, livestock, fruits
and vegetables, used cars, furs, fish, used goods,

------

[6]Cassady (1967).

antiques, and real estate.

Possibly of more importance to the United States'
economy than auctions are sealed bids. These are
used to purchase large items such as transformers
and steam turbines and many military contracts for
specific weapons such as ships, planes, tanks, or whole
systems. The sealed bid appears to be called for if
the manufacture of an item is large or valuable; also,
there is one seller or buyer and at most only a few
buyers or sellers. In such an instance the realities
of oligopolistic competition must be taken into account.

Sealed bids for large contracts usually do not
involve middlemen. However, open auctions and double-
auction markets like the New York stock exchange do.
Some indication of the economic importance or power
of the brokers and dealers is given by their fees,
which, as Cassady notes, in London were 10 percent
for pictures, rugs, jewels, etc., in lots more than
£100; 12.5 percent for smaller lots; 12.5 percent on
old coins and medals and 15 percent for books and
magazines.[7] He suggests that these figures are still
higher for New York and Los Angeles. Purebred cattle
at auction may yield 5 percent to the auctioneer.
Comparable figures exist for house brokers, and in

_____

[7]Cassady (1967).

the stock market commissions may range from a fraction
of a percent to 3 or 4 percent depending upon the size
and type of transaction. Cassady provides a valuable
bibliography of modern references on auctions and bidding and Talamanca on more historical information.
Stark and Rothkopf provide a detailed bibliography
on mathematical bidding models.[8]

REFERENCES

Cassady, R. (1967). Auctions and Auctioneering.
  Berkeley, Cal.: University of California.

Corrozet, G. (1550). Antiquex, Histoires et Singularitez de Paris, Ville Capitale du Royaume de France.

Janssen, J. J. (1975). Commodity Prices from the
  Ramasid Period. London: E. J. Brill.

Polanyi, K., C. M. Arensburg, and H. W. Pearson (eds.)
  (1957). Trade and Market in the Early Empires.
  Glencoe, Ill.: The Free Press.

Stark, R. and M. H. Rothkopf (1979). "Competitive
  Bidding: A Comprehensive Bibliography," Operations
  Research, Vol. 27, pp. 364-90.

Talamanca, M. (H. Ozbekhan, trans.) (1954). Contributi
  Allo Studio delle Vendite all'asta nel Mondo Classico,
  Series VIII, Vol. VI, Fascicolo 2, Academia Nasionale
  dei Lincei, Roma, p. 35.

---

[8]Cassady (1967); Talamanca (1954); Stark and Rothkopf
(1979).

Yang, Lien-Sheng (1950). "Buddhist Monasteries and
    Four Money Raising Institutions in Chinese History,"
    Harvard Journal of Asiatic Studies, Vol. 13, pp.
    174-91.

3

AN INTRODUCTION TO THE THEORY OF BIDDING
FOR A SINGLE OBJECT

Richard Engelbrecht-Wiggans

INTRODUCTION

The theory of auctions and bidding is currently receiving much attention.[1] During the past two decades, a variety of results have been derived for models of auctions of a single object. First for models in which different bidders have different values for the object, and each bidder knows his own value,[2] and later for models in which the object has the same uncertain value to each bidder.[3] Recent work provides

---

[1]Stark and Rothkopf (1979); Engelbrecht-Wiggans (1980).

[2]Vickrey (1961, 1962).

a framework for unifying many of these results.[4]
This presentation will provide a unified overview
of the current theory of auctions for a single object.

The theory will be illustrated through two examples amenable to analytic solution. The examples
were not meant to model any particular auction, but
were constructed so that many quantities of interest
could be calculated in closed form. In the first
section, the examples will illuminate the role of
information in auctions and bidding models. Nash
equilibrium strategies are derived for the examples
in the second section.[5] The revenue equivalence of
various mechanisms also is illustrated.[6] Nonequilibrium strategies and the winner's curse are discussed
in terms of one of the examples in the third section.[7]

---

[3]Ortega-Reichert (1968); Rothkopf (1969); Wilson (1977)
Winkler and Brooks (1980).

[4]Milgrom and Weber (1981).

[5]Nash (1950).

[6]Milgrom and Weber (1981); Myerson (1981); Riley and
Samuelson (1979); Vickrey (1961, 1962).

[7]Capen, Clapp and Campbell (1971); Engelbrecht-Wiggans
and Weber (1981).

Finally, a classification scheme for auction models
is presented in the last section; this classification
is used to provide an overview existing results and
to identify areas requiring additional research.

MODEL

One object is to be sold at auction. There are
two or more individuals interested in bidding for the
object; these individuals will be referred to as "bidders" regardless of whether they actually submit a bid.
The object has certain characteristics which determine
its value to each of the bidders. For an oil lease,
these characteristics may include the actual amount of
petroleum reserves under the tract, the location of
the tract, the future market price of the recoverable
hydrocarbons, and the tax laws affecting the winning
bidder for the duration of the lease. For a rare painting, these characteristics may include whether or not
the painting is genuine and how well the painting fits
in the collection of paintings already owned by each
bidder.

In certain special cases, each bidder knows precisely his own value and each of the other bidder's
values for the object (and that everyone knows that
this fact is common knowledge). Such cases result

in relatively uninteresting auctions. Therefore,
we will consider only models in which at least one
bidder is uncertain about either his own value or
at least one of the other bidders' values for the
object. In order to analyze auctions with such uncertainty, we model what each bidder knows about himself and about each of the other bidders. A common
approach is to model the auction as a game with incomplete information.[8] Each bidder obtains a single,
typically imperfect, estimate of his value for the
object. Even if all bidders have the same, but unknown, value for the object, their estimates may be
different due to the fact that they do not have perfect information. Each bidder determines his bid,
and whether or not to bid, based on his estimate.

Assume that the relationship between the object's
characteristics and each bidder's value is commonly
known. Although this assumes a bidder knows how others
evaluate the object, a bidder may still be uncertain
about others' (and his own) values due to any uncertainty in the object's characteristics. Each bidder
has an estimate of the joint probability distribution
of the object's characteristics, each bidder's estimate, and any other uncertain quantities. (Other

---

[8] Ortega-Reichert (1968); Rothkopf (1969); Wilson (1977);
Winkler and Brooks (1980); Harsanyi (1967).

uncertain quantities may include the number of bidders
and the auctioneer's reservation price; often these
could be included as uncertain characteristics of the
object itself.) Consider only the symmetric case in
which all bidders have the same estimate for this
distribution. Finally, assume that all bidders know
all assumptions made in modeling the auction, including this one.

This model includes two, commonly studied, extreme
cases. The first, the case of "preference uncertainty,"
is a model in which each of the n bidders discovers
precisely what the object is worth to him.[9] Each bidder's estimate is always equal to his value for the
object. However, since a bidder may still be uncertain
about other bidders' estimates, he may still also be
uncertain about other bidders' values for the object.
A slight generalization of this case occurs when bidders do not discover their values precisely, but each
bidder's distribution of his value for the object
conditional on his estimate is independent of the estimates obtained by other bidders. To the extent
that each bidder considers his value for a painting
to be independent of other bidders' estimates, such
a model may be used for an art auction.

The following specific example of such a model

_____

[9]Vickrey (1961).

will be considered. Each bidder's estimate (and estimates are assumed to be equal to values) is drawn
uniformly from the interval [0,1] and independently
of all other bidders' estimates; the bidders are assumed to be risk neutral.

In the second case, "quality uncertainty," the
object has the same, unknown value to each bidder.[10]
Each bidder obtains a single estimate of this value.
The estimates are typically imperfect, resulting in
different bidders having possibly different estimates
and submitting possibly different bids. Oil lease
auctions are typically modeled in this fashion. Consider the following specific example: There are n
risk neutral bidders $(n \geq 2)$. Their estimates
$\underline{X} = (X_1, X_2, \ldots, X_n)$ and the object's value Z have
(or, equivalently, are estimated by each of the bid-
ders and by the auctioneer to have) the joint prob-
ability density $f_{\underline{X},Z}(\underline{x},z) = (k-1)/z^{n+k}$ if
$0 \leq x_i \leq z$ for all i and $z \geq 1$ and $f_{\underline{X},Z}(\underline{x},z) = 0$
otherwise (where k is a commonly known integer
greater than 2). This joint density may be interpreted
as follows. The true value Z has a density function
$(k-1)/z^k$ for $z \geq 1$ (and zero otherwise). The estimate X_i is the true value z multiplied by an error

---

[10]Rothkopf (1969); Wilson (1977); Winkler and Brooks
(1980).

$W_i = X_i/z$ which is uniformly distributed on $[0,1]$;
the errors W_1, W_2, W_3, ..., W_n are independent (and
their distribution is independent of z). Thus, this
is a specific example of an "independent-error" model.

In the two examples, the bidders' estimates are
viewed as functions of the object's characteristics.
In the preference uncertainty case, the characteristics
result in different bidders typically having different
values. In the quality uncertainty case, the characteristics determine the common, unknown, value of the
object to all bidders. This is an intuitive, and the
historical, approach to modeling auctions.

However, for strategic purposes, the only aspects
of concern are those which are known before bids are
submitted. In particular, bids are functions only
of the estimates revealed to bidders (and, of course,
of any common knowledge). Thus, one should be able
to model an auction without considering the object's
characteristics explicitly. Indeed, it is the preoccupation with describing the object's value in terms
of underlying characteristics which makes quality and
preference uncertainty models appear so different.
In fact, from the proper perspective, the quality
uncertainty example is very nearly also an example
of preference uncertainty; this perspective is the
key to the general model considered next.

A recent approach in modeling auctions is to
describe the uncertain aspects of the auction by a
joint probability distribution of the bidders' estimates.[11] Each bidder's expected value (or, more
generally, expected utility) for the object is specified as a function of all the bidder's estimates.
This approach captures preference and quality uncertainty as special cases. For example, the most general form of preference uncertainty occurs when each
bidder's expected utility for the object conditional
on this estimate is independent of all other bidders'
estimates. (Indeed this independence happens to be
the single characteristic which distinguishes preference
uncertainty auctions from other auctions; to better
reflect this, we will hereafter refer to such auctions
as "independent-estimate auctions.") With such independence, there is no strategy-related difference between a bidder knowing precisely his value for the
object as a function of his estimate and knowing his
expected utility as a function of his estimate (the
latter being the case in our example of preference
uncertainty). In models of quality uncertainty (and
more generally, in many symmetric models with dependent estimates), each bidder's expected utility is
a symmetric function of all bidders' estimates. In

---

[11]Milgrom and Weber (1981).

our example of quality uncertainty, the expected value
of the object to each (risk neutral) bidder is
$(n+k-1)/(n+k-2)$ times the maximum of $\{1, x_1, x_2,$
$x_3, \ldots, x_n\}$.

Each auction is conducted according to some rules
or mechanism. There are three major aspects of an
auction mechanism. The bidding format specifies how
bids are transmitted to an auctioneer. An allocation
rule determines, as a function of the bids, to whom
the object is awarded. Finally, a price function specifies how much each bidder, possibly including those
who have not won the object must pay as a function of
the bids and to whom the object was awarded. The
precise details of the mechanism used in any auction
are assumed to be known to all bidders.

A variety of auction mechanisms are possible.
In first-price sealed-bid auctions, the object is
awarded to the highest bidder at a price equal to the
amount of the highest bid; non-winning bidders pay
nothing. Federal offshore oil leases are typically
sold by means of first-price sealed-bid auctions. A
variation is the second-price sealed-bid auction which
is similar except the price is equal to the second
highest bid.[12] In either version, the auctioneer
may have a reservation price; in many cases it is

---

[12] Vickrey (1961).

appropriate to treat this reservation price as if it
were a bid submitted by the auctioneer.

Art works are often sold via ascending oral auctions in which the auctioneer raises the asking price
until there remains only one bidder willing to pay
that price. An extreme example of an ascending oral auction
occurs when the asking price starts at the auctioneer's
reservation price and is slowly (continuously) raised,
each bidder is required to publically announce when the
asking price is equal to the maximum he is willing to
pay, and the object is sold to the last remaining bidder at a price equal to the lowest asking price such
that the winner was the sold remaining bidder (and
non-winners pay nothing).[13]   This mechanism differs
strategically from the second-price sealed-bid mechanism
in that the level at which bidders drop out may cause
the remaining bidders to revise their estimates of the
object's value. However, if each bidder's expected
utility for the object is independent of the other
bidder's estimates, then the two mechanisms are strategically equivalent.

Flowers for export from Holland have been sold
via a descending oral auction. The asking price starts
high and is continuously lowered until someone agrees

---

[13]Milgrom and Weber (1981).

to pay the current asking price; the object is sold
to that buyer at that price. This mechanism is strategically equivalent to the first-price sealed-bid
mechanism.

Non-winning bidders may also incur costs. All
bidders might be required to pay entry fees (the cost
of a catalog at an art auction) or the costs of preparing a bid (the cost of assembling seismic data on
an offshore oil lease), which are incurred by all
bidders whether or not they eventually submit a bid.
Other costs are incurred by all bidders actually submitting bids (the cost of a courier delivering the
bid in an offshore oil lease sale). The magnitude
of such costs, relative to the amounts of the bids,
depends on the situation. Entry fees, bid preparation
costs, and bid submission costs are often independent
of the amounts to be bid.

Non-winner's costs may depend on their bids.
Certain models of animal conflict may be viewed as
ascending oral auctions.[14] Each individual continues
to expend resources (such as time and energy) until
it decides to drop out. The last individual to stay
in wins the object (a nesting territory or a war, for
example). However, if the level at which an individual
has paid the amount of its bid (except the winner,

---

[14]Riley and Hirshleifer (1978).

which must only pay an amount equal to the second highest bid).

Multistage mechanisms are also possible. The winner of the first of two stages may obtain the right of first refusal to any offers resulting from the second stage. Paperback book rights have been sold at two-stage auctions.

Sometimes, for example in the case of defense contracts, the object is awarded to the lowest bidder. However, if one adopts the convention that the price represents the amount paid by the winner to the auctioneer, then all bids on a contract would typically be negative. In such cases, awarding the object to the bidder whose bid has the smallest absolute value corresponds to awarding the object to the highest bidder. Thus, high-bid-wins auctions include many cases of what would commonly be thought of as low-bid-wins auctions.

(Unless otherwise stated, we shall assume that the auctioneer has a reservation price of zero, and this fact is known to all bidders. The object, if sold, is always awarded to a highest bidder, but the object will not be sold if the auctioneer's reservation price exceeds each of the other bids. Only the winning bidder makes any payments.)

Having formed an estimate of the object's value

to himself, a bidder must only decide whether to bid,
and, if he decides to bid, how much he should bid. A
bidder is not explicitly concerned with how much he
would have bid had he obtained a different estimate.
However, consider auctions in which each bidder's
expected utility for the object is dependent not only
on his own estimate, but also on other bidders' estimates. As long as a bidder has some idea of how competitors translate their estimates into bids, the mere
fact that a bidder is awarded the object reveals additional information to the winner about his expected
utility for the object; each bidder knows he will win
the object only if all competitors receive estimates
which result in their bids being less than his own.
In such auctions, a bidder is therefore concerned with
how each competitor would bid in any particular situation.

A model of such an auction must describe what
each bidder knows about how others would bid in any
situation. The common approach is to deal in terms
of bidding strategies; a bidder's strategy specifies
how he will bid as a function of each possible estimate. Each bidder is assumed to know precisely each
of the other bidder's strategy. Of course, each bidder
knows his own bidding strategy. Thus, it is common
to talk of a bidder choosing a strategy (which he can
choose before observing his estimate just as well as

after) even though in practical situations each bidder must only choose a bid based for the case of the
estimate actually obtained. It is traditional to talk
of bidders' strategies even in those cases where each
bidder's optimal bid does not depend on the bidders'
bids; when such "dominant" strategies exist, it may
be unnecessary to consider strategies.

While a bidder rarely knows precisely what strategies competitors have chosen, the assumption that he
does is more plausible for symmetric models in which
all bidders might be assumed to use the same (or, at
least, very similar) strategies. Consider the follow-
ing general symmetric model: Let $\underset{\rightarrow}{x}_{-i}$ denote the
vector $(x_1, x_2, \ldots, x_{i-1}, x_{i+1}, \ldots, x_n)$. Then let
$u_i(x_i, \underset{\rightarrow}{x}_{-i})$ be the expected utility to bidder i as
a function of all the bidders' estimates. The general
symmetric model is obtained by assuming first that each
bidder's expected utility is a symmetric function of
his competitors' estimates.[15] That is, $u_i(x_i, \underset{\rightarrow}{x}_{-i})$
$= u_i(x_i, \underset{\rightarrow}{x}^*_{-i})$ where $\underset{\rightarrow}{x}^*_{-i}$ is any vector obtained by
permuting the components of x_{-i} . In addition, as-
sume each bidder has the same expected utility function
with respect to his own estimate and competitors'
estimates in the sense that $u_i(x_i, \underset{\rightarrow}{x}_{-i}) = u_j(y_j, \underset{\rightarrow}{y}_{-j})$

---

[15]Milgrom and Weber (1981); von Neumann and Morgenstern
(1953).

whenever $y_j = x_i$ and $\underset{\rightarrow-j}{y} = \underset{\rightarrow-i}{x}$. Both of our examples have this general form of symmetry. It is
therefore natural to consider the case in which all
bidders adopt the same bidding strategy. However,
if each bidder assumes that all other bidders are
similar to himself and therefore likely to make an
analysis similar to his own in adopting a bidding
strategy, he may also assume that each other bidder
is likely to adopt a strategy similar (if not identical)
to his own. In such cases, a bidder, knowing his own
strategy, at least can make a good estimate of each
other bidder's strategy. (For general symmetric models,
we only consider those cases in which all bidders use
the same strategy.)

   In our examples, each bidder's expected value
for the object is a nondecreasing function of his and
his competitors estimates. It is therefore not surprising that all optimal strategies subsequently derived for these examples are nondecreasing in the
bidder's estimate. If all bidders use the same nondecreasing strategy and the object is always awarded
to a highest bidder, then the winner will always be
(except, possibly, in the case of tied high bids) the
bidder with the highest estimate. If, furthermore,
only the winner makes any payments, each bidder is
interested only in his expected value conditional on

winning; that is, conditional on having the highest
estimate. Note that in our example of quality uncertainty, the expected value of the object to the bidder
conditional on the bidder having the highest estimate
is independent of the other bidders' estimates. Thus,
if all bidders use the same nondecreasing strategy,
the object is always awarded to the highest bidder;
if only the winner makes any payments, our example of
quality uncertainty is essentially also one with independent estimates. (The only differences between the
example and independent-estimate auctions are from the
perspective of nonwinning bidders, and they are of no
strategic consequence when nonwinners neither win the
object nor make any payments.) This example will under-
score the importance of distinguishing between independent versus dependent estimate models rather than
between preference and quality uncertainty.

Bidders may have complete freedom in choosing
their bidding strategy. One common assumption is that
each bidder, knowing the strategy chosen by each of
the other bidders, chooses a strategy which maximizes
his expected utility. Such a strategy is called a
best response to the competitors' strategies. A set
of strategies, one for each bidder, is called a "Nash
equilibrium" if each bidder's strategy is a best response to the competitors' strategies.[16] A Nash

---

[16]Nash (1950).

equilibrium is symmetric if, at the Nash equilibrium,
each bidder uses the same strategy. (In appropriately
symmetric models, we will only consider symmetric
Nash equilibria even though the model may also have
asymmetric Nash equilibria.) There are also less
frequently considered, alternate assumptions on how
bidders choose their strategies.[17] These will not
be explored in this presentation.

In certain cases, bidders may be restricted in
the strategies from which they can choose. For example,
a number of authors assume, without any equilibrium
analysis as justification, that each bidder choose a
multiplicative strategy. (A strategy is multiplicative if it has a bidder bidding the same multiple of
his estimate regardless of what estimate the bidder
has of the object's value.) Models restricting attention of bidders to "optimal percentage markup policies"
for bidding on contracts or "optimal bid fraction"
of estimated value for oil leases are examples. In
such cases, one might define a restricted Nash equilibrium (in the above case, a multiplicative Nash
equilibrium) as a set of strategies satisfying the
restriction, such that each bidder's strategy is a
best response (among strategies satisfying the restriction) to the other bidder's strategies. Such restricted

---

[17] Smith and Case (1975); Wilson (1967).

equilibria strategies would not necessarily be (and indeed, are often not) in equilibrium if bidders' strategies were unrestricted.[18]

Finally, one might consider what would happen if each bidder simply makes a bid on the basis of an unbiased estimate of the object's value to him. If there is a particular multiple of a bidder's estimate resulting in an unbiased estimate of the object's value, this is a particular case of multiplicative strategies (though, such strategies are typically not even multiplicative equilibrium strategies). In symmetric models with imperfect estimates (and a technical assumption on the positive associativeness of estimates),[19] each bidder bidding an unbiased estimate leads to the phenomenon known as the "winner's curve."[20] The winner is the bidder who overestimated the object's value the most and thus on average pays more than the object is worth.

In the following sections, some of the main results of auction theory are illustrated using the two specific examples presented above. Thus, the discussion will be in terms of models with only one object

---

[18]Engelbrecht-Wiggans (1978).

[19]Milgrom and Weber (1981).

[20]Capen, Clapp, and Campbell (1971).

for sale and in which all bidders are risk neutral. Discussions of auctions of more than one object[21] and the effects of risk aversion in auction theory[22] appear elsewhere in this volume. In the examples, each bidder obtains only a single estimate; bidders each obtaining more than one estimate substantially complicates the analysis in that an appropriate single sufficient statistic of the estimates is often diffi- cult to discover (the statistic sufficient for the object's value is in general not sufficient for the purpose of the bidder.[23] Bidding strategies of more than one variable have received very little attention.[24] There are also only relatively few results for auction models with only asymmetric equilibria.[25] The number of bidders is assumed to be fixed; the effects of the number of bidders on the auctioneer's expected revenue has, however been investigated.[26]

---

[21] Weber (1981).

[22] Maskin and Riley (1981)

[23] Engelbrecht-Wiggans and Weber (1980).

[24] Samuelson (1981); Stark (1974).

[25] Engelbrecht-Wiggans, Milgrom, and Weber (1981); Ortega-Reichert (1968); Wilson (1969).

[26] Griesmer, Levitan, and Shubik (1967); Matthews (1979); Milgrom (1977); Wilson (1977).

EQUILIBRIA

Sometimes, a Nash equilibrium may be discovered by inspection. In particular, in a second-price sealed-bid auction with the object (if awarded at all) going to a high bidder and only the winner making any payments, it may be verified that in many cases a Nash equilibrium results if each bidder i bids $v_i(x_i, x_i)$ where $v_i(x,y)$ denotes the expected value to bidder i as a function of his own estimate x and of the maximum estimate y obtained by any of the other bidders.[27] If $v_i(x,y)$ is only a function of x, then this strategy is also a dominant strategy.

For example, in the independent estimate example $v_i(x_i, y) = x_i$ consider the strategy in which a bidder simply bids his estimate. That that is indeed a dominant strategy depends heavily on the fact that in second-price auctions, a bidder can affect only whether or not he wins (but not the price when he wins) through his bid. If a bidder were to bid more than his estimate, he runs a chance of winning the object at a price greater than his value for the object. If he bids less than his estimate, he runs a change of not winning the object in a situation where the price was strictly less than his value. In either case, changing

---

[27]Milgrom (1978a, 1979).

the bid affects only whether or not the bidder wins,
but the change does not alter the price. Thus, bidding one's estimate is a dominant strategy and each
bidder using his dominant strategy results in a Nash
equilibrium.

In the example of quality uncertainty,
$v_i(x_i, x_i) = \text{Max}(1, x_i)(n+k-1)/(n+k-2)$. This quantity may be interpreted as the expected value conditional on just barely winning. With this interpretation, an argument like the one used above indicates
why each bidder i bidding $v_i(x_i, x_i)$ might result
in a Nash equilibrium. (That this results in an equilibrium in the example may also be formally verified
quite easily.)

In many cases, the following systematic approach
is useful in deriving Nash equilibria.[28] Consider
only those strategies which satisfy a relatively restrictive necessary condition for a Nash equilibrium.
In particular, consider the expected profit to a bidder i who bids B when $X_i = x$ and assumes that
each of the other bidders j bid $b_j(X_j)$. A necessary condition for a Nash equilibrium is that the
derivative (with respect to B) of this expected
value at $B = b_i(x)$ is zero. Applying this condition
to each bidder results in a system of (possibly

---

[28]Milgrom and Weber (1981); Wilson (1969); Wilson (1977).

differential) equations for the bidding strategies
b_1, b_2, ..., b_n . Any solutions of this system may
be examined to determine if they result in a Nash
equilibrium. If only symmetric equilibria are sought
in a general symmetric model, then the above system
of equations reduces to a single equation in terms
of the jointly used bidding strategy; each bidder
using this strategy is a candidate for a Nash equilibrium.

The approach just described will be used to derive Nash equilibria in the two examples for the first-
price, sealed-bid mechanism. In first-price, sealed-
bid auctions which award the object (if awarded at
all) to a highest bidder the expected profit

$$E[\$_i \,|\, X_i = x, \text{ i bids B, j bids } b(X_j) \forall j = i]$$

$$= \int_{y:b(y) \leq B} (v_i(x,y) - B) f(y\,|\,x) \, dy$$

where $f(y\,|\,x)$ denotes the density function of the
maximum estimate obtained by bidder i's competitors
conditional on $X_i = x$; $F(y\,|\,x)$ will denote the
corresponding cumulative distribution function. (In
the example of independent estimates, $f(x,y)$
$= (n-1)y^{n-2}$ for $0 \leq y \leq 1$ and zero otherwise;
whereas, in the example of quality uncertainty,

$$b(x) = \int_{w=-\infty}^{w=x} v(w,w)\, \delta(w)\, dw / F(x)$$

where

$$F(x) = \int_{w=-\infty}^{w=x} \delta(w)\, dw$$

This particular solution also satisfies the boundary condition, appropriate in our examples where the auctioneer has a reservation price of zero, that the expected profit to a bidder (at the equilibrium resulting from each bidder using this strategy) is positive if and only if the bidder submits a positive bid. For the independent estimates example, $b(x) = x(n-1)/n$; it may be verified directly that this strategy indeed results in a Nash equilibrium if the strategy is used by each bidder.

In the quality uncertainty example, the necessary condition simplifies to the following differential equation: $(n+k-1)/(n+k-2) = b(x)/x + b'(x)/n$. It may be verified that the solution $b(x) = (n+k-1)[1 + (n-1)x^n]/[n(n+k-2)x^{n-1}]$ for $x \geq 1$ and $(n+k-1)/[n(n+k-2)]$ otherwise results in a Nash equilibrium. Notice if all bidders obtain less than one, there will be tied high bids. If the bidders use the Nash equilibrium strategies in such cases,

each bidder expects zero profit and it, therefore,
does not matter how such ties are resolved.

Recall that descending oral auctions are in general strategically equivalent to first-price auctions.
Also note that since in both examples (and with independent estimates in general), the expected value of
the object to the winner conditional on winning is
independent of the other bidders' particular (lower)
estimates, the second-price auction is strategically
equivalent to the ascending oral auction. Thus, the
equilibria derived for the examples under first- and
second-price sealed-bid mechanisms are illustrative
of a number of other mechanisms as well.

Having derived sample equilibria, the natural
next question is what are the expected profit to a
bidder and expected revenue to the auctioneer when
bidders bid according to a Nash equilibrium. Under
a first-price mechanism, the expected profit to a
bidder is the expected difference between his value
for the object and the amount he bid when he wins
the object; the expected revenue to the auctioneer is
the expected amount of the highest bid. In the example
of independent estimates, the a priori expected profit to a bidder (that is, before he obtains his estimate of the object's value) is $1/n$ or $(1 - (n-1)/n)$
times the expected value of the maximum of the bidders'

estimates; the 1/n arises from the fact that all
bidders, on average, have an equal chance at winning,
while the factor $(1 - (n-1)/n)$ corresponds to the
amount by which the winner scaled down his estimate
to obtain his bid. Since the expected value of the
maximum of n independent random variables each is
distributed uniformly on the interval [0,1] is
$n/(n+1)$, each bidder's a priori expected profit is
$1/[n(n+1)]$.

At the first-price, sealed-bid Nash equilibrium
for the quality uncertainty example, the expected
profit to a bidder with an estimate x is zero if
$x \leq 1$ and $[k(x^n - 1)]/[n(n+k-2)x^{n-1}]$ if $x \geq 1$.
The a priori expected profit to each bidder is
$[(k-1)k]/[(n+k-2)^2(k-2)]$. The expected revenue to
the auctioneer is the expected amount of the common
value of the object to all bidders less than total
bidders' expected profits: $(k-1)/(k-2)$
$- n[(k-1)k]/[(n+k-2)^2(k-2)]$. The expected revenue
to the auctioneer is the expected amount of common
value of the object to all bidders less than total of
all of the bidders' a priori expected profits:
$(k-1)/(k-2) - n[(k-1)k]/[(n+k-2)^2(k-2)]$.

At the dominant-strategy, second-price Nash equilibrium in independent estimate auctions, the expected
profit to each bidder is 1/n of the expected differ-

ence between the highest and second-highest bids
(which are equal to the highest and second-highest
estimates); the expected revenue to the auctioneer
is the expected amount of the second-highest bid
(that is, the second-highest estimate). In the independent-estimates example, the a priori expected
profit to each bidder and the auctioneer's expected
revenue are the same at the second-price equilibrium
under the second-price mechanism as at the first-price
equilibrium under the first-price mechanism. This
expected revenue and profit equivalence also holds
for the strategically equivalent ascending and descending oral auctions. In the quality uncertainty
example, the expected profit to each bidder conditional
on his estimate, the a priori expected profit to each
bidder and the expected revenue to the auctioneer are
the same under equilibrium bidding in the second-price
mechanism as under equilibrium bidding in the first-
price mechanism.

This equivalence of expected revenue and profit
at equilibrium under a variety of mechanisms illustrates a quite general revenue equivalence theorem.[29]
Consider independent-estimates auctions in which the
auctioneer does not subsidize the bidders. That is,

---

[29]Vickrey (1961, 1962); Myerson (1981); Riley and
Samuelson (1979).

assume that a bidder who obtains the least favorable
possible estimate of the object's value to himself expects zero profit at equilibrium. Assume also that
the bidders are risk neutral. Then, the expected revenue to the auctioneer is a function only of the
probability (as a function of each bidder's estimate)
that each bidder is awarded the object. If one only
considers mechanisms in which the object is always
awarded to the highest bidder, then at no symmetric
Nash equilibrium of the independent-estimates example
is the auctioneer's expected revenue greater than under
the first or second-price sealed-bid mechanism. This
is true even for a multistage mechanism or for one
which requires entry fees or other payments by nonwinning bidders.

The probability of each bidder winning the object
is affected by the probability that the auctioneer
does not award the object to any of the bidders. The
auctioneer can affect his expected revenue through
his choice of a reservation price; the larger the
reservation price, the higher the probability the
object is not awarded.[30] For strictly positive reservation prices, the chance a bidder faces of not winning
the object because his bid is less than the reservation price (even though he may be the highest bidder)

---

[30]Myerson (1981).

results in more aggressive bidding at equilibrium in
first-price auctions than for a zero-reservation price.
(Treating the reservation price as a publically known
bid by the auctioneer reveals that the expected price
of the object in a second-price auction also increases
with the reservation price when all bidders use their
dominant strategies; sometimes, however, the object is
"sold" to the auctioneer.) Clearly the more aggressive bidding (or higher expected price when the object
is awarded to the bidder) is of no benefit to the auctioneer if the reservation price is so great that the
auctioneer never awards the object to a bidder. There
is, however, in general, some strictly positive reservation price which maximizes the expected revenue.
For independent-estimate auctions with risk neutral
bidders, an appropriate reservation price in a first-
or second-price auction results in an expected revenue
at least as large (at equilibrium) as that possible
under any other mechanism which never subsidizes bidders. Other mechanisms, including an appropriate use
of entry fees in first- or second-price auctions,
also result in the maximum possible expected revenue.[31]
(If bidders are risk averse, the simultaneous use of
both an appropriate reservation price and entry fee
results in a greater expected revenue than could be

---

[31]Riley and Samuelson (1979).

gained by imposing either an entry fee or reservation
price.[32]

The revenue equivalence is, in general, not true
for auctions other than those with independent estimates. If each bidder's estimate is statistically
dependent on other bidders' estimates, then there in
general exist mechanisms resulting in arbitrarily
small expected profits to each bidder.[33] In particular, consider a mechanism which requires a form of
bet so that a bidder expects to loose an arbitrarily
large amount unless he bets precisely the expected
value of the winning bid conditional on his own estimate. However, such a bet in general reveals the
bidder's estimate to the auctioneer, who in turn can
use this information about bidders' estimates (and
therefore values) to award the object to the bidder
with the highest value at the price arbitrarily close
to the winner's value for the object. Such mechanisms
are possible in quality uncertainty auctions when one
can use mechanisms which may require payments to or
from nonwinners.

In the example of quality uncertainty, a bidder's
estimate conditional on all competitors' estimates
being less than or equal to any number itself less than

---

[32]Maskin and Riley (1981).

[33]Myerson (1981).

or equal to his own estimate is independent of the
other bidders' estimates. Because of this special
property, the revenue equivalence of different mechanisms in independent estimate auctions extends to
this example if the auctioneer is restricted to mechanisms requiring only payments to or from the winner.
However, this particular form of independence is quite
unusual outside of true independent-estimates models.

Attention thus far has been focused on equivalence
results for a large class of mechanisms applied to a
very restrictive type of auction. Although the results
hold for all independent-estimates auctions, independence of estimates is in itself a very restrictive
assumption. The assumption is not satisfied if the
bids of others on an oil lease reveal even the slightest amount of additional information to a bidder about
the resale value of the lease or if the bids of others
on a painting reveal even the slightest amount of additional information to a bidder about its authenticity.

Comparisons can be made between the expected revenue at equilibrium for a few specific mechanisms
applied to a broad class of auctions. Consider general symmetric auctions and assume that the object is
always awarded to the highest bidder (that is, there
is a reservation price of zero and no entry fees) and
the only payments made are by the winner. (In addition, certain technical assumptions are necessary.)

With risk-neutral bidders, the expected revenue at equilibrium in a first-price auction is at least as great as at equilibrium in a second-price auction.[34] This relationship need not hold for risk-averse bidders; in a first-price auction, the more risk averse a bidder, the higher (and closer to the corresponding second-price equilibrium bid) he will bid in order to reduce the risk of not winning the object at all.[35] With constantly risk-averse bidders (which includes risk-neutral bidders as a special case), the expected revenue in specific ascending oral auctions is at least as great as in second-price auctions.[36]

In symmetric auctions, theorems on revenue equivalence have implications for bidders' expected profits. In particular, before observing his estimate, each bidder in a symmetric auction has the same expected profit at equilibrium as any other bidder. The total amount of all bidder's expected profits is the expected value of the object (to the bidder who values it most highly) less the expected revenue obtained by the auctioneer. Thus, if the expected revenue to the auctioneer can be compared for two mechanisms applied to a symmetric auction, then the inverse

---

[34] Milgrom and Weber (1981).

[35] Riley and Samuelson (1979).

[36] Milgrom and Weber (1981).

relationship holds for bidders' a priori expected
profits.

Very little is known about equilibria for asymmetric models. However, some results have been obtained for the following extreme case of an asymmetric
auction. Assume that all the information known by
some "poorly" informed bidder is also known to some
"well" informed bidder and that all bidders have the
same (unknown) value for the object. (For example,
the poorly informed bidder's estimate is distributed
independently of the true value while the well-informed
bidder's estimate might be correlated to the true
value.) In certain cases, it is possible to derive
equilibrium strategies. In general, the poorly informed bidder has an expected profit of zero at equilibrium.[37]

DISEQUILIBRIA

Bidders often use strategies which, in our simplified models, are not in equilibrium. A bidder's imperfect understanding of the relationship between his
estimate for the object's value and an optimal bid
would likely result in suboptimal bidding. Several
possible nonequilibrium strategies will be examined

---

[37] Engelbrecht-Wiggans, Milgrom and Weber (1981).

in order to obtain insights into at least the qualitative relationship between estimates and optimal
bids and how these relationships depend on the type
of auction model and mechanism. While we will speak
as if bidders were actually, or considering, using
such nonequilibrium strategies, this is not meant to
imply that such strategies have ever actually been
used or seriously considered. Rather, they will serve
to illustrate certain aspects of strategies which
would result in suboptimal bidding.

In second-price, independent-estimate auctions,
the dominant strategy equilibrium is for each bidder
to bid his expected value for the object. In first-
price, independent-values auctions, each bidder bidding
his expected value for the object is not in equilibrium. However, bidding one's expected value in the
first-price, independent-estimates auction is a "safe"
strategy in the sense that, on average, one will do
no worse than if one had not bid at all. (Indeed,
this strategy would, on average, result in zero profits; to make a positive expected profit, one could
simply bid slightly less than one's estimate of the
object's expected value.) These properties of bidding
one's expected value are a direct consequence of the
independence of bidder's estimates.

A bidder who bids his expected value for the object (or even just slightly less) in a first-price

auction with dependent estimates may, on the average,
do considerably worse than if he had not bid; a bidder tends to win (that is, be the highest bidder) in
only those cases when he overestimated the object's
value.[38]   To illustrate this "winner's curse" phenomenon, consider a particular class of first-price quality-
uncertainty auction. Nature chooses the (unknown)
true value of the object according to a known probability distribution. Independently for each bidder,
nature then chooses an unknown "error" for each bidder,
all errors have the same known distribution. Each
bidder is then told an estimate for the object's true
value; the estimate revealed to a bidder is the product of the unknown true value and his unknown error.
(Such multiplicative-error models have received considerable attention in the literature relating to offshore oil lease auctions.[39]

Assume that each bidder bids his expected value
for the object in such a first-price multiplicative-
error auction. Each bid is then an unbiased estimate
of the unknown true value. The object is, however,
awarded to the highest bidder. The highest bid will
on average be for more than the value of the object
because the maximum of several unbiased estimates is

---

[38]Capen, Clapp, and Campbell (1971).

[39]Rothkopf (1969); Reese (1978); Teisberg (1978).

always biased toward the high side. In particular,
the fact that a bidder is told he won the object in-
forms him that all other bidders had lower estimates
for the object's value than he did. This suggests
that he won the object because this just happened to
be one of those cases in which his expected value
of the object was higher than the true value. Although,
on average, each bidder's bid is equal to the expected
value, he tends to win in those cases when he bids
above the true value and does not recoop his losses
when his bid is less than the true value because someone else is likely to be the winning bidder.

The source of the winner's curse is revealed
when one examines a bidder's expected value for the
object as a function of not only his own estimate,
but also of all other bidder's estimates (which, of
course, are not known to him at the time of bidding).
In multiplicative-error auctions bidders' estimates
and expected values are positively associated; each
bidder's expected value for the object is an increasing function separately of each bidder's
estimate.[40] (Many symmetric nonindependent-
estimates auctions have this property of positively
association.) When preparing his bid, a bidder does
not know what estimates other bidders obtained and
must therefore average his expected value as a function
of others' estimates over all possible estimates the

---

[40]Milgrom and Weber (1981).

other bidders might obtain. When a bidder discovers
he was the high bidder, he must now average his expected value for the object over only those estimates
of other bidders which would result in his being the
high bidder; these are (assuming each bidder is nondecreasing function of his estimate) the lower possible
estimates and thus result in a lower expected value
for the object. Thus, in models with positive association, the "good" news that one has won the auction
is "bad" news with regard to one's revised expected
value for the object with respect to one's prior expected value.[41] It is this "good" news being "bad"
news which is the winner's curse, and in the case
where each bidder bids his expected value for the object results in the winner losing money on average.

    There are examples of auctions in which one or
all bidders are immune from the winner's curse. Of
course, in independent-estimates models, each bidder's
expected value is (by definition) independent of others
estimates and thus there is no curse to winning. In
an asymmetric two-bidder, additive-errors model (similar to multiplicative errors, except the obvious modification) in which one bidder's error is always very
close to twice as large as the others, the bidder with
the lower variance error has the higher expected value

---

[41]Milgrom (1978b).

for the object only when his expected value is less than his opponents; the bidder with the lower variance error actually benefits from the other bidder being affected by the winner's curse.[42] (In this case, the lower error variance bidder's expected value for the object as a function of both bidder's estimates is very nearly his own estimate less an amount equal to the other bidder's estimate minus his own estimate; this simplifies to twice his own estimate minus one the other bidder's estimate. This is a decreasing function of the other bidder's estimate and, therefore, the positive association property does not hold.) There are also symmetric examples in which there is no winner's curse (or even the opposite) due to the lack of positive association. (For example, an auction in which the bidders obtain independent identically distributed estimates and where each bidder's actual value for the object is equal to his own estimate minus the maximum of the other bidders' estimates.)

The magnitude of the winner's curse can be quite substantial. Consider what happens is each bidder bids his expected value for the object in our quality-undertainty example. In particular, a bidder with an estimate of x would bid $(k/(k-1))\max(1,x)$ and have an expected profit of $-(n-1)/(n(k-2)(n+k-1))$. The

---

[42]Winkler and Brooks (1980).

expected profit is always negative and decreases as
the number of bidders increases. For large numbers
of bidders, the combined expected loss of all bidders
approaches $1/(k-1)$ of the average true value of the
object.

In any practical situation, bidders may be presumed to compensate for the winner's curse in preparing their bids. The optimal bid may be quite small
when compared with a bidder's expected value for the
object simply due to the effect of the winner's curse.
In our quality-uncertainty example, all bidders make
a zero profit on average if each bidder bids
$((n-k-1)/(n-k-2))\max(1,x)$. In particular, in the
limit of many bidders, each bidder bidding $(k-1)/k$
on his respective expected value for the object results
in zero expected profit to each. Thus, if k is
equal to 2, each bidder bidding one-half his expected
profit; in an actual auction, one might expect bidders
to bid an even smaller fraction so that they may have
a strictly positive expected profit. (Oil companies
are rumored to bid between 30 and 60 percent of their
expected values for offshore oil leases.)

Each bidder bidding his expected value for the
object does not result in Nash equilibrium. Any bidder
would do better by not bidding at all and thereby
never losing (and never winning) money. It was observe

above that if each bidder bids an appropriate fraction
of max(1,x) , then nonnegative expected profits are
possible. This suggests there might be an "optimal
bid fraction" or "optimal markdown" of max(1,x) .
In particular, for the moment, assume that each bidder
i is restricted to choosing a constant B_i before
obtaining his estimate, and then must bid $B_i$max$(1, x_i)$,
where x_i is the estimate he eventually obtains;
bidders are restricted to multiplicative strategies.

A set of multiplicative strategies, one for each
bidder, is defined to be optimal if the strategies
form a Nash equilibrium when each bidder is restricted
to only using multiplicative strategies. The multiplicative-strategy Nash equilibrium is symmetric if each
bidder uses the same B_i . Such symmetric multiplicative-
strategy Nash equilibria exist for many examples.[43]
In particular, they have been derived for a class of
offshore oil lease models.[44] (There is no symmetric
multiplicative-strategy Nash equilibrium for our quality uncertainty example. This follows from the positive probability of tied high bids due to the possibility that all bidders obtain estimates less than
one. Thus, any candidate for such a strategy must
result in zero expected profit conditional on all

[43]Milgrom (1979); Rothkopf (1969); Teisberg (1978).

[44]Engelbrecht-Wiggans (1978).

bidders having estimates less than one. This is satisfied only by the Nash equilibrium strategy for the
second-price mechanism. However, using the second-
price strategy in the first-price auction results in
zero expected profit, and may be improved upon by any
one bidder who uses a slightly smaller fraction. Thus,
the only candidate after considering the effect of
tied bids does not result in a symmetric multiplicative-
strategy Nash equilibrium.)

Multiplicative-strategy Nash equilibria are rarely
in equilibrium if bidders are not restricted to multiplicative strategies. (Indeed, multiplicative-
strategy equilibria retain their equilibrium property
for unrestricted strategies only in very special cases,
including those in which a bidder has absolutely no
other information about the value of the object other
than the information conveyed through his single estimate of the object's value.[45] The multiplicative
strategies are, in certain cases, quite far from being
in equilibrium if strategies are not restricted to
being multiplicative. In a multiplicative error example based on offshore oil leasing data, a bidder
may improve his expected profits by 20 percent (approximately a one-half million dollar improvement) on each
lease if he may use any strategy while all the other
bidders are using multiplicative-strategy Nash equilibr

---

[45]Rothkopf (1980).

strategies.[46] However, despite the fact that they
are not optimum, multiplicative-strategy Nash equilibria have received considerable attention in the
optimal bidding literature.

OVERVIEW

Nash equilibria have been derived and studied
for a variety of auction models. In order to summarize the results for auctions of a single object with
risk-neutral bidders, and to identify those models
requiring additional work, we classify auction models
on the following two characteristics: bidders' evaluation of the objects and the relationship among different bidders' information about their values.[47]
Bidders' values are typically modeled in one of the
following three ways:

>   Private Values: Each bidder's value is indepen-
>   dent of each other bidder's value for the ob-
>   ject. This is related to the previously dis-
>   cussed preference uncertainty.
>   Common Values: All bidders have the same (typic-
>   ally uncertain) value for the object. This

----

[46]Engelbrecht-Wiggans (1978).

[47]This classification was suggested to me by Robert
J. Weber.

is the previously discussed case of quality
uncertainty.

General Symmetric Values: The joint distribution
of bidders' values is symmetric with respect
to bidders. This is the context within which
most of the results presented in this paper
were discussed and includes private values and
common value as special cases.

The information available to (or "signals" of) the bidders are typically assumed to be related in one of the
following three ways:

Independent Symmetric Signals: Each bidder's signal is independent of and has the same probability distribution as each other bidder's
signal.

General Symmetric Signals: The joint distribution
of bidders' signals is symmetric with respect
to bidders.

Asymmetric Signals: The joint distribution of bidders' signals is not symmetric with respect to
bidders.

It should be noted that the above categories are not
necessarily exclusive os each other, nor are they in-
clusive of all possibilities.

The simplest auction models are those involving
independent symmetric signals. The case of private
values is essentially equivalent to a private values

model in which each bidder knows his value of the
object precisely and each bidder's value is identically and independently distributed with each other
bidder's value. This model was studied first, and
in considerable detail, by Vickrey.[48] He showed
that at equilibrium the auctioneer's expected revenue
is the same under the first-price mechanism as under
the second-price mechanism. Rothkopf considered the
case of common values when the signals are assumed
to satisfy an additional constraint: the ratios of
the bidders' signals to the (unknown) common value
are assumed to be independent and identically distributed.[49] Milgrom and Weber have shown that Vickrey's
revenue equivalence of first- and second-price mechanisms extends to the case of general symmetric values
(and also include additional mechanisms).[50]

The next, more complex, class of models arise
under the assumption of general symmetric signals.
Riley and Samuelson and Myerson have described the
revenue equivalence of large classes of mechanisms
for a restricted class of symmetric signals (including independent symmetric signals) in the case of

---

[48]Vickrey (1961, 1962).

[49]Rothkopf (1971).

[50]Milgrom and Weber (1981).

private values.[51] Wilson and Milgrom also have shown
that the auctioneer's revenue converges to the object's
actual value as the number of bidders approached infinity under, respectively, first- and second-price
mechanisms in the case of common values.[52] Milgrom
and Weber have characterized equilibria and rank the
auctioneer's expected revenue (English, second price,
and first price in order of decreasing revenues) for
a variety of mechanisms in the case of general symmetric values.[53]

The third class, those models with asymmetrically
distributed signals, has received the least attention
and yielded the fewest results. Griesmer, Levitan
and Shubik and Ortega-Reichart studied specific examples of private-values models; the accuracy of some
of the analysis is suspect.[54] Vickrey obtained an
equilibrium for an asymmetric private values example
in which each of the two bidders knows their value
for the object precisely; this example illustrates
that mechanisms which always award the object to the
bidder having the highest value for it when bidders'

---

[51] Riley and Samuelson (1979); Myerson (1981).

[52] Wilson (1977); Milgrom (1977).

[53] Milgrom and Weber (1981).

[54] Griesmer, Levitan and Shubik (1967); Ortega-
Reichert (1968).

values are symmetrically distributed, do not necessarily retain this property when bidders' values (or
signals) are asymmetrically distributed.[55] Engelbrecht-
Wiggans, Milgrom and Weber characterized the first-
price equilibrium for those common value models in
which one of two bidders knows the other bidder's
signal.[56] The less-informed bidder expects zero profit from participating in the auction. There appears
to be no reported results for the case of general symmetric models.

The summary reveals several areas which have been
less than completely studied. First, with the exception of the above-mentioned asymmetrical example of
Vickrey, there appears to be nothing known about models
with asymmetrically distributed values; Vickrey's results suggest that the asymmetry results in important
differences from symmetric models. The case of asymmetrically distributed signals has also received very
little attention.

Two characteristics of auction models which I
have not considered are those of bidders' risk preferences and of the number of objects to be sold. Riley
and Samuelson and Milgrom and Weber have shown that an
increased risk aversion on the part of the bidders

---

[55]Vickrey (1961, 1962).

[56]Engelbrecht-Wiggans, Milgrom and Weber (1981).

makes the first-price mechanism more attractive (or,
less unattractive) as compared to the second-price
mechanism in regard to the auctioneer's expected revenue.[57]

Auctions of a number of objects may be classified
by whether the objects are interchangable or not, and
whether or not a bidder may obtain (or, alternatively,
wishes to obtain) more than one object. Until very
recently, there were very few published results concerning such auctions. The area is, however, currently
being significantly advanced in a variety of directions

CONCLUSION

The relationship between one bidder's expected
value for the object and his competitors' information
plays a key role in the theory of auctions and bidding.
Under the appropriate independence, dominant strategies
exist for bidders and these "optimal" strategies are
relatively simple to calculate. Such, relatively
unrealistic, models were analyzed extensively in the
earlier work on auctions and bidding. When a bidder's
expected value for the object is dependent on the
information known to other bidders, the situation is
complicated by what the bidder can infer about his

---

[57]Riley and Samuelson (1979); Milgrom and Weber (1981).

expected value from anything he discovers about the
information known to competitors. In particular, the
discovery that one was the high bidder reveals something about the information of other bidders; under
the appropriate positive associativeness of a bidder's
expected value with other bidders' information, the
"good" news that one is the winner is "bad" news with
respect to one's revised expectations about the object's
value and failure by a bidder to consider this winner's
curse phenomenon results in very poor bidding strategies. In addition, the derivation of optimal bidding
strategies is complicated by the fact that a bidder's
strategy now depends on how he believes competitors'
bids are related to their information. Finally, the
auctioneer can capitalize on this dependence in choosing an auction mechanism. Such models are beginning
to yield to analysis.

REFERENCES

Capen, E. C., R. V. Clapp, and W. M. Campbell (1971).
"Competitive Bidding in High Risk Situations," Journal of Petroleum Technology, Vol. 23, pp. 641-51.

Engelbrecht-Wiggans, R. (1978). "Bidding in Auctions
with Multiplicative Log-Normal Errors," Cowles Foundation Discussion Paper 500R, Yale University.

Engelbrecht-Wiggans, R. (1980). "Auctions and Bidding
Models: A Survey," Management Science, Vol. 26,
pp. 119-42.

Engelbrecht-Wiggans, R. and R. J. Weber (1980). "Estimates and Information," CMSEMS Discussion Paper, Northwestern University.

Engelbrecht-Wiggans, R., P. R. Milgrom, and R. J. Weber (1981). "Competitive Bidding with Proprietary Information," CMSEMS Discussion Paper, Northwestern University (to appear in Journal of Mathematical Economics, 1983).

Griesmer, J. H., R. E. Levitan, and M. Shubik (1967). "Towards a Study of Bidding Processes, Part IV," Naval Logistics Research Quarterly, Vol. 14, pp. 415-33.

Harsanyi, J. C. (1967). "Games with Incomplete Information Played by 'Bayesian' Players," Parts I, II and III, Management Science, Vol. 14, pp. 159-82, 320-34, 486-502.

Maskin, E. and J. Riley (1981). "The Gains to Making Losers Pay in High Bid Auctions" (these proceedings).

Matthews, S. (1979). "Information Acquisition in Discriminatory Auctions," Working Paper, Department of Economics, University of Illinois at Urbana-Champaign.

Milgrom, P. R. (1977). "A Convergence Theory for Competitive Bidding with Differential Information," Research Paper #400, Graduate School of Business, Stanford University.

Milgrom, P. R. (1978a). "A Bidding Model of Price Formation under Uncertainty," CMSEMS Discussion Paper #364, Northwestern University.

Milgrom, P. R. (1978b). "Good News and Bad News: Representation Theorems and Applications," CMSEMS Discussion Paper, Northwestern University.

Milgrom, P. R. (1979). The Structure of Information in Competitive Bidding. New York: Garland.

Milgrom, P. R. and R. J. Weber (1982). "A Theory of Auctions and Competitive Bidding," Econometrica, Vol. 50, pp. 1089-122.

Myerson, R. B. (1981). "Optimal Auction Design," Mathematics of Operations Research, Vol. 6, pp. 58-73.

Nash, J. (1950). "The Bargaining Problem," Econometrica, Vol. 18, pp. 1550-62.

Ortega-Reichert, A. (1968). "Models for Competitive Bidding under Uncertainty," Technical Report #8, Department of Operations Research, Stanford University.

Reese, D. K. (1978). "Competitive Bidding for Offshore Petroleum Sales," Bell Journal of Economics, Vol. 9, pp. 369-84.

Riley, J. and J. Hirshleifer (1978). "Elements of Theory of Auctions and Contests," Working Paper, UCLA.

Riley, J. and W. Samuelson (1979). "Optimal Auctions," Working Paper 152, Department of Economics, UCLA.

Rothkopf, M. H. (1969). "A Model of Rational Competitive Bidding," Management Science, Vol. 15, pp. 362-73.

Rothkopf, M. H. (1971). "An Addendum to 'A Model of Rational Competitive Bidding," Management Science, Vol. 17, pp. 774-77.

Rothkopf, M. H. (1980). "On Multiplicative Bidding," Operations Research, Vol. 28, pp. 570-75.

Samuelson, W. (1981). "Competitive Bidding for De-
    fense Contracts" (these proceedings).

Smith, B. and J. Case (1975). "Nash Equilibria in a
    Sealed Bid Auction," Management Science, Vol. 22,
    pp. 487-97.

Stark, R. M. (1974). "Unbalanced Highway Contract
    Tendering," Operational Research Quarterly, Vol.
    25, pp. 373-88.

Stark, R. M. and M. H. Rothkopf (1979). "Competitive
    Bidding: A Comprehensive Bibliography," Operations
    Research, Vol. 27, pp. 364-90.

Teisberg, T. J. (1978). "A Model of Rational Compe-
    titive Bidding," unpublished Ph.D Thesis, Univer-
    sity of California, Berkeley.

Vickrey, W. (1961). "Counterspeculation Auctions and
    Competitive Sealed Tenders," Journal of Finance,
    Vol. 41, pp. 8-37.

Vickrey, W. (1962). "Auction and Bidding Games,"
    Recent Advances in Game Theory, Papers delivered
    at a Meeting of the Princeton University Conference,
    October 4-6, 1961. Philadelphia: Ivy Curtis Press.

von Neumann, J. and O. Morgenstern (1953). Theory
    of Games and Economic Behavior, 3rd ed. Princeton,
    N.J.: Princeton University Press.

Weber, R. J. (1981). "Survey of Multi-Object Auctions"
    (these proceedings).

Wilson, R. B. (1967). "Competitive Bidding with Asym-
    metrical Information," Management Science, Vol. 13,
    pp. A816-A820.

Wilson, R. B. (1969). "Competitive Bidding with Disparate Information," Management Science, Vol. 15, pp. A446-A448.

Wilson, R. B. (1977). "A Bidding Model of Perfect Competition," Review of Economic Studies, Vol. 44, pp. 511-18.

Winkler, R. L. and D. G. Brooks (1980). "Competitive Bidding with Dependent Value Estimates," Operations Research, Vol. 28, pp. 603-11.

4

BIDDING THEORY:

THE PHENOMENA TO BE MODELED

Michael H. Rothkopf

This paper presents a management scientist's
rather than an economist's or game theorist's view
of the past and the future of bidding theory. Any
theory should be influenced by the questions it is
designed to answer, but management science seems to
have a particular need for sensitivity to this requirement. Phenomena of interest to management
scientists often must be modeled quite differently
depending upon the questions to be answered. Therefore, this paper starts by examining the operational
decisions that management scientists want to use
bidding theory to answer.

The original questions addressed by the management science bidding literature were questions faced

by "firing line" bidders, especially the question of
how much to bid.[1] This is an important question to
bidders. Often, large changes (relative to profit
margins) in winning bids would not change the results
of an auction. Although recent work has paid more
attention to questions faced by bid takers, how much
to bid is still the dominant question addressed by
the bidding literature. The question may be limited
to a single auction or it may include groups or sequences of auctions.[2] In each auction, the bid may
be a single amount or a vector of prices.[3] Another
concern of potential bidders that has received some
attention in the literature is whether or not the
necessary work to prepare a bid is justified.[4] Finally, bidders must sometimes decide whether to submit
a solo bid or to attempt to form or join a coalition
and sibmit a joint bid.

Bidding theory also addresses questions faced
by bid takers. These questions include whether an

---

[1]Friedman (1956).

[2]Friedman (1956); Kortanek, Soden and Sodaro (1973);
Oren and Rothkopf (1975); Stark (1974); Stark and
Mayer (1971).

[3]Stark (1974).

[4]Flueck (1967).

auction should, in fact, be held at all,[5] the rules
for an auction,[6] which bidders to invite to participate in an auction, and which bids to accept.[7]   An
example of the type of operational question faced by
bid takers was faced by a client for a large construction project that had sent specifications to
three construction companies (as required by company
policy).   These companies had agreed to prepare bids.
Well into the bid preparation period, one of the construction companies gave notice that it had just won
a large contract and that it was unable to make a
bid.   The client then had to decide whether to delay
the project to allow a new third bidder to prepare
a bid or to proceed with the better of the two bids
it was about to receive.   The cost of delay was easy
to estimate, but what was the cost of doing with out
a third bidder?   Indeed, why three bidders in the
first place?

Recently, a third category of questions, ones
faced by government agencies, particularly by prose-
cutors, has been discussed in the literature.   By

---

[5] Shubik (1970).

[6] Brimmer (1962); Reece (1979); Smith (1966).

[7] Bracken and McCormick (1966); Reece (1976); Stanley,
Honig and Gainen (1954).

examining the records of competitive bidding situations, these agencies seek to detect collusion or
other illegal activity.[8]

Those are some of the practical concerns of potential users of bidding theory. What phenomena must
bidding theorists understand and include in their
theories in order to address these concerns usefully?
There are many different phenomena. Some are more
prevalent and more critical than others. Some, and
not necessarily the same ones, are more often dealt
with than others. I have grouped the relevant phenomena into seven broad categories whose boundaries are
not always clear. They are

> 1) information,
>
> 2) valuation,
>
> 3) interrelationships,
>
> 4) "semirational" behavior,
>
> 5) effects upon other activities,
>
> 6) bid taker economics, and
>
> 7) collusion.

The activity of competitive bidding is associated
with a variety of information situations. The partic-
ulars of the information situation play a critical role
in the analysis of the questions addressed by bidding

---

[8] Comanor and Schankerman (1976); Kuhlman (1974); Pollock and Maltz (1978).

theory. Bidding theories depend upon what the bidders know and how each bidder's information is related
to that of each other bidder. Some questions also
depend upon what the bid taker knows and when he knows
it. Modeling assumptions about information situations
can be both subtle and critical in their implications.
Work on realistic information structures has greatly
expanded bidding theory's usefulness. Further work
in this area may well have a similar effect.

Friedman's early and much followed work in bidding theory represented a bidder's knowledge about
the value of the subject of the auction and his knowledge about the magnitude of the best competitive bid
with independent random variables.[9] This led to a
theory that indicated that it is advantageous for a
bidder to bid more aggressively when the competition
increases, that is, when there are more competitors
and/or more aggressive bidding by competitors. A
useful and qualitatively different theory emerged when
this independence assumption was replaced by a different one. When the value of the subject of the auction
is assumed to be the same (or in a known proportion)
for each bidder and each bidder is assumed to make
independent estimating errors, the "winner's curse"
phenomenon arises.[10] The theory that has been developed

---

[9]Friedman (1956).

[10]Capen, Clapp and Campbell (1971).

under these assumptions indicates that it is advantageous for bidders to bid <u>less</u> aggressively when
the competition increases beyond a relatively low
level.[11]

Bidding theorists also have begun to study situations involving dependent estimating errors[12] and
situations involving asymmetric information.[13] However, there is still much to learn about the effects
of imperfect information and about how and why bidders
gather information. Estimating and bid preparation
play a key role in bidding. Many of the bid takers'
decisions cannot be effectively modeled without modeling the bidders' estimating process. In addition
the bidding coalition formation process cannot be
effectively modeled without modeling the information
exchange implicit in it and in unsuccessful attempts
to arrive at joint bids. Work on information structures has concentrated on what bidders know about the
subject of the auction; what bidders know about each
other's knowledge is another important area for exploration.

---

[11] Capen, Clapp and Campbell (1971); Oren and Williams
(1975); Rothkopf (1969); Teisberg (1978).

[12] Winkler and Brooks (1980).

[13] Weverbergh (1979); Wilson (1967); Wilson (1969).

Another category of phenomena closely related
to bidding includes estimating and specifically valuation. Here is an example of the kind of complica-
tions that can be expected. I was once told by a
geologist of his experience in preparing an estimate
so that his employer could bid for certain exploration
rights. When the estimate came out to an amount less
than what both he and his management agreed was the
likely level of competition, he was instructed to
lower the cost of capital used in his evaluation so
that they could compete. He did, and his firm then
bid the amount of the estimate with the lower capital
charge. The moral is clear: "official" numbers
aren't always the real (that is, economically significant) ones.

Often, evaluation problems arise because of the
difference between accounting costs (or values) and
the economically significant opportunity costs (or
values). Data exists on the former, but the decision
should depend upon the latter. These problems are
at the heart of many of the estimating problems in
preparing a bid for a construction contract. It is
necessary not only to estimate the cost of the materials
specified and the labor cost, but also to estimate
the opportunity cost of the equipment and organizational assets to be employed and to estimate the profit to be made on the change orders that the winning

bidder may receive. In many situations, items are
purchased at auctions with the intention, or at least
the possibility, of reselling them afterwards. This
is certainly true of Treasury bills or oil leases.
When the value of what is won depends upon the resale
price and the selling effort required, a model of
the resale market as it will be after a successful
bid is required. If failing to win an auction will
lead a firm to buy in the resale market, then the
resale market as it will be after an unsuccessful
bid must also be modeled. The relationship of what
is won in an auction to other parts of a firm's
business must also be considered. Many of the phenomena in this whole category of evaluation difficulties are largely subjective and undocumented.
This does not make them unreal or unimportant, just
difficult.

Bidding theory originated with models of single
auctions; however, there are a number of important
phenomenon that have to do with the interrelationship
of different auctions. There has been some modeling
of bidding in simultaneous auctions.[14] However, additional work is needed, especially in the analysis
of the effects on simultaneous auctions of the existence of aftermarkets. The sequential effects of

---

[14]Friedman (1956); Rothkopf (1977).

one auction on the ones that follow need to be modeled.
These sequential effects may be internal to the bidding
firm[15] or they may be external competitive effects.[16]
The internal effects may depend upon limitations in
the firm's resources, or upon the interrelated values
(including risk) of the items being sold in different
auctions, or perhaps upon the feedback from the results
of one auction to the estimating process for future
ones.

The external effects of one auction on others
can be critical, as in the attempt of a chemical company to apply a simple, one-shot bidding model like
Friedman's[17] to a situation in which the company periodically bids to sell a particular chemical to government agencies. The company manufactured this high-fixed-
cost, low-variable-cost chemical as did the one other
company that regularly bid against it. The only other
competition in these auctions was an occasional bid by
a reseller of some of the product originally purchased
for the commercial market. A company analyst had carefully subtracted out the freight cost differential between the tender requests and the effects of certain

---

[15] Kortanek, Soden and Sodaro (1973); Stark and Mayer
(1971).

[16] Oren and Rothkopf (1975).

[17] Friedman (1956).

other differences. He was left with a rather narrow
distribution of the best competing bid. Using this
analysis he recommended a bid slightly lower than
the company would otherwise have made. His model
predicted that the bid he recommended would be, on
the average, substantially more profitable. The analyst's management was uneasy about the analysis, but
was unable to state why until it realized that the
reason the proposed bid had a much higher expected
profit was that the probability of winning had gone
from near 50 to about 99 percent. Once the management
realized that, it had no doubt about what was missing
from the analyst's model. They were quite sure that
the other manufacturer was not about to let them win
99 percent of the government business.

Another category of bidding behavior that needs
to be modeled can be called "semirational" behavior
because such behavior is unexplainable when looked at
as straightforward profit maximization. There are a
variety of reasons why bidders behave in what appears
to be an irrational manner. These reasons may be
organizational (only the preparers of winning bids
get promoted), informational ("Oh! I didn't realize
it has to be built underwater."), computational (pro-
portionality assumptions in cost estimating), competitive (preventing entry), emotional ("He got me last
time! Now I'm going to make him suffer!"), or rationa.

anticipation of semirational behavior by competitors
("He won't get me again."). These phenomena are important for many bidding related questions. For example, a decision as to whether or not to publish
losing bids may depend critically on the organizational
effect of revealing to the winning bidder's organization the amount of money he left on the table, and the
effect of this pressure on the executives who prepare
bids.

Another cause of "semirational" behavior may be
a bidder's disbelief that the rules of the auction
will always be followed. Sometimes the submission
of bids is known to be just the first step in a negotiation process. However, even when this is not so,
a bidder may believe that it is or that by his bid
he can make it so. While it was not a formal auction,
the following incident may be illuminating. In 1955,
Congress set up a commission that was directed to
sell competitively and _individually_ _by_ _unit_ a number
of government owned synthetic rubber plants built
during World War II including a plant with three units
located in Torrance, California. Shell Chemical Company made an offer for the entire Torrance plant that
turned out to be substantially higher than the sum
of the high offers on the individual units. When commission representatives told Richard McCurdy, the
President of Shell Chemical Company, that the law

did not allow Shell to bid on the entire plant, he
responded that Shell was telling the government that,
to Shell at least, the plant as a whole was worth
much more than its individual units, and that the
commission should attempt to get Congress to accept
Shell's offer. The commission did recommend this
to Congress and Shell's offer was accepted. Shell
operated the entire plant for many years, and McCurdy
went on to become president of Shell Chemical's corporate parent, Shell Oil Company.[18]

Another phenomena that may have to be modeled
is the effect of auction-related decisions on other
decisions. For example, Mead describes a situation
in which the choice of rules used in government timber
auctions was affected by government concern about
lumber mill investment.[19]

The analysis of the decision of which bids to
accept will depend upon the evaluation of the economic situation faced by the bid taker. This can involve the analysis of transportation costs, quality
differences, and what ever else it takes to put alternative tenders on a comparible basis.[20] It may also

---

[18]McCurdy (1981).

[19]Mead (1967).

[20]Bracken and McCormick (1966); Stanley, Honig and
Gainen (1954).

involve the analysis of the value to the bid taker
of not accepting any bid[21] and of the effect on future
bids of such a decision.

Finally, the study of collusion in competitive
bidding requires that its mechanisms be modeled.
Comanor and Schankerman apparently have written the
only paper that deals with collusion.[22]   They discuss
a cartel's balancing its desire to control precisely
the allocation of market share and its desire to minimize the illicit communication necessary to coordinate
bids.

We have identified a number of phenomena that
arise in competitive bidding and are important enough
to be worthy of research efforts but that have not,
as yet, been modeled. Other important phenomena have
been modeled in ways that are unsatisfactory or incomplete. Finally, some phenomena have been effectively
modeled by themselves but not in combination with
other important phenomena.

---

[21]Reece (1976).

[22]Comanor and Schankerman (1976).

REFERENCES

Bracken, J. and G. P. McCormick (1966). "Bid Evalu-
    ation," Chapter 3 in Selected Applications of Non-
    linear Programming. New York: John Wiley & Sons.

Brimmer, A. F. (1962). "Price Determination in the
    United States Treasury Bill Market," Review of
    Economic Statistics, Vol. 44, pp. 178-83.

Capen, E. C., R. V. Clapp, and W. M. Campbell (1971).
    "Competitive Bidding in High-Risk Situations,"
    Journal of Petroleum Technology, Vol. 23, pp. 641-51.

Comanor, W. S. and M. A. Schankerman (1976). "Ident-
    ical Bids and Cartel Behavior," Bell Journal of
    Economics, Vol. 7, pp. 281-86.

Flueck, J. A. (1967). "A Statistical Decision Theory
    Approach to a Seller's Bid Pricing Problem under
    Uncertainty," Ph.D Dissertation, School of Business,
    University of Chicago.

Friedman, L. (1956). "A Competitive Bidding Strategy,"
    Operations Research, Vol. 4, pp. 104-12.

Friedman, M. (1963). "Price Determination in the United
    States Treasury Bill Market, A Comment," Review of
    Economic Statistics, Vol. 45, pp. 318-20.

Kortanek, K. D., J. V. Soden, and D. Sodaro (1973).
    "Profit Analysis and Sequential Bid Pricing Models,"
    Management Science, Vol. 20, pp. 396-417.

Kuhlman, J. M. (1974). "Inferring Conduct from Per-
    formance: An Analysis of a Price Fixing Case,"
    Working Paper, Department of Economics, University
    of Missouri-Columbia.

McCurdy, R. C. (1981). Private communication.

Mead, W. J. (1967). "Natural Resource Disposal Policy --Oral Auction Versus Sealed Bids," Natural Resource Journal, Vol. 7, pp. 194-224.

Oren, M. E. and A. C. Williams (1975). "On Competitive Bidding," Operations Research, Vol. 23, pp. 1072-1079.

Oren, S. S. and M. H. Rothkopf (1975). "Optimal Bidding in Sequential Auctions," Operations Research, Vol. 23, pp. 1080-90.

Pollock, S. M. and M. D. Maltz (1978). "Bid Rigging Patterns and Methods of Analysis," ORSA/TIMS Bulletin, Vol. 6, p. 44.

Reece, D. K. (1976). "Bid Rejections in Federal Offshore Petroleum Sales," Paper at ORSA Western Section Meeting, Los Angeles.

Reece, D. K. (1979). "An Analysis of Alternative Bidding Systems for Leasing Offshore Oil," Bell Journal of Economics, Vol. 10, pp. 659-69.

Rothkopf, M. H. (1969). "A Model of Rational Competitive Bidding," Management Science, Vol. 15, pp. 362-73.

Rothkopf, M. H. (1977). "Bidding in Simultaneous Auctions with a Constraint on Exposure," Operations Research, Vol. 25, pp. 620-29.

Shubik, M. (1970). "On Different Methods for Allocating Resources," KYKLOS Internacionale Zeitschrift fur Sozialwissenschaften (International Review of Social Sciences), Vol. 23, Fasc. 2, pp. 332-37.

Smith, V. L. (1966). "Bidding Theory and the Treasury Bill Auction: Does Price Discrimination Increase Bill Prices?" Review of Economic Statistics, Vol. 48, pp. 141-46.

Stanley, E. D., D. P. Honig, and L. Gainen (1954). "Linear Programming in Bid Evaluation," Naval Research Logistics Quarterly, Vol. 1, pp. 48-54.

Stark, R. M. (1974). "Unbalanced Highway Contract Tendering," Operational Research Quarterly, Vol. 25, pp. 373-88.

Stark, R. M. and R. H. Mayer (1971). "Some Multi-Contract Decision Theoretic Competitive Bidding Models," Operations Research, Vol. 19, pp. 469-83.

Teisberg, T. J. (1978). "A Bidding Model of the Federal Oil and Gas Lease Auction," Ph.D Dissertation, Department of Economics, University of California, Berkeley.

Weverbergh, M. (1979). "Competitive Bidding with Asymmetric Information Reanalyzed," Management Science, Vol. 25, pp. 291-94.

Wilson, R. B. (1967). "Competitive Bidding with Asymmetrical Information," Management Science, Vol. 13, pp. A816-20.

Wilson, R. B. (1969). "Competitive Bidding with Disparate Information," Management Science, Vol. 15, pp. 446-48.

Winkler, R. L. and D. G. Brooks (1980). "Competitive Bidding with Dependent Value Estimates," Operations Research, Vol. 28, pp. 603-13.

5

BIDDING, ESTIMATING,
AND ENGINEERED CONSTRUCTION CONTRACTING
Robert M. Stark
Thomas C. Varley

The professional gatherings from which the papers
comprising this volume have emerged attest to the
growth of research interest in competitive bidding.
There is a certain satisfaction in this development
among those of us who have decades of research in
this field. However, our satisfaction is muted by an
awareness, cultivated over the last ten years, that
cost and value estimating for buildings, dams, ships,
and the like (upon which bidding models are based)
is not nearly as competent as one can be led to assume. It is not simply a matter of adjusting for a
"wrong number"! The deficiencies in estimating competence undermine the tendering for which the bidding

models were formulated. Some of the ideas we advance
are controversial to some people. We will endeavor
to state them in a way that can result in light rather
than heat.

Martin Shubik has traced the development of bidding elsewhere in this volume so that repetition here
is not warranted. We note that in the late 1960s
Edward Capen and Robert Clapp emphasized the uncertainties in the value of the object of the bidding
and its corrosive effect upon the relevance of bidding models. They drove the point home by appearing
at professional meetings with a jar of coins. People
were asked to estimate their value; the coins being
awarded to the closest estimate. Having provided an
incentive for obtaining some $20 worth of coins, they
would draw attention to the remarkable variance in
the estimates. On another occasion, Capen provided
data on bids from an Alaskan oil sale in which companies had shared geologic information. A plot of
the bids on normal probability paper, suggests that
the parties viewed the value of parcels quite differently despite the presumed commonality of their technical information. These are not isolated examples!

Brian Fine of a London firm bearing his name
with a long history of scholarship and experience
in engineered construction tells of making 20 copies
of a structural design, labelling half of them as

"Royal Theatre" and the other half as "barn" and send-
ing them to contracting engineers for estimates. The
estimates received were grouped about two figures
which differed by a factor of about 10. Again, it
suggests, as Fine puts it, that bidding is determined
more by "a socially accepted price" than by our estimating competencies.

Bid rigging is common! Large cost overruns tend
to support the observation that the challenge is to
"get the job," whatever the price; the actual payment
will, in effect, be negotiated later. Reasons for
such actions are due to laws and directives, which
encourage the choice of a low bidder; a lack of well-
defined statements of work and/or design packages
or knowledge of what is to be procured; depressed
industry looking for work at a very low profit or
at cost to pay for the fixed cost and maintain a functioning firm; rates of inflation which were not properly accounted for in the bid. Concepts for eliminating
many of these actions are possible, but they require
a well-established acquisition strategy at the beginning of a major project.

The deeper issue in contracting for engineered
construction that emerges is not the bidding--but,
rather, the estimating. This is not to say that there
is not tactical advantage in observing bidding patterns.
The point is that formal bidding models have not been

of primary concern to the managers; only the bid price
has been, and models probably will not be until improvement in estimating capabilities are achieved.

It is a beginning to recognize that professional
estimating organizations and documentation concluding
with figures stated to orders of accuracy clearly beyond the capability of measurement or prediction tend
to obscure the incompleteness of our knowledge. The
intent, of course, is not to demean anyone's competence. It is to suggest that there are no tools to
use to do the job better. Some modesty is appropriate here! We cannot advance a comprehensive framework
for a science of estimating. But our research enables
us to arrive at some solutions. Two examples will illustrate; taking care to clarify that these may not
be the only, or even the best examples. They do,
however, come from our sponsored research; hence,
we are in a reasonable position to represent them.

The first example, derived from engineering designs represented as stochastic geometric programs,
is described at length in a subsequent part of this
volume. The fascinating result of that research is
the implication that estimates that are made before
a design is made or construction is begin are samples
from a distribution tending to lognormal while the
actual costs incurred are samples from a distribution
tending to normal.

Cost estimates can differ from actual costs because they should--on scientific grounds--and not
necessarily because of ad hoc explanations of unanticipated peculiarities of labor or weather, among other
variables. Indeed, cost esitmates which equal actual
costs could be looked upon with suspicion. Now, this
does not fully explain the matter because we frequently
encounter differences in estimates and actual costs.
These are also likely to be rare events according to
our analyses.

One of the researcher's problems is that reliable information is elusive; even with cooperation.
It is a common practice for a site superintendent to
misallocate charges. For example, a site superintendent responsible for two jobs has one that is being
completed without serious problems, let us say, and
the other is meeting with problems. What does this
mean? This means that one job is well within the
estimates and the other is not--even as, already noted,
the estimates are not necessarily something in which
one can have complete confidence. Frequently, equipment used to rescue the faltering job has a tendency
to be charged to the job doing well. That helps the
reports to the home office "look better," exemplify-
ing a principle well-known to management scientists:
The movement of information from one managerial level
to another invites its modification (often in subtle

ways).

Another impediment to acquiring reliable information is the tendency, already noted, of the desire
"to get the job at any price." "We can deal with the
quantity surveyor later." The change order process
is an unfailing source of negotiation to recover
costs. The way it works is that contracts and specifications are drawn for, say, a ship and agreed to
by the contracting parties. The contractor discovers
that he can do the welding of some plates less expen-
sively by another means. About that time the client
decides that some room on the ship should be larger
--and there are thousands of change orders during
the course of construction so there is ample opportunity to alter designs. The contractor can plead
that he cannot easily change the room size; however,
if the client will permit the altered welding maybe
a deal can be struck. This is the practical means
by which ships, buildings, dams, and the like can be
built. Again it suggests that the contracting parties
simply do not have a clear idea of what they are contracting for in advance.

This leads to our second example.

Much, if not most, contracting is done by the
bill of quantities. Here is a copy of an advertisement. The client, the Delaware Department of Highways
in this instance, has engineers estimate items and

TABLE 2. DELAWARE DEPARTMENT OF HIGHWAYS. 23·06 miles, KENT COUNTY

18 ft surface treated roadway on 6 in. soil cement base. Completion date: 210 working days

Item No.	Quantity	Item
1	L.S.	Clearing and grubbing Road No. 184
2	L.S.	Clearing and grubbing Road No. 186
3	L.S.	Clearing and grubbing Road No. 187
4	L.S.	Clearing and grubbing Road No. 189
5	L.S.	Clearing and grubbing Road No. 199
6	L.S.	Clearing and grubbing Road No. 201
7	L.S.	Clearing and grubbing Road No. 218
8	L.S.	Clearing and grubbing Road No. 219
9	L.S.	Clearing and grubbing Road No. 223
10	L.S.	Clearing and grubbing Road No. 225
11	L.S.	Clearing and grubbing Road No. 226
12	L.S.	Clearing and grubbing Road No. 258
13	L.S.	Clearing and grubbing Road No. 299
14	L.S.	Clearing and grubbing Road No. 300
15	1000 C.Y.	Excavation
16	168,400 C.Y.	Borrow
17	1000 C.Y.	Select borrow
18	264,500 S.Y.	Soil cement base course
19	26,450 bbls.	Portland cement
20	178,500 gal	RC-250 asphalt
21	5100 tons	Coarse aggregate
22	4800 L.F.	12 in. R.C. pipe
23	3800 L.F.	15 in. R.C. pipe
24	900 L.F.	18 in. R.C. pipe
25	300 L.F.	24 in. R.C. pipe
26	350 L.F.	36 in. R.C. pipe
27	160 L.F.	42 in. R.C. pipe
28	160 L.F.	48 in. R.C. pipe
29	60 L.F.	54 in. R.C. pipe
30	210 L.F.	60 in. R.C. pipe
31	70 L.F.	58 in. × 36 in. C.M. pipe bit. C. and P.
32	1 each	Type "PW" catch basin
33	100 L.F.	Wire rope guard fence (wood post)
34	4 each	End post attachments
35	20,000 L.F.	Lateral ditching
36	30 tons	Calcium chloride for dust control
37	220 S.Y.	Grouted riprap
38	1 each	Standard junction box
39	L.S.	Removal of existing structures
40	121,756 L.F.	Seeding and mulching
41	23·06 miles	Grading and reshaping roadway
42†	0·0 L.F.	30 in. R.C. pipe

† The need for 30 in. R.C. pipe was not anticipated and this item did not appear in the advertisement.

quantities. Prospective bidders enter unit prices
(bill rates) and quantity × rate = item sum which,
summed over the items, is the bid. The job usually
goes to the lowest bidder. However, the total bid
is in some sense irrelevant once the contract is
awarded because payment is made on the basis of measured work as it is completed and at the unit prices.
Actually, the variation in unit bids is about the
same. The unit price for the first item varies from
$2900 for Bidder H to $8123 for Bidder I, and so on.

Some interesting observations can be made. The
lowest bid does not mean the client will pay the lowest final price. There are overruns, underruns, change
orders, and omitted items, among other problems.
One reason that unit prices vary is to improve cash
flow. Note, however, that cost is assumed to be linear
related to quantity. Our experience as management
scientists is that costs are rarely linear except by
decree. In effect, the tendering process requires
that you do not "tell it like it is." Later, we will
liken it to a Taylor expansion to first-order terms--
and we do not even seem to agree on the first term.
The pretense is that the cost of the roadway is the
sum of the cost of the ingredients. Who chooses a
bakery by the unit prices of the itemized ingredients?
"The quality is in the baking." That is, the way in
which the job is executed is surely an important factor

TABLE 4. PUBLIC RECORD OF BIDS

Item No.	Bidder			
	F† ($)	G ($)	H ($)	I ($)
1	4000·00	3400·00	2900·00	8123·00
2	400·00	300·00	800·00	1832·37
3	1000·00	1000·00	500·00	901·55
4	3000·00	3400·00	2300·00	7384·00
5	1400·00	2600·00	2000·00	1560·00
6	700·00	2000·00	1000·00	2765·00
7	4400·00	3200·00	4100·00	7493·00
8	600·00	500·00	1500·00	750·00
9	400·00	2400·00	1400·00	594·10
10	1400·00	1000·00	2000·00	1930·00
11	1400·00	800·00	2400·00	2598·00
12	1900·00	1800·00	2000·00	2499·00
13	1400·00	1500·00	1300·00	591·00
14	2000·00	2200·00	1400·00	1479·00
15	0·96	1·00	1·00	0·70
16	1·02	1·10	1·18	0·99
17	2·00	1·50	1·50	1·95
18	0·24	0·25	0·26	0·27
19	4·85	4·60	4·15	4·50
20	0·125	0·14	0·14	0·1275
21	6·00	6·50	6·00	5·85
22	3·00	3·00	3·00	2·73
23	5·00	4·00	5·00	4·45
24	6·00	5·00	5·50	5·95
25	9·00	8·00	7·00	7·89
26	14·00	17·00	12·50	13·18
27	18·00	20·00	15·00	16·68
28	22·00	26·00	18·00	22·77
29	28·00	33·00	24·00	27·27
30	35·00	37·00	28·00	30·44
31	25·00	32·00	24·00	22·20
32	300·00	500·00	250·00	482·00
33	2·70	3·00	2·65	1·90
34	50·00	50·00	45·00	50·00
35	0·70	0·90	0·75	0·60
36	70·00	50·00	80·00	40·00
37	12·00	10·00	10·00	10·00
38	300·00	400·00	200·00	375·00
39	600·00	1000·00	1000·00	900·00
40	0·14	0·15	0·14	0·14
41	1800·00	1500·00	1800·00	1500·00
42				
Total bids	585,946·84	598,528·40	600,993·34	580,327·21

† Winner.

Yet, current bidding practice does not usually make
explicit provision for it. One way to look at it
is that the current practice of estimating is not
even dimensionally correct. The proper units are resources per unit time and not simply the resources
themselves. What does this have to dö with estimating? The estimator is charged with determining the
unit prices. It is a time consuming job to say the
least. A handsome linear programming model is available which inexpensively provides optimal unit prices
so that the present worth of all future revenues is
a maximum. In effect, it undermines the estimator's
preoccupation with unit prices.

Why do that? Note, we did not say undermine
the estimator--only his preoccupation with unit prices.
Of course! To focus his attention on the essence of
estimating--How are we going to do the job? How will
it use recourses per unit time?

In the interests of brevity, one could say that
we imply that estimators never consider the mode of
executing the job. Of course, that is not always
so. However, it often is and, worse, current tendering practice fosters that attitude. Who is at fault?
Most likely if the buyer said we are going to include
in our evaluation how you use resources over time,
and what your past record has been (how good is the
bread), the bidder may put his bid together in a

different way.

Without going into a discussion of how sources
are selected and proposals evaluated, the bidder
needs to understand how the bids will be evaluated
and develop his model to reflect his best possible
chances for selection. That is, this is the way the
game is being played. If the bidder keeps this in
mind, he will have a fair chance of winning.

To sum up and suggest directions for research
and development, in a construction context, at least,
theories of bidding seem to miss a point. They con-
centrate upon guesswork and they do not do that well
enough, apparently, for management to employ bidding
models with confidence. Bidding models place more
emphasis upon an adversary process than seems useful.
A "constructive tension" is useful if it draws upon
construction management skill. There is a primitive
nonsense in a client feeling that he has the job at
a good price because the contractor lost money. And
likewise, if the contractor sees change orders, say,
as a lever to recover costs and a profit. This is
the difference between classical bidding and competence bidding (re-contracting). It is in the nature
of the partnership between the winning bid (contractors) and the buyer. The casual terms for the tension
are called win-lose when the buyer gets taken. Lose-
win when the bidder loses money but most often it

becomes a lose-lose situation for both. The need
for research is to develop the models, procedures
and schemes that produce a win-win situation.

To improve the science of estimating it can be
useful to look for analogues. Brian Fine (mentioned
earlier) empahsizes that "how the job can be executed"
has an analogy in seeking its "equations of motion."
Furthermore, equations of motion tend to hold in rather
controlled situations. They are not useful for tur-
bulent flow. The construction analogue is "variability"--and we largely use the same estimating practices
and construction technology when variability is promi-
nent as when it is not.

We could improve the means by which we sort the
highly variable from the less variable. This should
better enable a study of means for reducing variability. To many this is called risk assessment or uncertainty and includes a means for judging the amount
of risk a project entails. Even some very simple
measures of risk are important first steps in distinguishing high variability from low.

Finally, for example, to stretch the phenomeno-
logically descriptive analogy, equations often occur
in pairs. One describes the motion, the other the
elastic properties of the materials, one with the
chemical balance and the other with the thermodynamics of the chemical reaction, and so on. Perhaps

the construction analogue is the cost as a function
of quantity relation. Recall, that we noted that we
assume (require) a linear or first-order relation.
A reasonable research direction is to explore the
effect of higher order terms.

These are useful research prospects that can
in time alter the competence brought to the management of constructing facilities. With the possible
exception of agriculture, construction is often cited
as the world's largest dollar volume industry. And
one of fundamental importance since it provides the
infrastructure for civilization!

PART TWO

ISSUES IN THE THEORY OF AUCTIONS

1

PRIVATE INFORMATION IN AN
AUCTIONLIKE SECURITIES MARKET*
Paul R. Milgrom

Students of auction theory usually restrict the
scope of these analyses to include only those settings
where a single seller offers items for sale or a single
buyer solicits delivery price offers. A large volume
of trading takes place in settings of this kind, but
an even larger volume is conducted in settings where
there are both many buyers and many sellers making bids
and offers. The major securities market and commodities
and options exchanges are mostly of this second kind.

---

*The main ideas expressed in this paper evolved during
discussions with Larry Glosten. Any errors in this
presentation, however, are entirely my responsibility.
This research was supported by the U.S. Office of Naval
Research and by National Science Foundation grant
SES-8001932.

There is a reasonably acceptable economic theory
of securities markets for the hypothetical case where
all investors and traders have identical information.
This theory is an extension of the Arrow-Debreu competitive equilibrium theory, and as such it leads to the
usual kinds of conclusions about the existence and efficiency of equilibrium. However, like the competitive
equilibrium theory, the securities markets theory has
little to say about how prices are formed. This omission is particularly disturbing in extensions of the
theory in which some traders have private information.
In those extensions, the equilibrium prices typically
reflect more information than was available (when the
markets opened) to any individual trader. This is a
puzzling prediction of the theory, since someone must
set the prices! Far from explaining this puzzle,
traditional analyses have generated many doubtful
propositions, including the following ones: Traders
with inside information may be unable to profit from
concealing and using that information.[1] Traders'
beliefs about security prices--beliefs that are based
partly on past and present prices--can be extremely
sensitive to small variations in the prevailing prices,
and the prices themselves are so sensitive to small
shifts in demand that a single small trader can some-

---

[1]Grossman (1976).

times completely control price levels.[2] Moreover,
equilibrium prices must sometimes reflect information
that is not available to any active trader![3]

In contrast to the theory of securities markets
and to competitive equilibrium theory, auction theory
deals simply and directly with the issues of how prices
are determined, how bidders use and benefit from their
private information, and how private information affects prices. The insights summarized below, which
are gleaned from the study of auctions, suggests some
new ideas and approaches for security market theory.

Consider a sealed-bid auction in which a single
object is offered for sale to n bidders. In general, the amount a bidder is willing to pay for the
object depends on his personal preferences and the
characteristics of the object. In a charity auction
where a Carribean vacation for two is being sold, each
bidder can determine an appropriate value for himself
by introspection, and he can then make an intelligent
bid based on that value and on his beliefs about how
others will bid. In contrast to this case is the
case where oil rights on an offshore tract of land
are being offered: An appropriate value cannot then
be determined by introspection because some major

---

[2]Milgrom (1981).

[3]Tirole (1980).

value determining characteristics—the amount of recoverable oil, its depth, pressure, etc.—are unknown.
Experienced bidders base their bids on their estimate
of the value, but they also bid cautiously to counter-
act a phenomenon known as the winner's curse. The
winner's curse is the tendency of a winning bidder
to find that he has overestimated the value of the
prize he wins at auction. The curse arises because
a bidder is more likely to win an auction when he has
overestimated the value of the prize than when he has
underestimated it. (Economists may recognize the winner's curse as a variant of the phenomenon known as
adverse selection.)

Experienced bidders escape the ill effects of
the winner's curse in auctions for oil, gas, and mineral rights by reducing their bids to allow a margin
for estimation error and by carefully gathering and
analyzing geological data to reduce that error. In
those settings, it is clear that private information
can be useful to a bidder in choosing his bid.

In addition to its value in decision making,
private information can have a kind of strategic
value in auctions. Bidders facing a well-informed
competitor are particularly susceptible to the winner's curse. Consequently, the mere fact that a bidder has good information may lead the other bidders

to bid more cautiously, a response that benefits the
well-informed bidder.[4]

The question of how much of the bidders' private
information gets reflected in the selling price is a
subtle one. One might think that the price resulting
from a sealed-bid auction cannot reflect more information than was available to the winning bidder when
he made his bid, since that bid determines the price.
This reasoning, however, is incorrect. When the bid
made by the winning bidder is known, it can be inferred
that the other n-1 bidders made lower bids. The
information which this inference conveys about the
probable value of the mineral rights was unavailable
to the winning bidder when he made his bid. Thus,
the price resulting from a sealed-bid auction may reflect more information than was originally available
to any individual bidder, a prediction which is in-
triguingly close to the predictions of the securities
markets theories.

The essential feature that distinguishes bidding
models from existing securities market models is not
that there is competition on only one side of the
market or that the objects being sold are indivisible
nor even that the number of bidders is generally small:
the essential feature is that the process of price

_____

[3]Milgrom and Weber (1982a).

determination in bidding models is explicit. By examining this process, one is able to see how information can be used, why it is valuable, and how it
affects prices.

In the remainder of this paper, a simple model
of a competitive securities market is sketched in
which the bid and ask prices are set by a group of
market makers. When all traders have identical information, the equilibrium bid and ask prices are
constant over time and equal to each other and to
the price predicted by competitive equilibrium theory.
However, when some traders have private information,
the equilibrium ask price always exceeds the bid
price. If the informed traders are speculators with
no transactions motive for trading, then the market
makers lose money to the informed traders but profit
from the uninformed. The spread between the ask and
bid prices generally results in a reduced volume of
trade and an inefficient allocation of securities.
Information has positive value to individual traders
and prices come to reflect some or all of the information used by the informed traders.

Let there be a single marketed security offering
a random gross return $\underset{\sim}{R}$. Let each of the n traders
(indexed by i) be endowed with one share of the
security and one unit of a nonstorable commodity money

and let each be risk neutral. Trader i observes
two random variables X_i and Y_i : the variable
X_i represents the utility available to i from immediate consumption and Y_i represents information
about R . The X_i's are assumed to be independent
and identically and non-atomically distributed, and,
initially, they are also assumed to be independent
of $(R, Y_1, \ldots, Y_n)$. To capture the anonymity of
the market, it is further assumed that the joint distribution of $(R, Y_1, \ldots, Y_n)$ is invariant under
permutations of the indices. The numbers 1 through
n designate the order in which traders arrive at
the market.

The k market makers are assumed to be risk
neutral, and to have sufficient supplies of money
and securities that any k-1 of them could accommodate the traders' net demands along any price path
in the range of the equilibrium price function computed below. The market makers have no private information; even the ticker tape (the history of trading H_{i-1} when trader i arrives) is assumed to be
known by trader i . The market makers alternative
investments yield $X_0 = 1$, and 1 is also in the
support of the distribution of the X_i's .

The market operates as follows. When a customer
arrives, each of the k market makers simultaneously

announces a bid price and an ask price. The trader,
given his private information, his utility of current
consumption and these prices, chooses among three
options: to buy at the lowest ask price, to sell at
the highest bid price, or to stand pat and consume
his endowment. He makes the choice that maximizes
his expected payoff. Borrowing and short-sales are
prohibited.

The competition among the market makers resembles
the well known Bertrand competition in oligopoly theory
and the Bertrand arguments show that, at equilibrium,
the highest bid price b_1^* is equal to the highest
price at which a market maker can at least break even
in expectation. Similarly, the lowest ask price a_i^*
is the lowest break-even selling price.

If trader i faced bid and ask prices b and
a with $a \geq b$, he would sell at b if
$b\underset{\sim}{X}_i > E[\underset{\sim}{R}|\underset{\sim}{H}_{i-1}, \underset{\sim}{Y}_i]$ and he would buy at a if
$a\underset{\sim}{X}_i < E[\underset{\sim}{R}|\underset{\sim}{H}_{i-1}, \underset{\sim}{Y}_i]$. Calling the first of these
random events "i sells at b" and the second "i
buys at a," the equilibrium prices can be written
as follows:

$$b_i^* = \sup b\{E[\underset{\sim}{R}|\underset{\sim}{H}_{i-1}, \text{ i sells at b}] > b\}$$

$$= E[\underset{\sim}{R}|\underset{\sim}{H}_{i-1}, \text{ i sells at } b_i^*] \;, \quad \text{and}$$

$$a_i^* = \inf a\{E[\underset{\sim}{R}|\underset{\sim}{H}_{i-1}, \text{ i buys at a}] \le a\}$$

$$= E[\underset{\sim}{R}|\underset{\sim}{H}_{i-1}, \text{ i buys at } a_i^*] \;.$$

Notice that there is a tendency for traders to buy when they believe $\underset{\sim}{R}$ is high and to sell when they believe $\underset{\sim}{R}$ is low. Thus, the market makers are faced with a variation of the winner's curse. To avoid losing money, the market makers must build a margin of safety into their price quotations. It can be shown that if the density f_i of $\ln \underset{\sim}{X}_i$ satisfies $d^2 \ln f_i/dx^2 \le 0$ and if $(\underset{\sim}{R}, \underset{\sim}{X}_1, \ldots, \underset{\sim}{X}_n)$ are affiliated (see Milgrom and Weber for the definition and properties of "affiliation"), then the equilibrium prices specified above satisfy this requirement; that is, $b_i^* \le E[\underset{\sim}{R}|\underset{\sim}{H}_{i-1}] \le a_i^*$. For example, if the $\underset{\sim}{X}_i$'s have lognormal distributions and if the $\underset{\sim}{X}_i$'s are independent estimates of $\underset{\sim}{R}$ with the monotone likelihood ratio property, then these requirements are satisfied.

There are three cases which serve to illustrate the qualitative predictions of this model. In the first case, the $\underset{\sim}{X}_i$'s are degenerate, and convey

---

[5] Milgrom and Weber (1982b).

no information about R . It is then plain from the
formulas given above that $a_i^* = b_i^* = E[R|H_{i-1}] = E[R]$:
all trading takes place at the competitive equilibrium
price. In the second case, the X_i's are degenerate
and all equal to 1, but the χ_i's are non-degenerate.
Comparing the price formula in this case with the
trader's trading rule, it is clear that no trade can
take place. The equilibrium bid price is set so low
and the ask price so high that all potential traders
are discouraged. The third case arises when we assume
that trader i gets information about R only if he
has no transactions motive for trading with the market makers, i.e., only if $X_i = 1$. In this case,
it can be shown that if any trading involving the
informed traders takes place, then these traders impose losses in expectation on the market makers.
Since the market makers break even in expectation
overall, they must profit from trading with the uninformed.

The foregoing theory has some testable implications concerning security prices and trading volumes.
It predicts, for example, that closely held firms
(where there are relatively many traders with private
information) should exhibit larger bid-ask spreads
and less active trading among outsiders than comparable firms where insider holdings are small.

The model described in this paper is very specialized, but it seems likely that the qualitative conclusions can be extended to much more general settings. Once the process of price determination is made explicit, many of the contradictions and apparent paradoxes that plague the traditional theories of securities markets disappear, and a coherent alternative theory begins to emerge.

REFERENCES

Grossman, S. (1976). "On the Efficiency of Competitive Stock Markets Where Traders Have Diverse Information," Journal of Finance, Vol. 31, pp. 573-85.

Milgrom, P. (1981). "Rational Expectations, Information Acquisition and Competitive Bidding," Econometrica, Vol. 49, pp. 921-43.

Milgrom, P. and R. Weber (1982a). "The Value of Information in a Sealed-Bid Auction," Journal of Mathematical Economics, Vol. 10, pp. 105-14.

Milgrom, P. and R. Weber (1982b). "A Theory of Auctions and Competitive Bidding," Econometrica, Vol. 50, pp. 1089-122.

Tirole, J. (1980). On the Possibility of Speculation under Rational Expectations. Cambridge, Mass.: Massachusetts Institute of Technology Press.

2

THE BASIC THEORY OF OPTIMAL AUCTIONS
Roger B. Myerson

The theory of optimal auction design has been developed in several recent papers.[1] I shall review this theory and present some of the conclusions that can be made. Given a single object to sell, a seller wants to find the type of auction which will maximize his expected revenue. This is the basic problem considered in the area of optimal auction design. Among all the possible auctions (such as the first-price, second-price, sealed-bid, sequential auctions) which will maximize the seller's expected profit?

Notice first that the selection of the most

---

[1]Harris and Raviv (1978); Myerson (1981); Riley and Samuelson (1981); Maskin and Riley (1981).

advantageous auction is a problem of decision
in the face of uncertainty. That is, if the seller
knew how much the object was worth to each bidder,
then his optimal auction would be simply to announce
a nonnegotiable price for the object at (or just below) the highest bidder's valuation. However, because
the seller does not know his bidder's true valuations,
he is forced to choose among auction mechanisms which
are almost surely going to give him less than this
perfect information optimum. In summary, the seller
is bound to regret either that he set his minimum
bid level too high (because the object failed to sell
at that price) or too low (because the winning bidder
got the object for less than he was willing to pay).
But good decisions under uncertainty are never expected to abolish regret; rather the decision maker
must assess his subjective probability distributions
for the unknown quantities, and he must find the decision which maximizes his expected utility, given
his current information. Thus, the central feature
of an auction design problem must be the probability
distribution over bidders' valuations for the object.
I will consider only the case in which bidders' valuations are perceived as independent random variables.

Let n be the number of bidders, whom we shall
think of as a numbered $i = 1, 2, \ldots, n$. We let
$\tilde{V}_i$ denote bidder i's valuation for the object.

Since the seller does not know $\tilde{V}_i$, he must think
of it as a random variable, with some probability
density $f_i(v_i)$ and a cumulative distribution $F_i(v_i)$.
That is, $F_i(v_i) = \Pr(\tilde{V}_i \leq v_i)$ and $f_i(v_i) = F_i'(v_i)$,
for any number v_i . Since we are assuming that the
bidders' valuations are independent random variables,
this implies that the probability distribution of
the n valuations is just the product of their separate distributions:

$$f(v_1, \ldots, v_n) = f_1(v_1) \ldots f_n(v_n) .$$

Each bidder's valuation is not only unknown to
the seller; it is also unknown to the other bidders.
What one bidder thinks his competitors are likely
to do will influence how he bids in an auction, so
our model must also specify what subjective probability distribution is assessed by each bidder about
each other bidder's valuation for the object. We
assume here that each bidder assesses the same distribution on his competitors' valuations as the
seller does. That is, bidder j perceives his competitors' valuations as independent random variables,
with $f_i(v_i)$ as the probability distribution for
valuation of the bidder i .

Two other important assumptions which limit the
scope of our model must be pointed out. We shall

assume that the seller and the bidders are all <u>risk</u>
<u>neutral</u>. We also shall assume that each bidder's
valuation for the object depends only on his own personal information, so that he would not revise his
true valuation for the object after learning about
his competitors' valuations. Of course, he might
well revise his bidding strategy in an auction if
he could learn about his competitors' valuation.
We only assume here that his true trade off between
the object and money would not change if he knew more
about the other bidders' information. This assumption
rules out any "winner's curse" effect. The model
solved by Myerson in 1981 does allow for some forms
of value interaction and "winner's curve," but we
shall ignore these issues in this paper.

Within this structure, we can explicitly characterize the optimal auctions that maximize the seller'
expected revenues. This result may seem remarkable
since none of our assumptions has imposed any restriction on the <u>form</u> of the auction mechanism which the
seller may use. The auction rules may allow for an
arbitrarily large number of bidding rounds, and the
rules and bidding strategies in each round may be as
complex as desired.

In general, the seller faces only three kinds
of restrictions in designing his auction. First,
the auction must give each bidder a nonnegative

expected profit, whatever his valuation may be. This
restriction prevents the seller from ordering the
bidders to pay more than they expected to gain from
winning the object (because the bidders would refuse
to participate in such an auction). Second, the outcome of the auction cannot depend directly on the bidders'
true valuations, except in so far as each bidder's
valuation affects his strategy in playing the auction
game. This restriction must hold because the seller
cannot directly observe the bidders' true valuations.
Third, the bidding strategy which we expect each bidder to use in the auction game must be optimal for
him, among the class of all strategies available to
him. That is, for any bidder and any possible valuation, we must expect that the bidder will use the
bid that maximizes his expected profit in the auction game, given his valuation, and given the way
he expects the other bidders to bid as a function
of their valuations. When the bidders use bidding
strategies which all satisfy this rationality restriction, then we say that the strategies form an equilibrium.

The key insight which makes the problem of designing an optimal auction tractable is that the
seller may, without loss of generality, restrict
himself to incentive-compatible direct auctions.
We say that an auction is direct if each bidder is

only asked to report his valuation to the seller.
Thus, for example, any sealed-bid auction is direct.
A direct auction is <u>incentive compatible</u> if the optimal strategy for each bidder in the auction is to
report his valuation honestly (given that the others
are planning to report honestly). In other words,
a sealed-bid auction is incentive compatible if the
honest bidding strategies form an <u>equilibrium</u>.

Certainly most auctions are not incentive compatible. For example, in a first-price sealed-bid
auction, the optimal bid is generally lower than the
true valuation, so a first-price auction is not incentive compatible. But for any equilibrium of
strategies in any auction game, there is an equivalent incentive-compatible direct auction. To implement this equivalent direct auction, the seller simply
asks each bidder to report his valuation, then the
seller computes what would have been the bidder's
optimal bidding strategy in the given equilibrium of
the original auction game, and then the seller delivers the object and charges the bidders exactly as
he would have done in the original auction game if
the bidders had used these strategies. When all bidders are honest, this direct auction is equivalent
to the given equilibrium of the original auction game.
Furthermore, this direct auction is incentive compatible. If it were rational for any bidder to lie

in the direct auction, then it would have been rational
for him to lie to himself in carrying out his equilibrium strategy in the original game, which is impossible!

Thus, there is no loss of generality in restricting attention to incentive-compatible direct auctions.
That is, the optimal auction among the incentive compatible direct auctions is also optimal among all types
of auctions. This fact is valuable to us because the
set of all incentive-compatible direct auctions is
easy to characterize mathematically. A direct auction
is characterized by a list of two outcome functions,
denoted by $p_i(\cdot)$ and $x_i(\cdot)$, for each bidder i .
We let $p_i(v_1, \ldots, v_n)$ denote the probability that
bidder i gets the object, and we let $x_i(v_1, \ldots, v_n)$
denote the expected cash payment from bidder i , if
$(v_1, \ldots, v_n)$ is the vector of valuations reported
by the bidders 1, ..., n . Then the functions
$p_1(\cdot), \ldots, p_n(\cdot), x_1(\cdot), \ldots, x_n(\cdot)$ completely describe the direct auction. So the optimal auction de-
sign problem can be reduced to choosing 2n functions
to maximize the seller's expected revenue, which is

$$E[\sum_{i=1}^{n} x_i(\tilde{v}_1, \ldots, \tilde{v}_n)] \tag{1}$$

Here the expected-value operator $E[\cdot]$ treates

$\tilde{V}_1, \ldots, \tilde{V}_n$ all as random variables, with probability distributions $f(\cdot)$ as above.

There is only one object to distribute, so the $p_i(\cdot)$ outcome functions must satisfy, for every possible list of valuations $(v_1, \ldots, v_n)$,

$$\sum_{i=1}^{n} p_i(v_1, \ldots, v_n) \leq 1 \tag{2}$$

and all $p_i(v_1, \ldots, v_n) \geq 0$. That is, the bidders' probabilities of winning cannot sum to more than 1. Finally, it is easy to express mathematically the constraints that the auction must be incentive-compatible for the bidders and must give the bidders nonnegative expected profits. If bidder i were to report a valuation $\hat{v}_i$ when v_i was his true valuation, his expected profit would be

$$\begin{aligned} U_i(\hat{v}_i | v_i) = E[v_i \cdot p_i(\tilde{V}_1, \ldots, \hat{v}_i, \ldots, \tilde{V}_n) \\ - x_i(\tilde{V}_1, \ldots, \hat{v}_i, \ldots, \tilde{V}_n)] \end{aligned} \tag{3}$$

(Here the expected-value operator $E[\cdot]$ treats $(\tilde{V}_1, \ldots, \tilde{V}_{i-1}, \tilde{V}_{i+1}, \ldots, \tilde{V}_n)$ as random variables, but v_i and $\hat{v}_i$ are fixed.) Then the incentive-compatibility restriction asserts that bidder i should not gain by reporting $\hat{v}_i$ if v_i is his true valuation. In mathematical terms, this means

$$U_i(v_i | v_i) \geq U_i(\hat{v}_i | v_i) \qquad (4)$$

must hold for every bidder i and every two possible
valuations v_i and $\hat{v}_i$. To guarantee that every
bidder can get nonnegative expected profits, we must
add the constraints

$$U_i(v_i | v_i) \geq 0 \qquad (5)$$

for every bidder i and every possible valuation v_i .
    So the problem of designing an optimal auction
has been reduced to a mathematical optimization problem: to choose 2n functions ($p_i(\cdot)$ and $x_i(\cdot)$
for i = 1, ..., n) so as to maximize (1) subject
to the constraints (2) through (5). This mathematical problem is quite tractable. (In fact, if the
distribution of the $\tilde{V}_i$ random variables were dis-
crete, it would reduce to a linear programming
problem.)
    Given any possible valuation v_i for bidder
i , let

$$c_i(v_i) = v_i - \frac{1 - F_i(v_i)}{f_i(v_i)}$$

where $f_i(\cdot)$ is the probability density of the random variable $\tilde{V}_i$ and $F_i(\cdot)$ is the corresponding

cumulative distribution. We call $c_i(v_i)$ the _priority level_ associated with the bid v_i. Notice that the priority level is always less than the true valuation.

We say that the auction design problem is _regular_ if the priority level $c_i(v_i)$ always increases as v_i increases. Our main result is then as follows:

Fact 1. If the auction design problem is regular then, in the optimal auction, the seller must deliver the object to the bidder with the highest positive priority level. If all priority levels are negative, then the seller must keep the object, even though the valuations themselves may be positive; that is, $v_i > 0 > c_i(v_i)$.

Fact 1 only describes half of the optimal auction, since it tells us who should get the object, but it does not tell us how much he should pay. To complete the description of an optimal auction, we need one more construction, which generalizes the notion of a second-price auction. Given any list of reported valuations $(v_1, \ldots, v_n)$ from the n bidders, let $z_i(v_1, \ldots, v_n)$ be the lowest valuation for bidder i such that he could have changed his reported valuation from v_i to z_i and still won the object under the rules in Fact 1, if every other bidder j kept his reported valuation fixed at v_j. That is, $z_i(v_1, \ldots, v_n)$ satisfies $c_i(z_i) \geq 0$, and

$c_i(z_i) \geq c_j(v_j)$ for all $j \neq i$, and is the smallest such number.

Fact 2. For a regular auction design problem, the auction described here is incentive compatible and maximizes the seller's expected revenue among all possible auctions. Ask all bidders to report their valuations simultaneously. If $(v_1, \ldots, v_n)$ is the list of reported valuations, then deliver the object to the bidder with the highest priority level $c_i(v_i)$ and charge him $z_i(v_1, \ldots, v_n)$, provided that $c_i(v_i) \geq 0$. If all $c_i(v_i)$ are negative, then keep the object. Bidders who do not get the object pay nothing.

For a simple example, suppose each bidder's valuation is a uniform random variable on the interval from zero to 100. Then

$$f_i(v_i) = \frac{1}{100} \text{ and } F_i(v_i) = \frac{v_i}{100}, \ 0 \leq v_i \leq 100$$

So

$$c_i(v_i) = v_i - \frac{1 - v_i/100}{1/100} = 2v_1 - 100$$

In our optimal auction, bidder i wins only if his valuation $\tilde{v}_i$ satisfies

$$0 \leq 2\hat{\hat{V}}_i - 100 = \underset{j=1,\ldots,n}{\text{maximum}} (2\hat{\hat{V}}_i - 100)$$

With a little algebra, we see that this is equivalent to

$$50 \leq \hat{\hat{V}}_i = \underset{j=1,\ldots,n}{\text{maximum}} (\hat{\hat{V}}_j)$$

That is, the winner is the highest bidder, provided that his bid is at least 50. The winner pays either 50 or the second highest bid, whichever is higher (because this is the lowest valuation which he could have reported and still have won). This optimal auction is equivalent to a second-price auction (in which the high bidder wins and pays the second highest bid) where the seller himself submits a bid of 50. As in the usual second-price auction, this auction is incentive compatible, which means that each bidder's best bid is his true valuation.[2] Because of the seller's bid of 50, the seller must keep the object if all bids are less than 50 even though the object is worth nothing to the seller. This inefficient outcome will happen with probability $(1/2)^n$. However, if the high bid is above 50 and the second highest bid is below 50, then the winning bidder pays 50, rather than the second highest bid. So putting in a seller's bid of 50 is a gamble for the seller: it may be better

---

[2] Vickrey (1961).

or worse for him than a bid of zero, depending on
what the bidders' valuations are. This gamble is
worth taking for the seller. As was emphasized earlier, auction design involves making a decision under
uncertainty and, as such, involves accepting a positive probability of regret.

To see why the seller must accept a positive
probability of keeping the object even when the bidders are willing to pay more than zero, consider the
case of one bidder (n = 1) . In this case, the optimal auction for the example discussed above simply
reduces to a nonnegotiable offer to sell the object
for 50. Since the bidder's valuation is a uniform
random variable on the interval on the interval from
zero to 100 there is a 50 percent chance that the
buyer may refuse to buy at this price. The seller
would then be tempted to lower his price, say to 25,
since getting 25 is better than receiving nothing.
But such a strategy would <u>lower</u> the seller's expected
revenues because the rational bidder should anticipate the price reduction and refuse the first-round
price of 50, even if his valuation is above 50. To
command a price of 50, the seller must irrevocably
commit himself to not selling at any lower price,
and thus he must bear a risk of not selling the object at all, unless he can fool the bidder into
thinking that 50 is a final offer when it really is

not.

For a second example, suppose that there are
two bidders, the first bidder's valuation $\tilde{v}_1$ is
a uniform random variable on the interval from zero
to 100, and the second bidder's valuation $\tilde{v}_2$ is
a uniform random variable on the interval from zero
to 200. Thus, although we know that the first bidder's valuation is not more than 100, there is
reason to hope that the second bidder might be willing to pay as much as 200 for the object. It is
easy to check that, for this example,

$$c_1(v_1) = 2v_1 - 100 \quad \text{and} \quad c_2(v_2) = 2v_2 - 200$$

That is, if the two bidders had the same valuation,
the optimal auction would give the object to bidder
1 rather than bidder 2 (provided that $\tilde{v}_1 \geq 50$),
because bidder 2 would have the lower priority level.
In fact, for bidder 2 to win the object, the valuation of bidder 2 must be at least 50 more than the
valuation of bidder 1. We discriminate against bidder 2 because we hope that it may encourage him to
admit that he has a high valuation. If we simply
held a nondiscriminatory first-price auction, bidder
2 would never offer to pay more than 100, since he

knows that bidder 1 would never bid higher than 100. However in the optimal auction, because we discriminate against bidder 2, he may be forced to pay as much as 150 to get the object.

REFERENCES

Harris, M. and A. Raviv (1978). "Allocation Mechanism and the Design of Auction," Working Paper, Graduate School of Industrial Administration, Carnegie-Mellon University.

Maskin, E. and J. G. Riley (1980). "Auctioning an Indivisible Object," Discussion Paper No. 87D, Kennedy School of Government, Harvard University.

Myerson, R. B. (1981). "Optimal Auction Design," Mathematics of Operations Research, Vol. 6, pp. 58-73.

Riley, J. G. and W. F. Samuelson (1981). "Optimal Auctions," American Economic Review, Vol. 71, No. 3.

Vickrey, W. (1961). "Counterspeculation, Auctions, and Competitive Sealed Tenders," Journal of Finance, Vol. 16, pp. 8-37.

3

MULTIPLE-OBJECT AUCTIONS[*]

Robert J. Weber

1. INTRODUCTION

The received theory of auctions has a principal focus on the sale of a single object. However, a great number of observed auctions involve the sale of more than one object, sold either simultaneously or sequentially. We shall take a brief look at some of the issues which arise in the study of multiple-object auctions; a number of these issues simply do not arise when the sale of only one object is being

[*]This research was supported in part by the U.S. Office of Naval Research, the Xerox Corporation, and the Center for Advanced Studies in Managerial Economics at Northwestern University.

considered.

We classify the auctions we will discuss into three categories. A simultaneous-dependent auction is one in which the bidders are each called upon to take a single action, subsequent to which the objects will be distributed among the bidders and payments will be made. An example of such a sale is the weekly auctioning of United States Treasury bills. A special case of such a sale, which we choose to view separately, is a simultaneous-independent auction, in which the bidders must simultaneously act in several different auctions of individual items, and in which the outcome of each sale is independent of the outcomes of the others. The sale of mineral rights on federal land by the United States Department of the Interior frequently takes this form. It should be noted that such a sale may force a bidder to expose himself to the risk of obtaining more items than he desires. Finally, a sequential auction is just what the name suggests: the sale of one item at a time, perhaps with the public release of information concerning the outcome of a round prior to the beginning of the next. Examples of such sales are estate auctions at which a collection of objects such as stamps, coins, antiques, or the like, are sold.

2. BIDDERS WITH LIMITED CONSUMPTION CAPACITY

Perhaps the most elementary situation occurs when
a number of identical objects are to be sold, but each
bidder desires only one of them. Even in this setting,
much of the richness of the multiple-object environment
appears.

2.1. The Independent Private Values Model. We initially assume that each bidder knows the (identical)
values of the objects to himself (this is the private
values assumption), and that the values of the different bidders are independent observations of a nonnegative random variable X with a commonly known continuous
distribution. Let there be a total of n risk-neutral
bidders, and let X_1, ..., X_n be their valuations
(which we will also refer to as their types). Finally,
assume that a total of k objects are to be sold.
For the sake of notational ease, but with no real loss
of generality, we restrict our consideration to the
case $k < n$.

Let $X_{(1)} \geq X_{(2)} \geq \cdots \geq X_{(n)}$ be the order statistics of the n types. For any particular bidder,
the order statistics of the opposing types are central
to his decision problem. Therefore, taking the perspective of bidder 1, we define Y_1, ..., Y_{n-1} to
be the order statistics of X_2, ..., X_n .

First-price and second-price auctions are two
well-known procedures that are used to sell a single
object. In each, the bidders submit nonnegative sealed
bids; the highest bidder receives the object, and
pays either the amount of his own bid (first price)
or the highest of the opposing bids (second price).
Both can be generalized to simultaneous dependent
sealed-bid auctions in which each of the k highest
bidders receives an item. In the discriminatory auction
each of the k highest bidders pays the amount he
bid. In the uniform-price auction, each pays the
amount of the highest rejected ($(k+1)^{st}$ highest)
bid.

A strategy for a bidder in either of the auctions
under consideration is a function which associates a
bid with each of his possible types. When discussing
symmetric models, we are primarily concerned with
symmetric equilibria.

Theorem 1. In the independent private values model:

(a) Let $b^D(x) = E[Y_k | Y_k < x]$. Then $(b^D, \ldots, b^D)$
is the unique symmetric equilibrium of the discriminatory auction.

(b) Let $b^U(x) = x = E[Y_k | Y_k = x]$. Then
$(b^U, \ldots, b^U)$ is the unique symmetric equilibrium of
the uniform-price auction.

(c) The total expected revenue of the seller is

the same in both the discriminatory and uniform-
price auctions, and equals $k \cdot E[X_{(k+1)}]$.[1]

   Recent studies have set the "revenue equivalence"
result of Theorem 1(c) in a broad context. Consider
any auction mechanism which delivers at most one object to each bidder. Given fixed strategies for n-1
of the bidders, the selection of any bid by the remaining bidder determines a particular probability p of
his obtaining an item, and a particular expected payment e . Since the types are independent, the (p,e)-
pair associated with any bid does not depend on his
own type. The bidder's decision problem, when his
type is x , is to choose a bid b which maximizes
$x \cdot p(b) - e(b)$.

   The equilibrium assumption (that each bidder follows a strategy which is optimal given the strategies
of the others) yields for each bidder i a differential condition relating the p_i and e_i functions
he faces. Consequently, at equilibrium the n functions e_i , and hence the seller's expected revenue,
are fully determined by the n functions p_i and
n boundary conditions. A convenient set of boundary
conditions is provided by the expected payment made
by each of the bidders when he is of his lowest possible type. The preceding discussion motivates the

---

[1]Vickrey (1962); Ortega-Reichert (1968).

following theorem.[2]

Theorem 2. Consider any auction mechanism in the
k-object, n-bidder, independent private values setting.
Assume that an equilibrium point is given, such that
the bidders with the k highest types are certain
to receive items, and such that a bidder with the
lowest possible type has an expected payment of zero.
Then the seller's expected revenue at this equilibrium
is $k \cdot E[X_{(k+1)}]$.

A sequential auction may be viewed as a simultaneous dependent auction, albeit one in which a bidder's
"action" may be very complex (since it must specify
his intended action at every stage, conditioned on
the information revealed in previous stages). Consequently, Theorem 2 applies to sequential sales. Here
we consider two such sales, the first-price sequential
auction and the second-price sequential auction, each
based on the corresponding single-object procedure.
In each round, the bidders who remain (those who have
not yet been awarded an item) submit sealed bids. The
highest bidder is awarded an item and pays according
to the corresponding single-object pricing rule. A
public announcement is made concerning the outcome
of that round, and the procedure is then repeated

---

[2]Myerson (1981); Milgrom and Weber (1982).

(until all k objects have been sold).

   We shall consider two types of announcements.
The first is simply: "An object has been sold."
This provides each bidder only with information which
must be available to him at the start of the next
round. The second type of announcement is: "An object has been sold at the price p " (where p is
indeed the price at which the sale was made). In
the sequential first-price procedure, this announcement permits each remaining bidder to draw certain
inferences about the distribution of types of the
other remaining bidders. In the sequential second-
price auction, this announcement actually discloses
the bid made by one of the remaining bidders. A remarkable fact is that symmetric equilibrium strategies
for either auction are the same under either announcement policy.

Theorem 3. In the independent private values model:

   (a) Let $b_\ell^F(x) = E[Y_k | Y_\ell < x < Y_{\ell-1}]$
$= E[X_{(k+1)} | X_{(\ell)} = x]$ for $\ell = 1, \ldots, k$, and let
$b^F = (b_1^F, \ldots, b_k^F)$. Then $(b^F, \ldots, b^F)$ is the unique
symmetric equilibrium of the sequential first-price
auction.

   (b) Let $b_\ell^S(x) = E[Y_k | Y_\ell = x] = E[X_{(k+1)} | X_{(\ell+1)} = x]$
for $\ell = 1, \ldots, k$, and let $b^S = (b_1^S, \ldots, b_k^S)$.
Then $(b^S, \ldots, b^S)$ is the unique symmetric equilibrium
of the sequential second-price auction.

In both cases, $b_\ell(x)$ is the bid made by a bidder of type x in the ℓth round, if he has not yet received an item. In Theorem 3(a), Y_0 is interpreted to be infinite.

Both parts of the theorem can be proved recursively by working back from the final stage of the auction. A crucial consequence of the independent assumption is that

$$E[X_{(k+1)}|X_{(\ell)}, X_{(\ell-1)}] = E[X_{(k+1)}|X_{(\ell)}]$$

$$\text{for} \quad \ell = 1, \ldots, k$$

It is this which makes the equilibrium strategies independent of the type of announcement.

From Theorem 3, it is not difficult to see that the (unconditional) expected selling price at each stage is $E[X_{(k+1)}]$. But how does the sequence of actual prices behave? In the sequential first-price auction, the expected price in the ℓth stage, given that the $(\ell-1)^{st}$ price is p , is:

$$E[b_\ell(X_{(\ell)})|b_{\ell-1}(X_{(\ell-1)}) = p]$$
$$= E[E[X_{(k+1)}|X_{(\ell)}]|X_{(\ell-1)} = b_{\ell-1}^{-1}(p)]$$
$$= E[E[X_{(k+1)}|X_{(\ell)}, X_{(\ell-1)}]|X_{(\ell-1)} = b_{\ell-1}^{-1}(p)]$$
$$= E[X_{(k+1)}|X_{(\ell-1)} = b_{\ell-1}^{-1}(p)]$$
$$= b_{\ell-1}(b_{\ell-1}^{-1}(p)) = p \ .$$

Hence, the sequence of prices is a martingale; that
is, on average, prices drift neither up nor down over
time.   A similar result can be established in the
same manner for the sequential second-price auction.

The independent private values model can be generalized through the introduction of uncertainty concerning the number of bidders. Assume that the number
N of bidders is a random variable that is independent
of the bidders' types and is almost surely finite.
Let the types of the bidders present at the auction
be X_1, ..., X_N . Extend this finite list of types
by adjoining an infinite number of zeroes and define
the sequences $X_{(1)}$, $X_{(2)}$, ... and Y_1, Y_2 ... of
order statistics as before. Then Theorems 1, 2 and
3 remain valid as stated, and the martingale property
again holds for both the first-price and second-price
sequential auctions.

Another generalization of the independent private
values model arises when the private values assumption
is relaxed. Let the value of an object to bidder i
be V_i . Assume that there is a nonnegative real-
valued function u of n variables, such that for
every i , $V_i = u(X_i, \{X_j\}_{j \neq i})$. (That is, assume
that each bidder has the same "valuation function,"
and that the other bidders' types enter his function
in a symmetric manner.) Further, assume that u

is strictly increasing in its first argument and mono-
tone increasing in all of its arguments. Define
$v_k(x,y) = E[V_1 | X_1 = x, Y_k = y]$. Then Theorems 1 and
2 are valid for this "independent types, symmetric
values" model, when $v_k(Y_k, Y_k)$ (or $v_k(X_{(k+1)}, X_{(k+1)}$
is substituted for Y_k (or $X_{(k+1)}$) before the
conditioning signs in the various expectations.

2.2. <u>The General Symmetric Model</u>. Clearly, the assumptions that drove the results of the previous section were symmetry and type independence. In this
section, we relax the independence assumption. The
following two paragraphs present what we call the
<u>general symmetric model</u>.

     Let S_1, ..., S_m, X_1, ..., X_n be real-valued
random variables. The first m variables represent
qualities of the (identical) objects not directly
observable by the bidders; the remaining variables are
the bidders private <u>estimates</u>. Let V_i be the value
of any object to the bidder i . We assume that there
is a nonnegative function u on R^{m+n} , such that
for each i ,

$$V_i = u(X_i, \{X_j\}_{j \neq i}; S_1, \ldots, S_m)$$

Consequently, the m state variables enter all of
the bidder's valuations in the same manner. We

further assume that   u   is nondecreasing in all argu-
ments, and that $E[V_1 | X_1 = x]$ is increasing in   x .

   Let   f(s,x)   denote the joint density of the
m+n   random elements of the model. Our final symmetry
assumption is that   f   is symmetric in its last   n
arguments. We also assume that the elements of the
model have a positive statistical linkage. Let   z
and   z'   be points in R^{m+n} ; let   z v z'   denote
the coordinate-wise maximum and   z ∧ z'   the coordinate-
wise minimum. Then   f   is <u>affiliated</u> if for all   z
and   z' , $f(z \vee z')f(z \wedge z') \geq f(z)f(z')$. Roughly,
this condition states that higher values of some variables make higher values of the others more likely,
a not unreasonable assumption in the kinds of situations we wish to study. A formal development of affil-
iation is presented in Milgrom and Weber.[3]

   In this general setting, the revenue-equivalence
result of the previous section fails to hold. (The
argument given before Theorem 2 breaks down due to
the dependence of the functions p_i and e_i on bidder   i's   signal.) Indeed, we have the following
result.

---

[3] Milgrom and Weber (1982).

<u>Theorem 4</u>. In the general symmetric model, the uniform-price auction generally yields greater expected revenues than the discriminatory auction.

The proof of this theorem is based on the idea that, when the price paid by a bidder reflects the estimates of other bidders, that price is more closely linked to his own estimate, even when his choice of a bid is held fixed. This extra linkage leads to a steeper expected payment (a function of his estimate) for each bidder. Since the expected payment functions associated with the two auction procedures are the same (at equilibrium) when a bidder has the lowest possible estimate, the extra linkage generates higher expected revenues.

There is a colorful history of debate surrounding the format used for the weekly United States Treasury bill auctions. Tradition has been to use a discriminatory auction, although a number of authors have argued for a change to uniform pricing. Many of the arguments presented deal with questions of bidder collusion, or with the degree to which one format or the other will attract a greater number of small-volume risk-averse bidders. (Indeed, current practice is to allow small-volume bidders to enter "noncompetitive" bids and to award them bills at the average of the accepted "competitive" bids.) It is natural to assume that the bidder estimates of economic trends are statistically linked.

Therefore, to the extent that the assumption that
bidders desire equal quantities of bills is valid,
Theorem 4 provides a new dimension to the debate.
It should be noted, however, that the introduction
of risk-aversion complicates matters.

Theorem 5. In the independent private values model,
if the bidders are equally averse to risk, then the
discriminatory auction generally yields greater expected revenues than the uniform-price auction.

Consequently, if arguments in favor of one procedure or the other are to be based on their revenue-
generating properties, one must decide whether the
statistical linkage of the bidders' estimates or the
aversion of the bidders to risk is the overriding
factor.

Another consequence of the linkage argument given
above is that when the seller expects to hold private
information of his own (such as when he will observe
one or more of the state variables S_1, ..., S_n prior
to the sale), a policy of fully and accurately reporting his information to the bidders will yield a higher
expected price than any other policy of information
management (such as censoring the information, or
garbling it prior to release) which he might adopt.
Even if he does not hold private information, he can
bring some of the bidders' information into the public

domain (gradually) through the use of a sequential
auction. The effect of this is illustrated by the
following result, which holds for either of the types
of between-stage announcements previously discussed.

Theorem 6. In the general symmetric model, the sequential first-price auction generally yields greater
expected revenues than the discriminatory auction.
At equilibrium, the sequence of prices generated from
a sequential sale will display upward drift (that is,
will be a submartingale).

2.3. Simultaneous Independent Sales. From time to
time, the United States Department of the Interior
leases the mineral rights on various federal properties. In this section, we focus on drilling rights
on offshore territory. These lease sales often involve
more than a hundred tracts, all in the same area.
Bidders are required to submit separate, non-retract-
able sealed bids for all tracts on which they wish
to compete and to submit a substantial downpayment
with each bid. All bids on all tracts are unsealed
on the same day, after the deadline for the submission
of bids is reached. The high bidder on each tract
receives the rights on that tract, and is required to
complete his payment to the level of his bid. (Actually, the government reserves the right to withdraw
a tract from sale if it finds the highest bid unsatis-

factory. Also, in addition to his bid, a winning bidder is required to pay a royalty on the petroleum he extracts. These complicating factors need not concern us here.)

Historically, the variance of the bids submitted on a tract has been quite high. Studies of sales conducted in the late 1960s found the winning bid to typically be twice that of the second-highest bid.[4] Substantial sums of money are involved here. Examples abound in which tracts selling for around $100 million drew second-high bids of less than $30 million. Consequently, the spread between the high bid and the second-highest bid (known in picturesque oil-industry parlance as "money left on the table") is of some concern to the competing bidders.

Some authors have cited the substantial uncertainty concerning the extractable resources present on a tract as a factor which makes large bid spreads unavoidable. However, there is another factor which can lead to sizable spreads.[5]

When a firm prepares to bid on tracts in a particular area, it has two conflicting concerns. It does not wish to be "shut out" of the area: a certain number of leases must be obtained in order to protect

---

[4] Capen, Clapp, and Campbell (1971).

[5] Engelbrecht-Wiggans and Weber (1979).

its competitive position and to provide a use for
its costly exploratory equipment. Yet it also does
not wish to win too many tracts: there are many
dangers inherent in an overcommitment of capital in
a single area. Competing firms face similar concerns.

If it were possible, a firm might wish to submit contingent bids: "If we win less than k of the
first ℓ tracts for which bids are opened, then our
remaining bids stay in submission; otherwise, those
bids are withdrawn." However, this is not allowed.

Assume that the supply of tracts is roughly equal
to the demand for them. This is a plausible assumption, since the government can regulate the supply,
and has as one of its goals to have tracts explored
and developed expeditiously. Then one possible strategy for a firm is to bid quite aggressively on some
tracts (in order to minimize the chance of being shut
out), and to bid much less aggressively on others,
expecting to win them only if the other firms also bid
unaggressively, and then to win them at a bargain
price.

Indeed, in a relatively simple model in which
all tracts are identical and there is no uncertainty
concerning the values of the tracts being sold,
Engelbrecht-Wiggans and Weber have shown that there
is an equilibrium in such aggressive/nonaggressive

strategies, and that the distribution of the spread
between the winning and the second-best bids at equilibrium is similar to that observed in practice.
While it is unarguable that a certain amount of the
variance in bids submitted in oil-lease auctions is
the result of bidder uncertainties about the state
of nature, the preceding discussion suggests that
the strategic variance in bids forced by the use of
a simultaneous-independent auction procedure might
be an important factor in explaining the large sums
of money left on the table in these auctions.

3.   SEQUENTIAL AUCTIONS

In Section 2.1, the results we described concerning sequential auctions in the independent
private-values model relied on an important property
of the equilibrium strategies. To wit, a bidder
never had to concern himself with how the other bidders' perceptions of him were affected by his actions,
since their equilibrium strategies were independent
of those perceptions.

When the bidders have dependent value estimates,
the situation becomes much more complicated. If a
bidder bids more conservatively in one round than his
estimate would appear to warrant, he might lead others
to believe that he has private information concerning

unfavorable aspects of the objects being sold. The
others would then bid more conservatively in future
rounds, enabling him to "steal" an item at a bargain
price. At equilibrium, of course, the temptation
of deception must somehow be accounted for.

3.1. <u>A Two-Stage Signalling Model</u>. Important insights into the nature of equilibrium behavior in
sequential actions were first provided by Ortega-
Reichert.[6] He considered a two-object, two-bidder,
first-price sequential auction in a private values
model. Assume that Nature chooses a state variable,
unobserved by the bidders but distributed according
to a commonly known distribution. Conditional on
this state variable, the private values of the first
item to the two bidders are independently determined.
Each learns his own value of the object, from which
he can draw inferences about the state of nature.
These inferences affect his beliefs about the other's
value, as well as his beliefs about the value of the
second item to him. However, this second value,
drawn from the same distribution as his first, will
not be revealed to him until the sale of the first
item is concluded and <u>both</u> bids have been revealed.

Incentives to deceive arise from the common
uncertainty about the state variable. If bidder 1

---

[6]Ortega-Reichert (1968).

could convince bidder 2 that his first-stage value
was low, then the second-stage beliefs of bidder 2
about the state variable (which are conditioned on
his two values and the information he thinks he possesses concerning the first-stage value to bidder 1) would be falsely conservative. Bidder 2
would therefore bid less aggressively in the second
stage than he otherwise might, thinking that bidder
1 has a second-stage value which would more likely
be lower than it actually is. This would afford bidder 2 a chance to turn a large profit in the second
stage.

Ortega-Reichert found that there is a symmetric
pure-strategy equilibrium for the game in question.
In the first stage, each bidder bids less than he
would were the auction composed of only that stage.
This is perhaps surprising. A pure strategy is in-
vertible in the sense that a bidder's value can be
deduced with certainty from the bid he makes. But
if his first-stage bid is fully revealing, what gain
is there in not making a bid which maximizes his expected return in that stage? The answer lies in the
inferences drawn by the other bidder. If bidder 1
makes a higher bid in the first stage, it is true
that his first-stage expected profit will be greater
than it is from his equilibrium bid. But bidder 2
will then incorrectly conclude that the value to

bidder 1 was higher than it actually was, will have
falsely high beliefs about the state variable when
he prepares to bid in the second stage, and hence
will bid aggressively, expecting bidder 1 to have
another high value. At equilibrium, the cost to bidder 1 from stimulating this aggression in the second
stage outweighs the gain to be had from the use of a
non-equilibrium bid in the first stage.

Milgrom and Roberts used a related two-stage
model, which has an equilibrium of a similar nature,
to give a cogent analysis of the phenomenon of limit
pricing.[7]

3.2. _An Asymmetric Model_. Assume that k identical
objects are to be sold to two bidders via a first-price
sequential auction. There is initial uncertainty
concerning the quality of the objects; they are either
all of high value (1) or of low value (0). The probability p that they are all of value one is known
to both bidders. The values of the objects are additive; that is, a collection of ℓ of them is worth
either ℓ or zero.

Just prior to the sale, bidder A learns the true
value of the objects. This fact is publicly known;
in particular, bidder B is aware of it. How will
this affect the auction?

---

[7] Milgrom and Roberts (1982).

For the single-object version of this model it has been demonstrated that, at (the unique) equilibrium, the expected profit of A is positive, and the expected profit of B is zero.[8] In fact, this result holds no matter what the distribution of the object's value is, as long as there is <u>some</u> initial uncertainty. If both know the value of the object for certain, then at equilibrium both have expected profits of zero (the object sells at precisely its value).

When k is greater than one, the game has multiple equilibria.[9] However, only one has the property that A always bids zero when that is the value of the objects. (At the other equilibria, he makes positive bids which are always beaten by B's bids. Formally, these equilibria are "imperfect.") At this equilibrium, B's expected profit is positive. Indeed, when k is sufficiently large, the expected profit of uninformed bidder B exceeds that of informed bidder A !

The explanation of this result is surprisingly straightforward. Although A may know that the objects are of high value, he can only claim a profit from that knowledge in one stage. At equilibrium,

---

[8] Engelbrecht—Wiggans, Milgrom, and Weber (1981).

[9] Engelbrecht—Wiggans and Weber (1983).

B never bids zero (although as long as A has bid
zero in all previous stages, B has a substantial
probability of making only a nominal positive bid).
Therefore, A cannot profit from his favorable knowledge until he makes a positive bid. But if he ever
enters a positive bid, he reveals his knowledge. In
all subsequent stages, both bidders will bid one,
and neither will profit. Consequently, A's expected
profit is bounded above by p (that is, by one when
the objects are valuable, and zero otherwise). A's
equilibrium choice of a time to act, when the objects
are of value one, is distributed rather evenly over
the k stages of the auction. Therefore, B is
quite likely to be able to claim a number of objects
at low prices in the early stages, and the expected
values of these objects at the times he claims them
are not much less than p .

The phenomenon appearing here can be viewed from
the perspective of bargaining under uncertainty.[10]
Bidder A is of either of two "types": One type
knows that the objects are valuable, and the other
knows they are not. These types are involved in a
sort of bargaining game (internal to A). The first
type wants the second to make positive bids occasionally, so as to cloud the informational content of his

[10]Myerson (1980).

own positive bids. But the first type can provide
no incentives to the second for such actions (since
the second wants nothing from the first) and hence
is in a disadvantageous position. This internal conflict between types works to the detriment of A ,
and, in the process, B reaps substantial benefits.

If the objects being sold can take more than
two distinct values, it appears that equilibrium behavior involves several of A's "types" randomizing
on overlapping intervals of bids in the early stages.
Such behavior is different from that observed in any
of the classical auction models.

4.   NONIDENTICAL VALUES

There are two basic manners in which the items
for sale can have different values to a bidder. Either
the items are identical, and the bidder's marginal
value from an item varies with the number he possesses,
or the items are truly different.

If the items are identical, the seller may wish
to elicit a price-quantity function from each of the
bidders. Several different schemes of this nature
have been studied for the case in which the bidders'
marginal values are decreasing. Perhaps the most
simple generalizes the uniform-price procedure: Each
bidder submits k bids, the highest k bids secure

items, and a bidder who receives ℓ items is charged
the sum of the ℓ highest rejected bids. If the
bidders' valuations are independent, then a dominant
strategy for each is to submit bids equal to his first
k marginal values.

A similar, but more complex scheme can be used
when the objects are different and there is no statistical linkage across bidders. Each bidder submits
a bid for every subset of the objects. The set of
objects is distributed among the bidders according
to the partition of the set which draws a maximum
total bid amount (summing over the high bids on the
elements of the partition). Each bidder is charged
the difference between the maximum total which would
have occurred had his bids not been submitted, and
the sum of the high bids placed on the subsets other
than the one he receives in the actual maximizing
partition. This procedure is a generalization of
the one described in the preceding paragraph (which
in turn generalizes the uniform-price auction), and
again, a dominant strategy for each bidder is to bid
his actual valuations.[11]

Other types of procedures have drawn little or
no theoretical work. We offer as an example the bid-
for-the-right-to-choose sequential auction, at each

---

[11]Vickrey (1961).

stage of which the bidders compete for the right to select one from among the as-yet-unclaimed objects. Even in the independent private values setting, the strategic issues associated with this procedure seem quite involved.

Another example is the table auction, in which bid sheets for the objects are posted in a central location. Bidders can observe the current high bid for each object, and enter a higher bid whenever they choose. Questions of timing seem important in this setting.

5. PROSPECTS

Much remains to be learned about the auctioning of several objects. Should similar objects be sold individually, or in indivisible batches? How can contingent bids be handled? (Cassady presents a fascinating example of "entirety bidding," in which contingent claims play an important role.)[12] What are the fundamental properties of auction-like two-sided markets?

To these and many other questions, we can currently give few answers. But the recent explosion of interest in auctions holds the promise that our

----

[12]Cassady (1967).

understanding will be increased substantially in the near future.

REFERENCES

Capen, E. C., R. V. Clapp, and W. M. Campbell (1971). "Competitive Bidding in High-Risk Situations," _Journal of Petroleum Technology_, Vol. 23, pp. 641-53.

Cassady, R., Jr. (1967), _Auctions and Auctioneering_. California: University of California Press.

Engelbrecht-Wiggans, R., P. R. Milgrom, and R. J. Weber (1981). "Competitive Bidding and Proprietary Information," CMSEMS Discussion Paper No. 465, Northwestern University.

Engelbrecht-Wiggans, R. and R. J. Weber (1979). "An Example of a Multi-Object Auction Game," _Management Science_, Vol. 26, pp. 119-42.

Engelbrecht-Wiggans, R. and R. J. Weber (1983). "A Sequential Auction Involving Asymmetrically-Informed Bidders," _International Journal of Game Theory_, to appear

Milgrom, P. R. and D. J. Roberts (1982). "Limit Pricing and Entry under Incomplete Information: An Equilibrium Analysis," _Econometrica_, Vol. 50, pp. 443-59.

Milgrom, P. R. and R. J. Weber (1982). "A Theory of Auctions and Competitive Bidding," _Econometrica_, Vol. 50, pp. 1089-1122.

Myerson, R. (1980). "Two-Person Bargaining Problems with Incomplete Information," CMSEMS Discussion Paper No. 527, Northwestern University.

Myerson, R. (1981). "Optimal Auction Design," _Mathematics of Operations Research_, Vol. 6, pp. 58-73.

Ortega-Reichert, A. (1968). "Models for Competitive Bidding under Uncertainty," Department of Operations Research Technical Report No. 8, Stanford University.

Vickrey, W. (1961). "Counterspeculation, Auctions, and Competitive Sealed Tenders," _Journal of Finance_, Vol. 16, pp. 8-37.

Vickrey, W. (1962). "Auctions and Bidding Games," _Recent Advances in Game Theory_ (conference proceedings), Princeton University, pp. 15-27.

PART THREE

RECENT DEVELOPMENTS IN THEORY AND APPLICATIONS OF
COMPETITIVE BIDDING

0226
0227

1

PRICING SCHEMES WHEN DEMAND IS UNOBSERVABLE

Milton Harris

This report summarizes a few types of monopolistic pricing schemes commonly used in the marketing of many different products.[1] The most common is the simple single-price strategy in which a seller posts a price and offers to sell to anyone wishing to purchase at this price. Another widely used marketing technique is some form of auction, for example, to sell Treasury bills and bonds, some corporate financial securities, art objects, oil leases, or government contracts. There are several types of auction procedures classified by the way in which bids are solicited (sealed-bid or open) and by the method for determining the

---

[1] Harris and Raviv (1981).

the final allocation as a function of the bids (such
as competitive or second-price auctions, and discrimi-
nating auctions). A third scheme is one in which
various prices are charged and buyers paying higher
prices are assigned higher priority in receiving the
product. We call this technique "priority pricing."
For example natural gas and electric power are sold
to some industrial consumers by means of priority
pricing (users paying lower prices are cut off before
those paying higher prices in times of shortage).
Another example is the close-out sale in which the
price is reduced over time and buyers willing to accept lower probabilities of obtaining the product may
be able to purchase it at lower prices. A third example is the way in which mail delivery is priced
by most post offices; lower priced third-class mail
is handled only after all first-class mail has been
serviced. Other examples include stand-by airline
tickets and theater tickets the price of which are
reduced on performance day.

     Our purpose is to derive endogenously the form
of an optimal marketing scheme in a context in which
almost any conceivable mechanism is feasible. We
thereby seek to provide an explanation of the use
of the types of schemes discussed above and to identify the conditions under which each particular scheme
will be used. For example, when would one expect

to observe a single-price strategy as opposed to some
form of auction?

Previous work in this area has imposed a given
pricing scheme and analyzed optimal valued for the
parameters of this scheme. The optimal single-price
allocation has been characterized for the single-price
scheme.[2] Another scheme has been described in which
quantity is set prior to the realization of demand
with price determined by ex post market clearing.[3]
Other studies have extended this type of analysis
to allow different prices to be set ex ante in different periods depending on the expected demand in
those periods. (This last type of pricing scheme is
generally referred to as peak-load pricing.)[4] Most
of these studies characterize optimal peak-load prices
and capacity, given the peak-load pricing scheme.
Also, it has been considered that price discrimination might be based on the quantity purchased, that
is, nonlinear pricing.[5] This results in optimal payment schedules which give the total cost to a consumer

---

[2]Baron (1971); Holthausen (1976); Leland (1972).

[3]Holthausen (1976).

[4]Sherman and Visscher (1978); Crew and Kleindorfer
(1978); Brown and Johnson (1969); Meyer (1975).

[5]Stiglitz (1977).

as a function of the quantity purchased. Another
pricing scheme analyzed in the literature is similar
to that we have called priority pricing. In this
scheme an interruptible service is priced according
to its reliability. Given this pricing scheme, these
studies characterize an optimal price-reliability
schedule.[6]

A separate literature analyzes auctions as a
method of marketing goods. Most studies in this area
analyze the properties of <u>given</u> auctions.[7] The object
of these studies was generally to compare two different
types of auctions based on some criterion such as seller's expected revenue. A somewhat broader view is to
search for an optimal auction design among the larger
class of feasible auctions.[8] Our approach to explaining pricing schemes is based on the presumption that
the observed marketing scheme is chosen optimally by
the seller from a large class of feasible allocation
mechanisms. This class contains the three pricing
schemes discussed above (single price, priority pricing, and auctions) as well as most other conceivable

---

[6] Marchand (1974); Tschirhart and Jen (1979).

[7] Baron (1972); Holt (1980), Matthews (1979); Riley
and Samuelson (1979); Wilson (1979).

[8] Vickrey (1961); Myerson (1978); Harris and Raviv
(1979).

schemes (such as nonlinear pricing). Thus, in contrast
to previous studies, we do not impose a particular
marketing technique, but instead derive an optimal
scheme endogenously. This deeper approach allows
us to explain observed marketing schemes. Our model
consists of a single, monopolistic seller and N
potential buyers. The seller produces a homogeneous
product with constant marginal production cost up to
a capacity limit. The limit on capacity may or may
not be binding. Each buyer is assumed to demand up
to one unit of the product at any price at or below
his reservation price. Buyers are identical except
for the reservation price. A central assumption of
the model is that there is asymmetric information
among the agents. In particular each buyer knows only
his own reservation price and not that of any other
buyer. The seller does not observe any buyer's reservation price. Each agent has Bayesian priors regarding reservation prices he cannot observe. Our approach
to deriving optimal marketing schemes is based on
the methodology suggested by Harris and Townsend.[9]

Our results consist of characterizing optimal
marketing schemes for the environment described above.
It turns out that the optimal marketing technique
depends critically on the assumptions regarding the

---

[9]Harris and Townsend (1981).

capacity limit. In particular we show that, when
potential demand exceeds capacity, the priority-
pricing scheme discussed above is optimal for the
seller. We show how the optimal priority prices depend on the exogenous aspects of the model, namely,
marginal cost, capacity, and the priors of the agents.
Another scheme which is optimal in some environments
is a modified, multiobject version of Vickrey's competitive auction. In this auction, buyers may submit
sealed bids above a minimum acceptable bid and a uniform price is charged to all accepted bids. The minimum acceptable bid is equal to the lowest priority
price. Again we show how the equilibrium price depends
on the bids and the exogenous aspects of the model.
When capacity exceeds potential demand, the single-
price scheme is optimal. The optimal price is determined by the usual "marginal revenue equals marginal
cost" condition modified to account for the specific
type of uncertain demand assumed in the model. Finally,
when capacity can be chosen by the seller, for sufficiently low cost of capacity, it is optimal to choose
capacity equal to maximum potential demand and charge
a single price.

   The explanation of the use of various pricing
schemes provided by these results appears to be consistent with the observations described above. In

particular we seem to observe priority pricing or auctions mainly when limits on capacity are important. However, we observe a single price mainly when the limits on capacity are not binding. Obviously oil leases, securities, rare art objects, and government contracts are sold by monopolists, and the potential demand for these products exceeds capacity. As mentioned above, these products are generally sold at auction as predicted by our analysis. Similarly, discontinued products or styles, natural gas, electric power, mail delivery, are also examples of products in which capacity is limited relative to potential demand. These products are often sold by priority pricing. Furthermore most products sold at a single price are products for which capacity limitations are unimportant or increases in capacity are relatively cheap.

REFERENCES

Baron, D. (1971). "Demand Uncertainty in Imperfect Competition," International Economic Review, Vol. 12, pp. 196-208.

Baron, D. (1972). "Incentive Contracts and Competitive Bidding," American Economic Review, Vol. 62, pp. 384-394.

Brown, G., Jr. and M. B. Johnson (1969). "Public
    Utility Output and Pricing under Risk," _American
    Economic Review_, Vol. 59, pp. 119-128.

Crew, M. A. and P. R. Kleindorfer (1978). "Reliabil-
    ity and Public Utility Pricing," _American Economic
    Review_, Vol. 68, No. 1, pp. 31-40.

Harris, M. and A. Raviv (1979). "Allocation Mechan-
    isms and the Design of Auctions," Working Paper
    #5-78-79, Graduate School of Industrial Administra-
    tion, Carnegie-Mellon University.

Harris, M. and A. Raviv (1981). "A Theory of Monopoly
    Pricing Schemes with Demand Uncertainty," _American
    Economic Review_, Vol. 71, No. 3, pp. 347-65.

Harris, M. and R. M. Townsend (1981). "Resource Allo-
    cation under Asymmetric Information," _Econometrica_,
    Vol. 49, No. 1, pp. 33-64.

Holt, C. (1980). "Competitive Bidding for Contracts
    under Alternative Auction Procedures," _Journal of
    Political Economy_, Vol. 88, No. 3, pp. 433-445.

Holthausen, D. M. (1976). "Input Choices and Uncer-
    tain Demand," _American Economic Review_, Vol. 66,
    pp. 94-103.

Leland, H. E. (1972). "Theory of the Firm Facing
    Uncertain Demand," _American Economic Review_, Vol.
    62, pp. 278-291.

Marchand, M. G. (1974). "Pricing Power Supplied on
    an Interruptible Basis," _European Economic Review_,
    Vol. 5, pp. 263-274.

Matthews, S. (1979). "Information Acquisition in Dis-
    criminatory Auctions," University of Illinois work-
    ing paper.

Meyer, R. A. (1975). "Monopoly Pricing and Capacity Choice under Uncertainty," American Economic Review, Vol. 65, pp. 326-337.

Myerson, R. (1978). "Optimal Auction Design," Graduate School of Management working paper, Northwestern University.

Riley, J. and W. Samuelson (1979). "Optimal Auctions," University of California, Los Angeles discussion paper #152.

Sherman, R. and M. Visscher (1978). "Second Best Pricing with Stochastic Demand," American Economic Review, Vol. 68, No. 1, pp. 41-53.

Stiglitz, J. E. (1977). "Monopoly, Non-Linear Pricing and Imperfect Information: The Insurance Market," Review of Economic Studies, Vol.45, pp. 407-430.

Tschirhart, J. and F. Jen (1979). "Behavior of a Monopoly Offering Interruptible Service," Bell Journal of Economics, Vol. 10, pp. 244-258.

Vickrey, W. (1961). "Counterspeculation, Auctions, and Competitive Sealed Tenders," Journal of Finance, Vol. 16, pp. 8-37.

Wilson, R. B. (1979). "Auctions of Shares," Graduate School of Business working paper, Stanford University.

0227

2

THE GAINS TO MAKING LOSERS PAY
IN HIGH-BID AUCTIONS

Eric Maskin

John G. Riley

A major theme of the recent theoretical advances in the theory of auctions is that auction rules which maximize expected revenue are not efficient ex post. That is, a seller exploiting his monopoly power to the maximum will design a scheme in which there is a finite probability that the agent with the highest valuation will not end up with the object for sale. Discussion of the issue to date has focussed on the simplest auction in which each buyer has a valuation which is perceived by others to be an independent random draw from some known distribution $F(\cdot)$. In his seminal paper Vickrey established that, with risk-neutral buyers, expected seller revenue is the same for high and second bid auctions.[1] While this conclusion holds

for any announced minimum price Vickrey focussed on
the case in which the minimum price is equal to the
value to the seller of the object. Since the winner
is the buyer with the highest valuation in excess
of the minimum price, both auctions are efficient.

Butters first posed the question as to the optimal design of an auction from the seller's viewpoint.[2] He showed that expected revenue was necessarily increased by announcing a minimum price in
excess of the seller's use value.

Independently Harris and Raviv, Riley and Samuelson, and Myerson have all considered optimal auction
design from the seller's viewpoint under successively
weaker assumptions about the distribution $F(v)$.[3]
From these papers we know that when buyers are risk
neutral and a mild restriction on $F(v)$ is satisfied,
there is no auction which yields greater expected
revenue than the high bid (or second bid) auction
with the appropriately selected minimum price.[4] Then,
for the revenue-maximizing auction, the inefficiency

---

[1]Vickrey (1961).

[2]Butters (1978).

[3]Harris and Raviv (1978); Riley and Samuelson (1981);
Myerson (1981).

[4]Maskin and Riley (1980).

is associated with the possibility that one or more
buyers have valuations between the seller's use value
and his announced minimum price.

Various authors have also shown that, when buyers
are risk averse, the high- and second-bid auctions
no longer generate the same expected revenue.[5] In
the second-bid auction, buyers bid their reservation
values whether or not they are risk averse. However,
in the high-bid auction, risk averse buyers place a
lower marginal valuation on larger gains. To understand the implications of this it is easiest to consider the open-auction equivalent of the high-bid
auction. In this "Dutch" auction the auctioneer calls
out successively lower prices. Loosely speaking, a
risk averse buyer has a greater fear of losing and so
signals to stop the auction more quickly than if he
were risk neutral. The resulting bids are therefore
higher on average. This conclusion holds regardless
of the preannounced price at which the seller will
withdraw the object. Thus, for any minimum price,
the high bid auction yields greater expected revenue
than the second-bid auction.

It is then natural to inquire as to whether the
high-bid auction can itself be improved upon. The

---

[5]E.g., Holt (1980); Matthews (1979).

answer turns out to be in the affirmative. For a broad
class of auctions which include the independent valuations auction and the "mineral rights" auction (with
mild additional restrictions) Maskin and Riley have
established that a seller can increase his expected
revenue if losers share the burden of payment with the
winner.[6] Making losers pay lowers the equilibrium
bids and thus raises the expected gains of the winner.
The outcome of the auction is thus more risky than
it is if only the winner pays. This exacerbates each
buyer's fear of loss. As a result bids are not lowered
by so much that the decline in expected revenue from
the winner completely offsets the revenue received
from losers.

    Since the analysis of the general case is compli-
cated the conclusion will be illustrated by means of
an example. In the following section we shall show,
for a simple two-buyer auction with risk averse buyers,
that the seller increases his expected revenue by
employing both a minimum price and an entry fee. General results are summarized in Section 2.

---

[6]Maskin and Riley (1980).

1. AN EXAMPLE

Consider two buyers, each with a valuation of some object $v_i \in [0,1]$ where v_i is an independent random draw from the uniform distribution: $F(v) = v$. Each buyer has the piecewise linear utility function

$$U(x) = \begin{cases} x & , \quad x \leq w , \quad 0 < \alpha \leq 1 \\ w + \alpha(x-w) & , \quad x > w \end{cases} \qquad (1)$$

The smaller is α the greater the kink at $x = w$ and hence the more risk averse are the buyers.

The seller announces that the object will be sold to the highest bidder who submits a bid above some minimum price m . Moreover each bidder must also submit an entry fee of c along with the bid. We wish to establish that the seller can raise more expected revenue by utilizing some pair $<m,c>$, with c strictly positive, than if he employs only a minimum price m . For any pair $<m,c>$ there is some valuation $\underline{v}$ below which there is no incentive to enter the auction. A buyer with the "entry valuation" $\underline{v}$ bids the minimum, m , and wins if the other buyer has a lower valuation, that is, with probability $F(\underline{v}) = \underline{v}$. With no entry fee $\underline{v} = m$. Therefore, with c sufficiently small, the wealth of the buyer,

if he wins, is less than w and the entry value satisfies

$$EU = \underline{v}(\underline{v}-m) - c = 0 \tag{2}$$

To determine the symmetric Bayesian equilibrium
bid function, b(v) , we begin by assuming that buyer
2 bids according to a bid function with the general
characteristics depicted in Figure 1. We then show
that there is some such function with the property
that buyer 1's best response is to employ the same
bid function. That is, with buyer 2 making a bid
$b_2 = b(v_2)$ buyer 1's best response $b_1 = b(v^*)$ is
to choose $v^* = v_1$. At this point it is useful to
note that expected utility is a function of buyer 1's
true valuation, his bid b and his probability of
winning p . That is, we may write

$$EU = U(-b, \ p, \ v_1) \tag{3}$$

In making a bid buyer 1 considers the trade off between
a higher bid, and hence a smaller increase in wealth
if he wins, and a higher probability of winning.
    Consider first the case in which buyer 1's valu-
ation is close to the entry value $\underline{v}$. Then, win
or lose, his wealth is less than w . Expected utility
is therefore

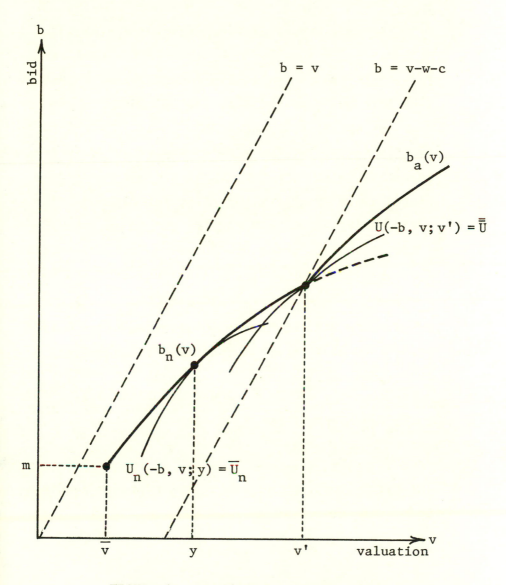

FIGURE 1.   Equilibrium Bid Function

$$U(-b_n(v), v; v_1) = v(v_1 - b_n(v) - c) - (1-v)c \quad (4)$$

where we have introduced the subscript n to denote that this holds in the risk neutral range.

The optimization problem of buyer 1 can then be thought of as choosing a point on the curve $b = b_n(v)$ to maximize $U(-b, v; v_1)$. This is illustrated in Figure 1. From (4) we may write the marginal rate of substitution of v for b as

$$MRS_n = \frac{-\partial U}{\partial v} \Big/ \frac{\partial U}{\partial b} = \frac{v_1 - b}{v} \quad (5)$$

Then for $b_n(\cdot)$ to be the equilibrium bidding strategy, the indifference curve must be tangential to this function at $b = b_n(v_1)$, that is

$$b_n'(v_1) = \frac{v_1 - b}{v_1} , \quad \text{for all } v_1 \geq \underline{v}$$

Integrating and making use of the boundary condition $b_n(\underline{v}) = m$ we obtain

$$b_n(v) = \frac{1}{2}v + \frac{m\underline{v} - \frac{1}{2}\underline{v}^2}{v} , \quad v \geq \underline{v} \quad (6)$$

Substituting from (2), we can rewrite expression (6) as

$$b_n(v) = \frac{1}{2}v + \frac{\frac{1}{2}v^2 - c}{v} , \quad v \geq \underline{v} \tag{7}$$

It is reasily confirmed that $b_n(v)$ is a strictly increasing function with slope less than $1/2$ for all c satisfying

$$0 \leq c \leq \frac{1}{2}\underline{v}^2 \tag{8}$$

If the successful bidder has valuation v, his final wealth,

$$v - b_n(v) - c = \frac{1}{2}v - \frac{\frac{1}{2}v^2 - c}{v} - c$$

is strictly increasing in v and rises from $\frac{c}{\underline{v}} - c$ to $\frac{1}{2}(1 - \underline{v}^2)$ as v rises from $\underline{v}$ to unity. If w exceeds $\frac{1}{2}(1 - \underline{v}^2)$ buyers remain always in the risk neutral range. We shall henceforth assume that (8) holds and, in addition,

$$c\left(\frac{1}{\underline{v}} - 1\right) < w < \frac{1}{2}(1 - \underline{v}^2) \tag{9}$$

Then risk aversion affects the behavior of high value bidders but not the behavior of low value bidders. We have already seen that with c satisfying (8), $b_n(v)$ has a slope less than $1/2$. Therefore, for

all c satisfying (8) and (9), there is some v'
such that $v - b_n(v) - c$ is less than w if and only
if $v < v'$. Then (7) describes the equilibrium
(throughout this paper we examine only first order conditions. See Maskin and Riley and Samuelson for a
treatment of the second order conditions)[7] for all
$v \leq v'$ where v' satisfies

$$\frac{1}{2}v' - \frac{\left(\frac{1}{2}v^2 - c\right)}{v'} - c = w \tag{10}$$

We now consider the slope of an indifference curve
within the risk averse region, that is, for
$b < v_1 - (w+c)$. With $b_a(v)$ the equilibrium bid
function, expected utility becomes

$$U(-b(v), v; v_1) = v[w + \alpha(v_1 - b_a(v) - w - c)] - (1-v)c$$

$$= \alpha v \left[\left(\frac{1-\alpha}{\alpha}\right)(w+c) + v_1 - b_a(v)\right] - c$$

where the subscript a denotes bidding in the risk
averse region. Then treating utility as a function of
v and b we may write the marginal rate of substitution of v for b as

---

[7] Maskin and Riley (1980); Riley and Samuelson (1981).

$$MRS_a = \frac{-\partial U_a}{\partial v} \bigg/ \frac{\partial U_a}{\partial b} = \frac{w + c + \alpha(v_1 - b - w - c)}{\alpha v} \qquad (11)$$

At the boundary of the risk averse region the term in parentheses is zero so the slope of the indifference curve is simply

$$MRS_a \big|_{b=v_1-w-c} = \frac{w+c}{\alpha v} , \quad \alpha < 1 \qquad (12)$$

Furthermore, from (5), the slope at the other side of the boundary is

$$MRS_n \big|_{b=v_1-w-c} = \frac{w+c}{v} \qquad (13)$$

Thus, as depicted, for all v_1 each member of the family of indifference curves has an upward kink at $b = v_1 - w - c$.

For $b_a(\cdot)$ to be the equilibrium bidding strategy in the risk averse range the indifference curve through $<v_1, b_a(v_1)>$ for buyer 1 with valuation v_1 must lie below the curve $b = b_a(v)$ for all $v \neq v_1$. This is also depicted in Figure 1.

Since the main aim of this section is merely to illustrate a general theorem we now introduce the further assumption that risk aversion is not too great. Specifically, we assume

$$\frac{w+c}{m+w+c} < \alpha < 1 \tag{14}$$

As before we set the slope of the bid function equal to the slope of the indifference curve at $<v_1, b_a(v_1)>$ and solve to obtain

$$b_a(v) = \frac{1}{2}v + \left(\frac{1-\alpha}{\alpha}\right)(w+c) + \frac{k}{v}$$

The constant of integration is determined by the requirement that the bid function be continuous at v'. Making use of (6) we then obtain

$$b_a(v) = \frac{1}{2}v + \frac{mv - \frac{1}{2}v^2}{v} + \left(\frac{1-\alpha}{\alpha}\right)\left(1 - \frac{v'}{v}\right)(w+c) \quad , \quad v > v'$$

$$\tag{15}$$

$$= b_n(v) + \left(\frac{1-\alpha}{\alpha}\right)\left(1 - \frac{v'}{v}\right)(w+c) \quad , \quad v > v'$$

The curves $b_a(v)$ and $b_n(v)$ are depicted in Figure 1 We have already seen that $b = b_n(v)$ intersects the line $b = v - w - c$ only once at v'. We now confirm that $b_a(v)$ lies below this line for all $v > v'$.

First we note that at v'

$$\frac{db_a}{dv}(v') = MRS_a = \frac{w+c}{v'}$$

$$= \frac{w+c}{\alpha(b_a(v') + w + c)} \quad , \quad \text{since } b_a(v') = v' - w - c$$

Also $b_a(v')$ must exceed the minimum bid m.
Then if (14) is satisfied the slope of $b_a(v)$ is
less than unity at v'. Since exactly the same argument holds at any intersection point of $b = b_a(v)$
and $b = v - w - c$ it follows that the latter always
has a greater slope. Then there can only be one such
intersection point.

To summarize, we have established that if (8),
(9), and (14) hold the equilibrium bid function is

$$b(v) = \begin{cases} 0 & , \ v < \underline{v} \\ b_n(v) & , \ \underline{v} \leq v \leq v' \\ b_a(v) & , \ v' < v \leq 1 \end{cases} \quad (16)$$

Since $b_a(v)$ $b_n(v)$, for all $v > v'$, it
follows immediately that the seller's expected revenue
is higher when buyers are risk averse. Moreover, as
the kink becomes larger (α declines) expected revenue
increases. Thus the more risk averse are the buyers
the greater is the seller's expected revenue. (These
results illustrate more general conclusions obtained
by Riley and Samuelson.)[8]

To determine the effects of introducing an entry
fee we are interested in perturbing the equilibrium

---

[8]Riley and Samuelson (1981).

from an initial situation in which there is no entry
fee.   The expected revenue of the seller is the sum
of the expected entry fees plus the expected high bid.
Since the high bid is made by the individual with the
high valuation and   Prob{high value is less than v}
$= F^2(v)$,   we may write expected revenue as

$$R_\alpha(m,\underline{v}) = 2 \int_{\underline{v}}^{1} cdF(v) + \int_{\underline{v}}^{1} b(v) dF^2(v) \qquad (17)$$

Substituting for $b(v)$ we obtain

$$R_\alpha(m,\underline{v}) = 2 \int_{\underline{v}}^{1} cdF(v) + \int_{\underline{v}}^{1} b_n(v) dF^2(v)$$

$$+ \int_{v'}^{1} (b_a(v) - b_n(v)) dF^2(v)$$

If $\alpha = 1$ (no kink so that buyers are everywhere risk
neutral) the third term is zero.   Moreover the first
two terms are independent of α .   Therefore we may writ

$$R_\alpha(m,\underline{v}) = R_1(m,\underline{v}) + \int_{v}^{1} (b_a(v) - b_n(v)) dF^2(v) \qquad (18)$$

Substituting from (2) and (7) we obtain

$$R_1(m,\underline{v}) = \int_{\underline{v}}^{1} (\underline{v}^2 + v^2)\, dv$$

Note that R_1 is independent of m . That is, when buyers are risk neutral, any pair $<m,c>$ yielding the same entry value, $\underline{v}$, yields the same expected revenue. Moreover, it is readily confirmed that R_1 takes on its maximum at $\underline{v} = 1/2$. Then from (2), any pair $<m,c>$ satisfying

$$c = \frac{1}{4} - \frac{1}{2}m$$

maximizes expected revenue. In particular expected revenue is maximized by the pair $<m,c> = <\frac{1}{2},0>$.

It remains to show that $R_\alpha(m,\underline{v})$ is strictly decreasing in m at $m = \underline{v}$. First of all, from (9) and (2) v' satisfies

$$\frac{1}{2}v' - \frac{(m\underline{v} - \frac{1}{2}\underline{v}^2)}{v'} - (\underline{v}^2 - m\underline{v}) = w$$

Holding $\underline{v}$ fixed we differentiate with respect to m to obtain

$$\left[\frac{1}{2} + \frac{m\underline{v} - \frac{1}{2}\underline{v}^2}{(v')^2}\right]\frac{\partial v'}{m} - \underline{v}\left(\frac{1}{v'} - 1\right) = 0$$

At $m = \underline{v}$ the bracket is positive then $\partial v'/\partial m$ is positive.

Under assumption (14) we can substitute (15) into (18) to obtain

$$R_\alpha(m,\underline{v}) = R_1(\underline{v}) + \left(\frac{1-\alpha}{\alpha}\right)(w+c)\int_{v'}^{1}\left(1 - \frac{v'}{v}\right)2vdv$$

Integrating and substituting from (2) we obtain

$$R_\alpha(m,\underline{v}) = R^1(\underline{v}) + \left(\frac{1-\alpha}{\alpha}\right)(1 - v')^2(w + \underline{v}^2 - \underline{v}m)$$

Differentiating by m we obtain finally

$$\frac{\partial R_\alpha}{\partial m} = \left(\frac{1-\alpha}{\alpha}\right)\left[-v(1 - v')^2 - 2(1 - v')\frac{v'}{\partial m}\right]$$

Since $\partial v'/\partial m$ is positive at $m = \underline{v}$ the bracket is negative. Thus at $m = \underline{v}$ expected seller revenue is strictly decreasing in m. From (2) $c = \underline{v}^2 - \underline{v}m$. Therefore, expected seller revenue strictly increases with the entry fee c in some neighborhood of $c = 0$.

2. GENERAL RESULTS

Maskin and Riley developed a general auction model
which encompasses a broad class of "one-shot" auctions.[9]
Rather than elaborate here on this general model, we
shall summarize the main conclusions for the two most
commonly studied models: the "independent values
auction" and the "common value" or "mineral rights"
auction. The former is precisely the model examined
in the previous section. Each agent has a valuation
v_i which is an independent draw from some known distribution $F(v)$. As in our illustration, it is
natural to introduce risk aversion by making each
buyer's return a concave function of the difference
between the gross gain (v_i for the agent with the
highest valuation and zero for the others) and any
payments due. For such a model it can be shown that
making some losers pay always raises expected revenue.
Formally, we have

<u>Proposition 1</u>. (Some losers pay in the independent-
values auction.) Suppose each of n buyers has a
valuation v_i , i = 1, ..., n , an independent draw
from the distribution $F(v)$. Suppose also that each
buyer's return can be expressed as

---

[9] Maskin and Riley (1980).

$U(v_i - w)$, if the object is awarded to agent i

$U(-w)$, otherwise

where w is wealth and $U(\cdot)$ is a concave function. Then it is always possible to raise expected revenue from a high bid auction by giving buyers a choice as to whether or not to pay an entry fee. "Free bids" are considered only if no buyer submits an entry fee.

The first step in the proof of Proposition 1 involves establishing that, for any v^* , there is an equilibrium bid strategy in which only those with valuations exceeding v^* have an incentive to pay the entry fee. The second step involves demonstrating that, for sufficiently high v^* , introduction of a small entry fee raises expected revenue.

The same general theorem of Maskin and Riley also results in the next proposition.

Proposition 2. (All losers pay in the independent-values auction.) Under the assumptions of Proposition 1 it is always possible to raise expected revenue from a high bid auction with a positive reserve price by lowering the latter and introducing a required entry fee.

As the example in section 1 makes clear, expected revenue is generally maximized by establishing auction rules such that those with sufficiently low valuations

in excess of that of the seller choose not to participate. The resulting auction is therefore inefficient, ex post, because there is a chance that some
buyer with a valuation in excess of that of the
seller remains out of the auction.

It might then be argued that in the sale of some
right to access by a governmental unit, which has no
alternative governmental use, an auction should be
designed so that any buyer with a positive valuation
has an incentive to bid. Accepting this argument,
Proposition 1 then implies that the governmental unit
can do better than utilize a high bid auction with
zero minimum price. Expected revenue is revised by
introducing a voluntary entry fee and giving priority
to those submitting the fee with their bids. (Note
that we cannot appeal to Proposition 2 for this result. A buyer with a zero valuation will never pay
an entry fee since his probability of winning is zero.)

Finally we turn to the "common value" auction.
Each of n buyers is assumed to observe a signal,
x_i , of which is jointly distributed with the true
value, s , according to the continuous density function $g(s, x_i)$.

A buyer's signal provides information about the
true value in the following sense. For any s ,
s' , x_i , x_i'

$$(s - s')(x_i - x_i') > 0 \leftrightarrow g(s, x_i)g(s', x_i')$$

$$\geq g(s, x'_i)g(s', x_i)$$

That is, for any pair of draws, (s, x_i) , (s', x_i') , it is more likely that $s - s'$ and $x_i - x_i'$ have the same rather than opposite signs. Following Milgrom and Weber we shall say that x_i and s are <u>positively related</u>.[10]

Suppose that buyer 1 has a signal or "estimate" x_1 and that the highest of the other n-1 signals is y_1 . If buyer 1 pays an amount b and wins the auction when the true value is s , his utility is assumed to be $U(s-b)$ where U is a concave function. Knowing only x_1 and y_1 , buyer 1's expected utility is therefore

$$v(x_1, y_1, -b) = E\{U(s-b) | x_1, y_1\}$$

Under our assumptions the joint distribution of s and $x_1, \ldots, x_n$ is

$$f(s, x_1, \ldots, x_n) = \prod_{i=1}^{n} g(s, x_i) / (\int_{-\infty}^{\infty} g(x,s)dx)^{n-1} \, ($$

———————————

[10] Milgrom and Weber (1980).

From eq. (20) the conditional density $f(s, x_3, \ldots,$ $x_n | x_1, x_2)$ can be calculated

$$v(x_1, y_1, -b) =$$

$$(n-1)\int_{x_3=-\infty}^{y_1} \int_{x_n=-\infty}^{y_1} \int_{s=-\infty}^{\infty} U(s-b)f(s,x_3,\ldots,x_n | x_1,y_1)dx_3,\ldots,dx_n ds$$

Knowing about the conditions described in eq. (20) buyer 1 can also compute the conditional density function $h(y_1 | x_1)$. In the high-bid auction buyer 1 wins if and only if he outbids all the others. Then if all but buyer 1 are utilizing the bid function $b(x)$ and buyer 1 bids $\hat{b}_1 = b(\hat{x}_1)$, his expected utility is

$$\phi(x_1, \hat{x}_1) = \int_{-\infty}^{x_1} v(x_1, y_1, -b(x_1))h(y_1 | x_1)dy_1$$

The equilibrium-bid function is then described by the requirement that, for all x_1, $\phi(x_1, \hat{x}_1)$ takes on its maximum at $x_1 = \hat{x}_1$. That is, when others are bidding according to $b(x)$ buyer 1's best response is to bid $b_1 = b(x_1)$.

Maskin and Riley derived the following result.

Proposition 3. (Some losers pay in the common-value auction.)[11] Suppose that the utility function U(·) satisfies conditions such that each buyer exhibits a nonincreasing absolute risk aversion. Then, if buyers are sufficeintly risk averse and the rate of absolute risk aversion does not decrease too quickly with wealth, it is possible to increase expected revenue from a high bid auction by giving buyers a choice as to whether or not to pay an entry fee and looking at bids without a fee only if there is no fee-paying buyer.

We also have the following counterpart to Proposition 2.

Proposition 4. (All losers pay in the common-value auction.) If buyers exhibit a sufficiently large and constant absolute risk aversion it is always possible to raise expected revenue from a high-bid auction with a positive reserve price by lowering the latter and introducing a required entry fee.

A few concluding remarks are in order concerning the role of our assumptions about risk aversion. First of all, it is critical that any buyer with a very favorable signal should have a lower marginal utility

---

[11]Maskin and Riley (1980).

of income if he submits the high bid than if he does
not. That is, a buyer with a favorable signal would
like to purchase fair insurance against losing out in
the bidding. In the absence of such insurance the
seller is able to exploit buyers' fear of loss by introducing payments for losers.

With constant absolute risk aversion all buyers
satisfy this "insurance condition." With decreasing
absolute risk aversion it is not satisfied by buyers
with sufficiently unfavorable signals. However, unless absolute risk aversion decreases rapidly the
insurance condition must be satisfied by buyers with
highly favorable signals.

To see how the degree of absolute risk aversion
plays a role we first define

$$\bar{v}_3(x_1) = \int_{-\infty}^{x_1} v_3(x_1, y, -b(x_1))h(y|x_1, y \leq y_1)dy$$

and

$$\bar{v}_{33}(x_1) = \int_{-\infty}^{x_1} v_{33}(x_1, y, -b(x_1))h(y|x_1, y \leq y_1)dy$$

In proving Propositions 3 and 4 it is assumed that
the following inequality holds for all those buyers

satisfying the insurance condition.

$$\frac{\overline{v}_{33}(x_1)}{\overline{v}_3(x_1)} \leq \frac{[v_3(x_1, x_1, -b(x_1)) - \overline{v}_3(x_1)]}{v(x_1, x_1, -b(x_1)) - U(0)}$$

With buyers' signals positively correlated it can be shown that the right hand side is negative. Thus the information effect, absent in the independent valuations model, makes it necessary to introduce the assumption that buyers are sufficiently risk averse.

REFERENCES

Butters, G. R. (1978). "Equilibrium Price Distributions and the Economics of Information," Ph.D Dissertation, Department of Economics, University of Chicago, Chicago, Illinois.

Harris, M. and A. Raviv (1978). "Allocation Mechanisms and the Design of Auctions," Working Paper, Graduate School of Industrial Administration, Carnegie-Mellon University, Pittsburgh, Pennsylvania.

Holt, C. A., Jr. (1980). "Competitive Bidding for Contracts under Alternative Auction Procedures," 99, pp. 433-445.

Maskin, E. S. and G. Riley (1980). "Auctioning an Indivisible Object," Discussion Paper, Kennedy School of Government, Harvard University.

Matthews, S. (1979). "Risk Aversion and the Efficiency of First and Second Price Auctions," Working Paper, Department of Economics, University of Chicago.

Milgrom, P. and R. Weber (1980). "A Theory of Auctions and Competitive Bidding," Working Paper, Kellogg Graduate School of Management, Northwestern University.

Myerson, R. B. (1981). "Optimal Auction Design," Mathematics of Operations Research, Vol. 6, pp. 58-73.

Riley, J. G. and W. F. Samuelson (1981). "Optimal Auctions," American Economic Review, Vol. 71, pp. 381-392.

Vickrey, W. (1961). "Counterspeculation, Auctions and Competitive Sealed Tenders," Journal of Finance, Vol. 16, pp. 8-37.

3

EFFICIENT ALLOCATION OF A STOCHASTIC SUPPLY: AUCTION MECHANISMS

Curt A. Monash

1. INTRODUCTION

Our society offers several different mechanisms for allocating resources. Depending upon the specific issue, one of two viewpoints usually predominates: 1) market forces allocate efficiently or, 2) market forces do not (or cannot) allocate resources efficiently or equitably, and hence the allocation should be performed administratively. A third option, as efficient (in theory) as a market, but often overlooked, is an auction. This paper tries, through an example, to illustrate the potential power of auction based policy initiatives.

Specifically, we will be interested in commodities like natural gas (water would be another excellent example), whose availability can be predicted only stochastically. These commodities usually are allocated according to historically or administratively determined patterns, by rules which do not necessarily produce economic efficiency. Merely permitting after-the-fact transfers--the "white market" --is insufficient to guarantee efficiency, since purchasers of these commodities must engage in costly preparation to use them; examples include the farmer who plants crops and then waits for his irrigation ditches to fill, the rancher who breeds cattle before knowing the feed harvest, and any firm which invests in capital goods which will require energy to operate.

The basic model is presented in Section 2. After developing the general theory of multicommodity auctions in Section 3, it is applied to our model in Section 4. In Section 5 we show how our model can illuminate real-world debates. In the first appendix, we carry the mathematical discussion into more detail, providing several different interpretations of the auction proposed. In the second, we outline the considerations involved in actually running such an auction on a computer. Finally, in Appendix 3, we give some of the legal and political background to the ongoing natural gas policy; market and auction systems are also compared. Appendices 1 and 2 may be regarded as extensions of Section 4; Appendix 3 is an extension of Section 5.

2. THE MODEL

Most industrial users of gas have the capacity to switch to Number 2 oil (distillate). Distillate is available primarily on one or more year contracts; spot supplies, when available at all, are typically much more expensive. Number 6 oil (resid) is cheaper and more plentiful; however, time and significant capital costs are necessary to acquire the capability to use it. Thus, efficiency requires not only that available gas be allocated correctly, but that all fuel-use choices (gas versus distillate versus resid versus electricity versus total shutdown) be made correctly in advance. (This point does not seem to be well-recognized; see however, McKay. McKay also provided a literature survey. The same point is raised by Monash. Also relevant is Leonard, Monash, and Zeckhauser.)[1]

In the models we will consider, each (risk-neutral)

---

[1] McKay (1978); Monash (1981), Leonard, Monash and Zeckhauser (1981).

user i can make one of a finite number of decision j . If he receives a unit of gas, it then has value to him g_{ij} ; if he does not receive the unit, he loses ℓ_{ij} (we assume an extra unit has no additional value). Thus the <u>marginal</u> value of that unit to him is $h_{ij} = g_{ij} + \ell_{ij}$. Describing the possible states of the world by some finite set K , we assume h_{ij} is independent of the state actually reached. The possible states can thus be assumed to be $Q = 0, 1,$ ..., N , where Q is the quantity of gas actually available; N , for convenience, is assumed to be strictly less than the number of users.

Our problem thus consists of efficiently allocating the contingent claims: One unit of "gas if $Q = 1$ two units of "gas if $Q = 2$," and so forth. But the allocation must in particular be efficient given the additional information that the users i make the efficient decisions $j(i)$. Thus, the good "gas if $Q = 1$ " must be awarded to the user with the highest $h_{ij(i)}$, and so forth. In particular, the user who gets good "gas if $Q = q$ " also must get good "gas if $Q = q^*$ " for $q^* = q+1, ..., N$. Thus, finally, we reduce our problem to the efficient allocation of N "tickets" "gas if $Q \geq q$," for $q = 1, ..., N$.

3. MULTICOMMODITY AUCTIONS

Consider now the general problem of allocating
N objects among N or more people. When N = 1 ,
the efficient solution is the Vickrey auction:[2] Ask
everybody to state his valuation for the object, and
award it to the highest bidder, charging him the second
highest price. Under these rules each bidder finds
it optimal to bid his true valuation; thus the object
is awarded efficiently to the bidder with the highest
true valuation.

For N objects, the procedure works similarly.
(This well-known generalization is difficult to find
in print. An excellent exposition is Leonard.)[3]
Each bidder submits a list of valuations for the objects. The prices are determined as follows: Ex-
cluding bidder i , compute the optimal allocation,
and its total value to the other bidders. For each
good q , repeat the calculation, but now assuming
that good q goes to bidder i , and hence is unavailable to the other bidders. The total value of
all-goods-except-q to the other bidders will of course
be less than or equal to the value to them of all
the goods combined. The difference between these

---

[2]Vickrey (1961).

[3]Leonard (1981).

two quantities becomes the price, to i , of q .
The procedure is that we allocate to each bidder the
q which maximizes his surplus (valuation - price).
These maximizations can be simultaneously performed,
since they are each equivalent to the <u>maximization</u>
<u>of</u> <u>total</u> <u>social</u> <u>welfare</u> (using the announced valua-
tions--see below).

Since the prices a bidder faces are <u>independent</u>
of the value he states, it is clear that his optimal
strategy is to announce his true values (so that the
maximization of his announced surplus will yield the
maximization of his true surplus). So now we need
only check that the allocation actually reached is
efficient. But each bidder maximizes

value (to him) - price

> = value (to him) - (constant - value (to
>   everybody else))

> = total value of the allocation - constant

which of course is equivalent to maximizing the total
value of the allocation. Thus the auction we have
outlined is <u>incentive</u> <u>compatible</u>; that is, it obtains
honest bids, and it is efficient.

Consider the following example. Bidder A values
good 1 at 6 and good 2 at 1; bidder B values good 1
at 7 and good 2 at 2.5.

	Good 1	Good 2
A	6	1
B	7	2.5

Then the price A faces for good 1 is 7 - 2.5 = 4.5, while the price he faces for 2 is 7 - 7 = 0. Similarly, B faces price 6 - 1 = 5 for 1, and price zero for 2. Thus A chooses good 1, for his benefit 6 - 4.5 = 1.5 exceeds the benefit 1 of getting good 2 for free, while B chooses good 2 (since 2.5 - 0 = 2.5 exceeds 7 - 5 = 2). We check that this allocation gives total values 6 + 2.5 = 8.5, greater than the alternative 7 + 1 = 8.

Although this auction procedure sounds fairly complicated, it is remarkably easy to implement on a computer even for large N . For, when we solve the well-known "assignment" problem of determining the efficient allocation of the goods, the linear program automatically generates shadow prices. But these shadow prices are exactly the prices the successful bidder must pay; and so the entire program is solved. Difficulties arise only when we generalize away from the model of one person and one good (see Appendix 2), but even those should not prevent speedy and cheap computations in real-world situations.

4. EFFICIENT ALLOCATION OF GOODS IN STOCHASTIC SUPPLY

Let us now return to our model. There are N "tickets"; these tickets provide gas with probabilities $f_1, \ldots, f_N$, where $1 \geq f_1 \geq f_2 \geq \cdots \geq f_N \geq 0$. If he is risk-neutral, customer i values ticket q at V_{iq}, where $V_{iq} = \underset{j}{\text{Max}}(g_{ij}f_q - \ell_{ij})(1 - f_q))$; for if he knows he has ticket q, he then adjusts j optimally. For each i, V_{iq}, as a function of f_q, is increasing, piecewise linear, and concave up. Of course, at the time of the delivery of gas, i is fixed, and so bidder i perceives a unit of gas as simply worth h_i, where $h_i = g_{ij(i)} - \ell_{ij(i)}$ corresponds to the $V_{iq(i)}$ actually chosen.

Consider an example. Bidder A has only one option, with $g = 6$ and $\ell = 4$. B has two: either he can let $g = \ell = 7$, or he can let $g = 5$ and $\ell = 0$. Q will equal 1 or 2, with probability .5 of each event. Then there are two "tickets": 1, which gives gas with certainty, and 2, which gives gas with probability .5. Thus, assuming risk-neutralit‧ the value to A of ticket 1 is 6, the value to B of ticket 2 is 2.5 (the maximum of .5 × 5 - .5 × 0 and .5 × 7 - .5 × 7), and so forth. Summarizing in a table, we have:

	g	ℓ	.5g − .5ℓ	ticket 1	ticket 2
A	6	4	1	6	1
B option 1	5	0	2.5	7	2.5
B option 2	7	7	0		

The right-hand portion of the diagram is just the example of the previous section. Thus A gets ticket 1,
B gets ticket 2, and hence chooses option 1. Observe
that this result might not hold if the tickets were
auctioned sequentially, because B could outbid A for
ticket 1, by a margin of 7 to 6; in this case he would
(contrary to overall efficiency) choose option 2.

Suppose now that the bidders are risk-averse, but that
they have access to a perfect insurance market. Then
the bidder i who gets ticket q , which entitles
him to gas whenever $Q \geq q$, will immediately purchase a contract which gives him h_i dollars when
(and only when) $Q < q$ (and nothing otherwise); the
expected value of this contract--and hence its price
--is of course $h_i(1 - f_q)$. But, given the availability of these contracts, his valuation for the tickets
is exactly the same as if he were risk-neutral. So
the bidders can submit their g_{ij} and ℓ_{ij} and permit the auctioneer to compute the V_{iq} ; in particular,

the bidders <u>need</u> <u>not</u> <u>know</u> <u>the</u> <u>probability</u> <u>distribution</u>
f for the system to work. It is this feature which
makes the auction system potentially more attractive
than the information-intensive market alternative.

5. PRACTICAL CONSIDERATIONS

The real natural gas market in the United States
is, of course, much more complicated than the situation described above. Producers sell gas to pipelines,
who sell gas to distribution companies, who sell it
to end-users; pipelines and distribution companies are
both regulated monopolies (or oligopolies), subject
to different sets of regulations (see Appendix 3 for
more detail). We assume, however, for ease of discussion, that each distribution company has a fixed annual
supply of gas, at a fixed cost. We also assume that
the companies are so effectively regulated by their
respective state public utilities commissions that
they act as benevolent, efficiency-maximizing monopolists. Neither of these assumptions is widely unrealistic (see also Appendix 3).

Out of the supply (fixed) controlled by a distribution company, they are obligated by law and custom
to satisfy high-priority (chiefly residential) demand
first. It is the stochastic, weather-dependent nature

of their demand which introduces the uncertainties into the low priority supply. There are now two possibilities. Either the rate paid by residential customers is higher than the amount curtailed industrial customers would be willing to pay, or (the actual case) high-priority customers are receiving a subsidy. In the first case, distribution companies can play the role of insurer themselves. For every unit of gas not sold to a low-priority customer is sold to a high-priority customer--at a higher rate; thus enough revenues are automatically generated to cover the insurance payments. In the second case, it is natural to demand that the high-priority users, in return for their subsidy, play the role of insurer, especially since they, as consumers, reap the ultimate benefits from economic efficiency.

Some of the administrative features have already been outlined in this discussion. Customers would have to perform relatively few computations. Forecasting of gas supplies would remain centralized at the distribution company level, as it is now, rather than being forced upon individual customers. Distribution companies would receive accurate signals about storage, incremental supplies, and so forth (additional gas is worth $3 per mcf if and only if it displaces cash payments of $3 per mcf or more). (Of course, their incentive structure might be such as to lead them to respond inappropriately to these signals. See also Appendix 3.) For these—and other—reasons, we conclude that, whatever their ultimate merits, auction systems have been unjustifiably neglected in policy debates.

APPENDIX 1

We now attempt to justify the auction-derived prices on several heuristic grounds. Assume, for ease of notation, that tickets $1, \ldots, N$, are allocated to bidders $1, \ldots, N$, respectively. Let P_{qr} be the price the qth bidder faces for the rth ticket. Suppose bidder q relinquishes ticket q . One possible reallocation is

ticket 1 to bidder 1
$$\vdots$$
ticket q-1 to bidder q-1
ticket q   to bidder q+1
$$\vdots$$
ticket N-1 to bidder N
ticket N   to bidder N+1

Then bidder $q+1$ gains $h_{q+1}(f_q - f_{q+1}) = h_{q+1}F(q)$, where

$$F(q) = f_q - f_{q+1} = \text{Prob}(Q = q) \; ;$$

in general, bidder k gains

$$h_k(f_{k-1} - f_k) = h_k F(k-1)$$

for k = q+1, ..., N . Thus P_{qq} , the price actually
paid by the qth bidder for the qth ticket, is at
least $\sum_{k=q+1}^{N+1} h_k F(k-1)$. Indeed, in the case where the
bid of no one player influences the decision j of
any of the others, the reallocation we indicated is
precisely optimal (since tickets must be allocated in
strict order of the h_i), and so the formula

$$\sum_{k=q+1}^{N+1} h_k F(k-1)$$

is exact.

$$\sum_{k=q+1}^{N+1} h_k F(k-1)$$

can be regarded as the expected value of the qth
ticket. For, if there are exactly k-1 units of
gas available (an event which occurs with probability
F(k-1)) then the "value" of a unit of gas becomes
h_k . More precisely, h_k is the outcome of a (hypothetical) Vickrey auction of the available gas, as well as

being the lower bound of the interval $(h_k, h_k - 1]$ of (hypothetically) possible market-clearing prices.[4]

Our next observation is clearer if we change to the calculus notation. Consider a bidder determining which value of h to state. Let us say he is risk-averse, so he also purchases "insurance"; then his total expense is

$$\sum_{k=q+1}^{N+1} h_k F(k-1) + h_q(1 - f_q)$$

where $h_{N+1} = 0$, which, with obvious changes of notation, "equals"

$$-\int_q^{N+1} h\frac{df}{ds}ds + h(q)(1 - f(q))$$

This in turn, equals

$$h(q)f(q) - h(N+1)f(N+1) + \int_q^{N+1} f\frac{dh}{ds}ds + h(q)(1 - f(q))$$

$$= h_0 + \int_{h_0}^0 fdh \ , \quad \text{where } h_0 = h(q) = h_q$$

$$= h_0 - \int_0^{h_0} fdh = \int_0^{h_0} (1-f)dh$$

---

[4] Leonard (1981).

Assuming that h_0 is his true marginal valuation for gas, he is paying this price for a contract whose marginal value to him (either gas or cash) is exactly h_0.

Suppose he instead states h_1 h. Then the price increase is

$$\int_{h_0}^{h_1} (1-f)\,dh$$

while the increase in benefit is $(h_1 - h_0)(1 - f(h_1))$, since his new probability of receiving <u>cash</u> is $f(h_1)$. Since f is a decreasing function of h, the price increase exceeds the benefit increase, and so he is worse off. Similarly, he is worse off stating $h_2 < h_0$. So we have again checked the incentive-compatibility of our system.

For our final observation, assume that, below some base price H, demand becomes unlimited. Then

$$\int_0^H (1-f)\,dh = \int_0^H 1\,dh = H$$

So the price

$$\int_0^{h_0} (1-f)dh = h_0(1 - f(h_0)) + \int_0^H (1 - f(h_0))dh$$

$$+ \int_0^{h_0} (f(h_0) - f(h))dh$$

where $h_0(1 - f(h_0))$ = expected value of the insurance policy,

$\int_0^H (1 - f(h_0))dh = (1 - f(h_0))H$ = expected "base" value of gas received, and

$\int_H^{h_0} (f(h_0) - f(h))dh$ = premium for priority in the allocation.

APPENDIX 2

In real life, of course, bidders have more complicated demand functions than those we have postulated
The auction, as designed, will conform to buyers' incentives no matter what the range of demands (provided
a price is now computed for every bundle of tickets,
for every bidder). The main technical problem is com-
puting the optimal allocation for a complicated set
of bids. (If this can be solved, obtaining the necessary prices should be easy.)[5]

---

[5] Various private communications; Leonard (1981).

Write X_{ijkq} for the quantity of "gas if $Q \geq q$" bidder i is allocated for use as his k^{th} unit under his j^{th} option. Think of q as an index of priorities, so that there may be many tickets with probability $F(q)$. Call the numbers of such tickets $a(q)$. Let

$$V_{ijkq} = \begin{cases} F(q)h_{ijk} - \ell_{ij} & \text{if } k = 1 \\ F(q)h_{ijk} & \text{otherwise} \end{cases}$$

Then the allocation program may be written

$$\text{Maximize} \quad \sum_i \sum_j \sum_k \sum_q V_{ijkq} X_{ijkq}$$

subject to:

1. $\sum_i \sum_j \sum_k X_{ijkq} \leq a(q)$, for all q

2. $\sum_j \sum_q X_{ik} \leq 1$, for all i , q

3. $\sum_{q'=1}^{q} X_{ijk'q'} \leq X_{ijkq}$, for all $i, j, k < k', q$

4. $X_{ijkq} = 0$ or 1, for all i , j , k , q

These constraints have the following meanings.

1. limits the <u>total</u> number of q-tickets allocated;

2. indicates that i labels at most one ticket each as his 1st, 2nd, 2rd, and so on;

3. insures that i gets his k^{th} unit of q only if he first gets his 1st through $k-1^{st}$;

4. is self-explanatory.

The natural approach to solving this program is to relax 4, replacing it with

4'. $X_{ijkq} \geq 0$, for all i , j , k , q .

The hope is that this new program will have integer solutions, which will of course also be optimal for the original problem.

Unfortunately, if Condition 2 proves binding, this need not be the case. In practice, then, this suggests one class of algorithms: Try the relaxation, use the results to fix most of the allocation, and try some more powerful method on the remainder.

A second approach becomes attractive if we notice that many of the difficulties arise because of the disparity in sizes of the bidders, since Appendix 1 gives us a very fast algorithm in large-number cases. Thus many small bids could be aggregated into several large bids, and the resulting smaller program (now mixed integer) solved; the aggregated purchases would then be broken into smaller sub-allocations. This solution would provide information about the "true" aggregated demand functions, and could be iterated as necessary.

Finally, the program can be reformulated, possibly more naturally, as follows:

$$\text{Maximize} \quad \sum_i \sum_j \lambda_{ij}\left(-\ell_{ij} + \sum_k \sum_q F(q)h_{ijk}X_{ikq}\right) ,$$

subject to

1. $\sum_q X_{ikq} \leq 1$, for all i , k ;

2. $X_{ik'q} \leq X_{ikq}$, for $k < k'$, for all i , q ;

3. $\sum_j \lambda_{ij} = 1$, for all i ;

4. $\lambda_{ij} = 0$ or 1, for all i , j ;

5. $X_{ikq} = 0$ or 1, for all i , k , q .

Possible algorithms could be based upon various linear relaxations of constraints 4 and 5. It will be impossible to choose among these alternatives without some empirical testing. This is a fruitful area for further research.

APPENDIX 3

The natural gas market in the United States is
caught in a regulatory web. Producers sell to pipelines at legally regulated prices. Under the provi-
sions of the Natural Gas Policy Act of 1978, no "new"
gas will be regulated after 1985; in the meantime,
however, long-term contracts exist, with prices varying by two orders of magnitude. The pipelines sell
the gas to distribution companies; these transactions
are regulated by the Federal Energy Regulatory Comis-
sion (FERC). The distribution companies then sell gas
to end-users, subject to rate-of-return regulation
administered by state public utilities commissions.
Besides purchasing gas from pipelines, utilities
typically produce synthetic natural gas (SNG) or im-
port liquidied natural gas (LNG), both of which are
much more expensive than old domestic gas (currently,
however, LNG may not cost more than its oil equivalent)
To meet peak demand, they also store gas purchased
in the summer for winter use, subject to capacity and
cost constraints.

There are several reasons why an auction system
might be difficult to implement. First, there are
redistributional considerations. In theory, the revenues from the socially optimal allocation must be

sufficient to compensate the beneficiaries under the
current system. In practice, many powerful buyers
may oppose letting the reallocation genie out of the
bottle. Indeed, in the one state (Wisconsin) where
an auction system has been tried, it was scuttled
through legal and political opposition.[7]

Transaction costs, and administrative difficulties, would probably not turn out to be oppressive.
At least two classes of problems, however, may be
seen in deficiencies in our model. To begin with,
we have ignored the issue of the seller's incentives.
However, we argued that any efficient system must
allocate contingent claims to gas; this allocation
(even in a market), clearly depends upon beliefs
about the future. Insofar as the seller has superior
information then, as well as something resembling a
profit motive, it will likely be impossible to design
a theoretically tamper-proof pricing regime. Thus
the efficiency of the outcome will depend, in part,
on the effectiveness of the regulatory procedures
(primarily regulation by the public utilities commissions of the distribution companies); and so an overly
detailed theoretical discussion of incentive problems
seems a bit beside the point.

Another deficiency is that the quantities $a(q)$
are not truly fixed. Instead, any vector a has

some cost P(a) . Thus the allocation problem is
better rewritten:

$$\text{Maximize} \quad \sum_i \sum_j \sum_k \sum_q V_{ijkq} X_{ijkq} - P(a)$$

subject to the usual set of constraints. Technically,
the system can accommodate this feature, by charging
each bidder i the <u>total</u> cost (to the other bidders
and the seller) of his bid. In practice this would
entail charging marginal users for expensive marginal
supplies, but charging higher-priority users for the
costs of forcing the marginal users to resort to the
expensive sources. The resultant efficiency is extremely attractive, but again might cause some political redistributional battles. Technical problems
should be possible to overcome.

One attractive conjecture is that systems will
work better if the different levels of allocation are
performed simularly (for example, if the pipelines
auction gas to the distribution companies, who then
auction it to the end-users). Given our hypothesis
of effective regulation, however, such a conclusion is
not immediately obvious.

Now we come to the major flaw in the world model.
We have assumed that a bidder's marginal valuation
of a unit of gas, once his action k is chosen, is

independent of the quantity Q of gas actually realized. We can construct several plausible arguments
why this assumption would fail. For example, low Q
implies high residential demand, which implies cold
weather, which strongly suggests high demand for heat-
ing oil, which of course could lead to high prices
for distillate. On the other hand, sufficiently scarce
supplies of gas (and oil) depress the economy, also
reducing demand. In these cases the bids h_{ij} (or
h_{ijk}) no longer have the same meaning. It still
follows that our auction allocates priorities and
hedges risks more efficiently than any plausible administrative solution; thus a "white" after-market
would presumably show less activity in the auction
case. In particular, the h_{ij} submitted should be
very close to their true expected values.

Nevertheless, it now becomes reasonable to propose a market as an alternative. To alleviate thin-
ness, we suggest the company allocate claims of the
form "gas or $c," for a limited range of c . They
can also, if desired, allocate claims of the form
"gas or oil," for a specific grade(s) of oil. The
initial form of this allocation is not important, as
a market would arise. The distribution company would
promote efficiency by arbitraging among the different
sorts of claims, and adjusting its stockpiles of gas

oil, and cash accordingly. A detailed discussion of such a market is beyond the scope of this discussion. However, it seems clear that the theoretical and administrative features are comparable to those of the auction-with-aftermarket; the decisive variable will be legal and political feasibility.

REFERENCES

Leonard, H. (1981). "Elicitation of Honest Preferences for Positions When a Currency Is Available," mimeographed.

Leonard, H., C. Monash, and R. Zeckhauser (1981). "Efficient and Near-Efficient Allocation of Commodities in Stochastic Supply," mimeographed.

McKay, D. J. (1978). "Two Essays on the Economics of Electricity Supply," Ph.D Thesis, California Institute of Technology, Pasadena, California.

Monash, C. (1981). "The Valley of Wheat and Grapes: A Comment on the Efficient Allocation of Water Resources," mimeographed.

Vickrey, W. (1961). "Counterspeculation, Auction, and Competitive Sealed Tenders," Journal of Finance, Vol. 16, March, pp. 8-37.

4

WHEN A QUEUE IS LIKE AN AUCTION[*]

Charles A. Holt Jr.

Roger Sherman

I.   INTRODUCTION

Art objects, antique furniture, off-shore oil
leases, defense weaponry contracts, and many other
items are distributed on the basis of monetary bids
through price auctions. Other items are distributed
by means that resemble auctions more than we may realize. Tickets to the superbowl, the world series,
or college basketball games commonly are distributed
on a first-come-first-served basis; arriving early
to be near the front of the line corresponds to a

[*]This research was supported by the National Science
Foundation under grants SES-7923694 and SES-7914081,
and by the Sloan Foundation.

high bid at an auction. A specific opening time for
a retail sale can elicit similar queuing behavior,
as may advance commitment to obtain discount airline
tickets or resort hotel reservations, or queuing for
admission to a popular film. The rules of the queuing process may be important, as this report shows.[1]

> A fist fight broke out...inside the
> K-B Cinema Theatre on Wisconsin Avenue
> NW where "The Empire Strikes Back"
> is playing to sellout crowds. Fisti-
> cuffs erupted when two patrons tried
> to save theater seats for friends who
> had not shown up yet. "These other
> people had waited for 2-1/2 hours.
> They didn't think it was fair to save
> seats," a spokesman said.

Whenever an individual's decision about when to
join a queue depends on the anticipated arrival times
of others it is like a bid at auction. We can even
call such a queuing process a "waiting-line auction."
Other queues, like the one at a bridge toll gate or
the familiar checkout line at the supermarket, have
individuals joining and leaving all day long and are
not like an auction at all. To be sure, any person
in such a queue has to anticipate an extra delay,
but most of the rivalry of the waiting-line auction
is missing because the number of items is not limited

---

[1]Washington Post (1980).

to those being given away at a particular time. Instead there is a continuous queue with a predictable
expected waiting time that is the same for any participant. In contrast, the waiting-line auction will
have a queue that gradually lengthens until the time
when all the items people have been waiting for are
quickly distributed, with the result that different
persons wait for different periods of time. Earlier
arrival times at the waiting-line auction correspond
to higher bids at a price auction because they improve
the chances of winning.

In Part II, we present an equilibrium model of
waiting competition for the case of a queue that has
properties of an auction. (A thorough derivation of
the equilibrium in this model is available.)[2] The
aggregate transactions cost associated with waiting
in line can be significant, and we discuss factors
which affect this transactions cost in Part III. We
consider how changes in price level affect the waiting line auction and how the distribution of goods
through it compares with a lottery. We also consider
alternative arrangements that would seem to improve
the efficiency of waiting in line but are surprisingly
limited in that effect. Indeed, when very many persons know about a waiting-line auction we show that

---

[2]Holt and Sherman (1980).

all potential rents can be absorbed by the waiting
that results. Part IV contains a summary.

II. AN EQUILIBRIUM MODEL OF THE WAITING-LINE AUCTION

What one person will do in a waiting-line auction
depends on what others do, so it is reasonable to ask
whether there will be any equilibrium. Here we represent the evaluations of individuals in one very simple
function and then go on to present an equilibrium
arrival-time-strategy function which explains queuing
behavior in the waiting-line auction. Individuals
are assumed to know enough about the population of
other prospective bidders to judge the chances they
have of winning with particular arrival times. And
convenient regularities in evaluation are assumed; in
particular, the item to be awarded is valued more
by persons who also value their time more. The functions we employ are also assumed to be continuous and
differentiable functions, so convenient mathematical
operations can be performed.

One feature of the arrangements we examine is
that they often involve the distribution of many units,
let us call them prizes, rather than the one unit
that is usually the subject of an individual auction.
As compared to having a single prize, however, there

is no substantive difference when there are many prizes.
More prizes simply mean that the top ten, or 25, or
more generally any number m , of prizes go to an equal
number of top bids in a sealed-bid auction. All that
is necessary to make the problem interesting is that
the number of prospective bidders, n , exceed the
number of available prizes. We shall also assume
these bidders are neither fond of risk nor bothered
by it, in that they are willing to act on the expected
values of outcomes without giving separate attention
to the variances involved.

To simplify our representation of bidders' preferences we assume their valuations, or the amounts
they are willing to pay for a prize, can be represented
by a valuation function, $v(w_i)$, which depends only
on their opportunity costs of time, w_i (there are
n values of w_i for i = 1, ..., n persons). Thus
the values individuals attach to their time will be
related systematically to their interest in the prize.
Each bidder (queuer) knows his or her own value of
time, but with respect to other prospective bidders
knows only the population distribution of time values,
which we assume is given by the distribution function
G(w) , plus the fact that w_i for others will be
independent drawings from the population of time values.
We assume each bidder also knows n and m , the

number of prospective bidders and of prizes, although
these numbers can be random variables without affecting our results.[3]

   Now suppose there is no separate money price for
a prize that can be obtained by waiting in line. Let
t_i represent the amount of time the ith person
arrives <u>in advance</u> of the time prizes are awarded,
and let k represent a (constant) amount of time
every bidder must spend just to reach the place where
the auction is held. Let us also assume that after
m persons are in line for the m prizes, anyone else
who arrives will know at once that winning is impossible, with the result that they will not wait at
all. Then it is easy to see that a winner in the
waiting-line auction will receive the amount the
prize is worth, $v(w_i)$ for the ith person, less
the value of t_i plus k minutes that were required
to obtain it, $t_i w_i + k w_i$. The loser, in contrast,
who spends k minutes to reach the auction only to
learn he has lost, will have a payoff of $-k w_i$.
If we were thinking of a sealed bid auction, where
k was a fixed participation cost and t_i was a bid,
the payoffs to winners and losers would be similar
to those in the waiting-line auction, as Table 1 shows.

_____

[3]Holt and Sherman (1980).

TABLE 1

Payoffs for Participation

	Waiting-line Auction	Sealed-Bid Auction
Winner	$v(w_i) - t_i w_i - k w_i$	$v(w_i) - t_i - k$
Loser	$-k w_i$	$-k$

To identify an equilibrium strategy for the waiting-line auction we focus on a bidding function, $t_i = \sigma(w_i)$, which specifies equilibrium arrival times for all prospective bidders. (The equilibrium idea here is due to Nash.)[4] Roughly speaking, this equilibrium will survive an "announcement test"; if each of the other n-1 prospective bidders is known to select an arrival time according to the $\sigma(w)$ function, the ith person (where i can be anyone from i = 1, ..., n), acting individually, cannot increase his expected payoff by departing from $t_i = \sigma(w_i)$. We also define an elasticity of the valuation function with respect to time value as follows:

$$\eta = \frac{dv(w)}{dw} \frac{w}{v(w)} \tag{1}$$

[4]Nash (1951).

This concept of elasticity is useful when we impose restrictions on the value of η because whether the individuals' valuations tend to rise more or less than proportionately with the time value will determine whether those with higher or lower time values will wait in line. If $\eta < 1$, those with higher time values place a higher value on the prize but not by enough to warrant waiting in line, so we can expect those with lower values of time to be the earliest arrivals at the line. (To see this, note that the value of the prize in time units is $v(w_i)/w)/dw < 0$. As w becomes larger the time value of the prize, and hence the willingness to wait, becomes smaller.) For example, $\eta = 0$ if each prize is worth a fixed number of dollars. Sometimes banks give away dollar bills for promotional reasons, and those who wait in line the longest tend to have very low opportunity costs of time. This relationship between time values and arrival times will be reversed if $\eta > 1$.

We first consider the case in which $\eta < 1$. In this case, individuals choose earlier arrival times when they have lower values of time, and the equilibrium $t_i = \sigma(w_i)$ function is strictly decreasing in w_i. This means that individual i will win a prize if w_i is less than the mth smallest of the $n-1$ rival time values. To examine the properties of the

m^{th} smallest time value, suppose $F(w)$ is its distribution function and $f(w)$ is its probability density function. These functions $F(w)$ and $f(w)$ can
be derived from $G(w)$ for given n and m . (The
appropriate formula can be found in Hogg and Craig
and in most other mathematical statistics texts.)[5]
Then $1 - F(w)$ is the probability that the mth smallest of the $n-1$ rival time values is greater than
or equal to w . Since having the mth smallest
time value greater than or equal to one's own w_i
is precisely what is required to win a prize, this
means $1 - F(w_i)$ is the probability that individual
i will win a prize.

With the term $1 - F(w)$ indicating the probability a person with time value w will win a prize,
we can identify a time value above which persons will
not participate. The person who is barely willing to
participate will arrive just when the prizes are given
away, to avoid waiting. One who cannot recover enough
satisfaction from the prize to offset the cost kw_i ,
even after winning without waiting, will, of course,
not participate. Thus the time value of that person
who separates participants from non-participants will
be the time value w^* for which

$$[1 - F(w^*)]v(w^*) = kw^* \tag{2}$$

----

[5] Hogg and Craig (1978).

On the left-hand side of this expression is
$[1 - F(w^*)]v(w^*)$, the expected gain from participating, while kw^* on the right-hand side is the
cost of participating when there is no waiting. Those
with w below w^* are willing to arrive earlier
because $1 - F(w)$ is sufficiently larger to offset
the cost of some waiting, but no one with time value
above w^* will be willing to participate. (If w^*
exists it will be unique. We know that the probability of winning, $1 - F(w)$, declines as w rises,
and $\eta < 1$ implies that $d(v(w)/w)dw < 0$, so
$d\{[1 - F(w)]v(w)/w\}/dw < 0$. Thus $[1 - F(w)]v(w)/w$
will decline continuously as w increases and the
solution w^* occurs when it equals k in eq. (2).)

Using standard methods of analyzing equilibrium
behavior in auction games, it can be shown that the
equilibrium strategy function which specifies the
equilibrium relationship between the values of w and
the arrival times is

$$\sigma(w) = \frac{1}{1 - F(w)} \int_w^{w^*} \frac{v(y)}{y} f(y) dy \tag{3}$$

for $w < w^*$. (This equilibrium strategy function
is derived in Holt and Sherman. The $\overline{F}(w)$ and $\overline{f}(w)$
notation in that paper corresponds to the $F(w)$ and

f(w) notation in this paper.)[6] Note that $\sigma(w)$ approaches zero as w increases toward w^* ; that is,
"marginal participants" tend to arrive at the last
minute. (The equilibrium behavior of marginal participants is discussed in Holt.)[7]

The strategy function described in eq. (3) constitutes an equilibrium in the sense that, if the time
value and the arrival time for each participant are
known to be determined by eq. (3), then no individual
with $w < w^*$ can achieve a greater expected payoff
by unilaterally choosing an arrival time which is
inconsistent with eq. (3). This concept, based on
the Nash equilibrium, seems to be appropriate as long
as several of the potential recipients have had previous experience with similar waiting lines.

It can be shown that the $\sigma(w)$ function in eq.
(3) is a decreasing function of w . (It is straightforward to show that the sign of the derivative of
$\sigma(w)$ in eq. (3) is the same as the sign of the expression: $\sigma(w) - v(w)/w$. When $\eta < 1$, $v(w)/w$ is a
decreasing function of w , so eq. (3) implies that
$\sigma(w) < v(w)/w$. It follows from these observations
that $\sigma(w)$ in eq. (3) is a decreasing function of w .)

---

[6]Holt and Sherman (1980).

[7]Holt (1979).

Thus a participant with a time value of w will win
a prize if w is less than the mth smallest of
the rival time values. The probability of winning
for this individual is $1 - F(w)$, and since we are
considering the case in which only winners wait, the
expected waiting time for this person is $[1 - F(w)]\sigma(w)$
Let $T(w)$ denote the equilibrium expected waiting
time as a function of w . It follows from these observations and from eq. (3) that

$$T(w) = \int_{w}^{w^*} \frac{v(y)}{y} f(y)\,dy \qquad\qquad (4)$$

This expected waiting time will be important in subsequent discussions because it represents a transactions cost which is associated with the waiting line
allocation procedure.

A specific example may help clarify some of the
previous calculations. For this purpose let us make
particular assumptions about the distribution of
w , about m and k , and about $v(w)$. Suppose
that w is uniformly distributed on the open interval $(0,1)$. That is, the distribution function is
$G(w) = w$ and the density function is $g(w) = 1$ on
this interval. Let $m = 1$; it follows from well-
known properties of order statistics that the minimum
of $n-1$ realizations of w will have the following

distribution and density functions: $F(w) = 1 - (1-w)^{n-1}$
and $f(w) = (n-1)(1-w)^{n-2}$, for $0 < w < 1$. Now
let $v(w) = w - w^2$ for $0 < w < 1$, so $v(w)/w = 1-w$
and $\eta = -1$. Note that $\eta < 1$ in this example.
If $k = 0$, it follows from eq. (2) that $w^* = 1$;
that is, if there is no "fixed cost" for participation,
all potential recipients will participate. Making
the appropriate substitutions into eqs. (3) and (4),
one can show for this case that $\sigma(w) = (1-w)(n-1)/n$
and $T(w) = (1-w)^n(n-1)/n$. Obviously, if $n = 1$,
there would be no reason to waste time waiting. Then
$\sigma(w) = 0$ for all w .

   It is also possible to derive an equilibrium
strategy function when $\eta > 1$. In this case, valu-
actions of the prize rise more than in proportion to
the value of time, so individuals with higher values
for their time will arrive earlier and in equilibrium
strategy function $\sigma(w)$ will be an increasing function of w . Besides this change in the relationship
between arrival times and the individual's values for
their time, all that is needed to deal with the $\eta > 1$
case is to redefine the $F(w)$ and $f(w)$ functions.
This redefinition is necessary since the distribution
of the mth _largest_ of the $n-1$ observations that
might be drawn from the population of time values
will now determine the probability of winning. Given

this redefinition of F(w) and f(w) , Holt and
Sherman have demonstrated that an equation analogous
to eq. (2) determines the w* cutoff with the property that individuals who have time values which exceed w* will participate in the waiting-line competition.[8] Also, there is an equation analogous to eq.
(3) which determines the equilibrium arrival times,
but individuals with higher value for their time will
arrive earlier in this case.

A new possibility arises when those with the
higher values for their time line up earlier. Now
those who would wait might hire someone with a lower
value of his time to stand in their place. In many
cases such an agreement would be difficult to arrange,
and negotiating it could require more time than simply
joining the queue instead. In other cases, such as
the distribution of tickets to college sporting events,
procedures sometimes are intended to limit the use of
such substitutes in the queuing process. If hiring
substitutes should occur, however, the analysis presented here would have to be modified to take into
account the lower cost of queueing thus made available
for individuals who have high time values.

---

[8] Holt and Sherman (1980).

III.   THE TRANSACTIONS COSTS OF WAITING—LINE
       ALLOCATION MECHANISMS

     Much of the literature on traditional auctions
with monetary bids has been motivated by the search
for auction procedures which maximize the revenue of
the auctioneer or person selling the prize commodity.
The monetary bids in traditional auctions are proposed
transfer payments. In contrast, the bids in the waiting-
line auction use up a real resource (waiting time),
and high bids are typically not desirable from the
point of view of the person allocating the prizes.
The aggregate opportunity cost of the time spent waiting in line is a transactions cost associated with
distributing prizes. In this part, we consider the
factors which affect the level of this transactions
cost. Unless otherwise indicated, the arguments will
be made for the $\eta < 1$ case, but analogous arguments
apply to the $\eta > 1$ case.

Effect of Price Change. Recall that $v(w)$ is the
maximum amount an individual with a time value of w
would be willing to pay for a unit of the prize commodity. If winners must pay a nonzero money price for
a prize, in addition to the implicit cost of waiting,
then a one dollar increase in this price will reduce
$v(w)$ by one dollar for all values of w . An increase

in the price charged to winners will therefore reduce
the incentive to participate in the waiting-line auction. Specifically, as long as $k > 0$, so the participation cutoff is of interest, a one unit decrease
in $v(w)$ will reduce the value of w^* determined in
eq. (2). To verify this, note that $1 - F(w^*)$ and
$v(w^*)/w^*$ are decreasing functions of w^* when $\eta < 1$.
As a result, the price increase will reduce the interval of time values from which participants in the
waiting-line auction can be drawn. Thus a price increase which reduces $v(w)$ and w^* will reduce both
the value of the integrand for all w and the range
of integration on the right side of eq. (4). Therefore, the equilibrium expected waiting time is reduced
by a price increase. Similarly, it can be shown that
a price increase reduces the expected waiting time
for each participant when $\eta > 1$. These results are
not surprising because the transactions cost associated
with waiting arises only when the price is too low
to clear the market.

Comparison with Lottery. Waiting-line auctions are
resorted to when allocation according to a market-
clearing price either is not feasible or is unaccept-
able to the community involved. In such cases another
alternative to the use of market price is a lottery.
Although it is not possible to state generally whether

a lottery or a waiting-line auction is to be preferred for all possible purposes, some observations about the two procedures can be made.

The main advantage of a lottery is that it requires no waiting time. Its main disadvantage is that it makes no distinction among those who participate, whereas the waiting-line auction gives those willing to wait longer a greater probability of obtaining a prize. To be preferred over a lottery, however, a waiting-line auction must create enough benefit--through its iden- tification of those who are willing to wait--to offset the inefficient waiting it requires.

The waiting-line auction will identify consumers who realize greater benefit from the prizes, measured by their greater valuations, $v(w)$, when $\eta > 1$. If the differences in consumers' valuations are great, making those with high valuations more likely to be winners may be worthwhile. But if the differences among valuations are very small this advantage in identifying the higher $v(w)$ consumers and making them more likely winners of prizes may not offset waiting costs. When $\eta < 1$, those who value their time most highly will not be identified as more likely winners in the waiting-line auction. It is possible, however, that from a social welfare standpoint certain redistributional goals will favor the awarding of prizes

to those who do not value their time so greatly, particularly when the lower valuations are due to lower
incomes. In such cases, if $\eta < 1$, the waiting-line
auction can make awards to those socially desired
recipients more likely. Of course if income redistri-
bution is the goal when $\eta > 1$, or if maximum expected
private benefit is the goal when $\eta < 1$, the waiting-
line auction could be inferior to a simple lottery.

If both the lottery and a waiting-line auction
require the same fixed entry time, k , more participants can be expected in the lottery, and this is
consistent with the observation that the waiting-line
auction is more selective. To see this, recall that,
when $\eta < 1$, the cutoff for participation in the
waiting-line auction comes at the time value w^*
satisfying: $[1 - F(w^*)][v(w^*)/w^*] = k$, where
$1 - F(w^*)$ is the probability of winning obtained
by arriving just when the prizes are awarded and not
waiting at all. Recall also that a person with a time
value of w^* would be indifferent between arriving
at the award time and not participating. The payoff
for not participating is zero, so the expected payoff for a person with time cost w^* who arrives at
the award time is zero. Now suppose there is an un-
expected and unannounced switch to the lottery system.
A person who had planned to arrive at the award time

for the waiting-line auction would have under the
lottery a greater probability of obtaining a prize
than $1 - F(w^*)$. So, if the switch to a lottery
is not known in advance, it would cause a person with
time value w^* to have a positive rather than a zero
ex ante payoff. This would alter the participation
cutoff in subsequent lotteries toward more participation, until the expected payoff at the "marginal"
time cost is zero. Thus the expected number of participants would be greater in a lottery than in a
waiting-line auction with the same value of k . A
similar analysis applies when $\eta > 1$.

Waiting by Losers and Shared Waiting. Thus far we
have assumed that losers need not wait in line at all
because, when they arrive at the queue, they can be
told that persons already in line will take all the
prizes; thus they are spared waiting. Such a procedure is not always followed, either because it requires
effort the distributor is not willing to make or because the number of prizes cannot be known reliably
enough in advance that losers can be identified when
they arrive. (After first showing a film in a theater,
for instance, the number of vacant seats for the next
show is not reliably known unless the ushers empty
the theater after the first show.) Also, sharing
arrangements may allow reductions in the time actually

spent waiting in line. Such waiting-line auction arrangements can also be examined by altering the model
presented in Part I.

Payoffs for winning and losing will be modified
if losers must wait or if shared waiting is possible.
To accommodate such arrangements we can add waiting
time as a possibility in the loser's payoff from Table
1 and introduce parameters W and L in the winning
and losing payoffs to represent alternative waiting
requirements:

$$\text{Winner's Payoff} = v(w_i) - Wt_i w_i - kw_i$$

$$\text{Loser's Payoff} = -Lt_i w_i - kw_i$$

Now if W = 1 and L = 0 , we have the case in Table
1 when losers need not wait. But if W = L = 1 , the
losers also must wait in line before discovering they
have lost. An example when losers must wait occurs
when some of the persons waiting in a theater line for
admission do not learn they lost until they are denied
admission at film starting time. Sharing of waiting
time can also be accommodated by altering W and L .
If losers wait, for instance, but persons adjacent
in the queue can take turns holding one another's
positions so they can cut their waiting time in half,

the payoffs will be as above with $W = L = 1/2$.

It is straightforward to calculate the equilibrium strategy function for the model in Part I using
the more general winner's and loser's payoffs given
above, rather than the payoffs in Table 1. The equilibrium strategy function analogous to eq. (3) has
been derived in Holt and Sherman.[9] As before, let
$\sigma(w)$ denote this function. The expected waiting
time for a participant having time cost w can easily
be calculated from the winning and losing waiting
times, when combined with their respective probabilities of occurrence. With $T(w)$ representing this
expected waiting time, we thus obtain for the $\eta < 1$
case,

$$T(w) = W\sigma(w)[1 - F(w)] + L\sigma(w)F(w) \qquad (5)$$

where W and L are the parameters of the payoff
functions. When the equilibrium strategy function
that takes W and L into account is substituted
into eq. (5) to compute the expected waiting time in
equilibrium, it can be shown that the resulting expression for $T(w)$ is independent of W and L .[10]
Thus changes in the W and L parameters cause

---

[9]Holt and Sherman (1980).

[10]Holt and Sherman (1980).

changes in the equilibrium arrival times which maintain a constant $T(w)$ for each value of w. For
example, consider a switch from $(W = 1, L = 0)$
to $(W = 1/2, L = 0)$. This switch, which allows
people to hold a place for a neighbor in the line,
will result in arrival times which are exactly twice
as great as was the case before sharing was allowed.
When they can reduce their waiting times participants
simply arrive earlier. The expected waiting times
are unchanged for each value of w, so the aggregate expected transactions cost associated with waiting in line will be unchanged. Therefore, all potential recipients of prizes should be indifferent to
procedural changes which correspond to changes in
the W and L parameters. (More detailed examination of this effect of procedures on waiting time may
be found in Holt and Sherman.)[11] This neutrality result depend critically on the assumption that individuals are risk neutral.

Competitive dissipation of Rents. Suppose only one
person is informed that $1,000.00 will be given away
at a certain time to the first person who arrives and
waits at a specified location. The informed person
can arrive at the last minute and gain a net profit of
$1,000.00 minus the cost of travel. But if many peopl

[11]Holt and Sherman (1982).

are informed of this prize, the aggregate dollar amount
of the rent for informed people may be much less than
it was if only one informed person had been involved.

This competitive dissipation of rents can be
illustrated with the simple example presented in Part
I. In that example, $G(w) = w$, $g(w) = 1$, $m = 1$,
$k = 0$, $w^* = 1$, $v(w) = w - w^2$, $\eta < 1$, and
$T(w) = (1-w)^n(n-1)/n$. Thus there are n individuals
"drawn" from a uniform distribution of time values
who are informed of the prize to be given away. The
aggregate net rent is the value of the prize to the
winner minus the total opportunity cost of the time
spent waiting by the various participants. Instead
of considering the aggregate net rent for a specific
drawing of the n values of w , we are interested
in the ex ante expected value of this aggregate net
rent.

First, consider the expected value of the prize
to the winner. In this case the winner, that is, the
person who arrives first is the person with the lowest
of the n values of w . Recall that in this example
from Part I f(w) , the density function for the lowest of n-1 values of w , is $(n-1)(1-w)^{n-2}$ for
$0 < w < 1$. It follows that the density function for
the lowest of n values of w is $n(1-w)^{n-1}$ for
$0 < w < 1$, so the expected value of the prize for
the winner is computed

$$\int_0^1 (w - w^2)n(1-w)^{n-1}dw = n\int_0^1 w(1-w)^n dw$$

Next consider the expected aggregate cost of waiting in line. The expected waiting cost for an individual with time value w is $wT(w)$, so the expected aggregate waiting cost is computed

$$n\int_0^1 wT(w)g(w)dw = n\int_0^1 \frac{w(1-w)^n(n-1)}{n}dw$$

$$= (n-1)\int_0^1 w(1-w)^n dw$$

where we use the fact that $g(w) = 1$ and $T(w) = (1-w)^n(n-1)/n$ in this example. Now, if this expected aggregate waiting cost is subtracted from the expected value of the prize to the winner, it is possible to obtain the expected value of the aggregate net rent

$$\int_0^1 w(1-w)^n dw \tag{6}$$

Note that if there is only one potential recipient for the prize $(n = 1)$, then that person would not waste time waiting, and for this case eq. (6) is the expected value of a prize for one randomly selected person.

Now consider the effect of n on the expected aggregate net rent. It is apparent from eq. (6) and the fact that $0 < w < 1$ that aggregate net rent is a decreasing function of n in this example. Moreover, the fact that $0 < w < 1$ implies that the aggregate net rent in eq. (6) is less than

$$\int_0^1 (1-w)^n dw$$

The integral equals $1/(n+1)$, which means the expected aggregate net rent is bounded from above by $1/(n+1)$. However, since $1/(n+1)$ approaches zero as n becomes large, the expected aggregate net rent must converge to zero as n becomes large. Thus all rent is dissipated in the waiting competition as n goes to infinity. It can be shown that this dissipation of rent in the limit is a general property of the model in Part I.

IV.   CONCLUSION

Waiting-line allocation mechanisms are similar to sealed-bid auctions in the sense that an earlier arrival at the waiting line is a "bid" which has a

higher probability of securing a prize. The standard
methods for analyzing equilibrium behavior in sealed
tender auctions can be used to analyze the equilibrium
relationship between individuals' opportunity costs
of time and their arrival times at a queue. The relationship between opportunity costs of time and
equilibrium arrival times depends on the elasticity
of the value of a prize with respect to the value
(opportunity cost) of time.

In sealed-bid auctions the monetary bids are
proposed transfer payments, but the bids in waiting-
line auctions require the expenditure of real resources
(waiting time). The transactions costs associated
with waiting-line allocation procedures can be significant. Requiring successful participants to pay
a price for a unit of the prize commodity will reduce
the transactions cost. However, charging a price
for prizes will typically be inconsistent with the
distributional objectives which provide the rationale
for using willingness to wait as a basis for allocating prizes. The use of a lottery may also be unattractive for the same reason. Another possible way of
reducing the aggregate cost of waiting in line is to
allow individuals to hold a place for someone else
or to inform losers that there are no prizes so that

they do not wait needlessly. When individuals are risk neutral, however, these policies will result in earlier arrivals so that expected waiting times are unchanged.

The main purpose of distributing "free" commodities to those willing to wait in line is presumably to confer rents on those people, but this purpose may not be served if too many individuals are informed of the distribution of prizes. An example was presented in which the expected aggregate net rent converges to zero as the number of informed people goes to infinity. In general, the performance of waiting-line allocation mechanisms will deteriorate when the number of competitors for position in the line becomes large.

REFERENCES

Hogg, Robert V. and Allen T. Craig (1978). Introduc-
    tion to Mathematical Statistics, 4th ed. New York:
    Macmillan.

Holt, Charles A., Jr. (1979). "A Theory of Signalling
    Auctions," Discussion Paper No. 79-110, Center for
    Economic Research, University of Minnesota.

Holt, Charles A., Jr. and Roger Sherman (1980). "Wait-
    ing-Line Auctions," unpublished working paper, Uni-
    versity of Virginia, July.

Holt, Charles A., Jr. and Roger Sherman (1982). "Waiting-Line Auctions," Journal of Political Economy,
  Vol. 90, pp. 280-94.

Nash, John (1951). "Equilibrium in N-Person Games,"
  Proceedings of the National Academy of Sciences,
  Vol. 36, pp. 48-49.

Washington Post, July 3, 1980.

PART FOUR

EXPERIMENTAL AND EMPIRICAL RESULTS

1

EMPIRICAL ANALYSIS ON LEASE BIDDING
USING HISTORICAL DATA
James B. Ramsey

Notwithstanding the by now voluminous literature
on bidding and auctions, the number of empirical works
that have been published is surprisingly sparse as
is evidenced by this chapter's small bibliography.
Further, the gap between the concerns expressed in
the theoretical literature and those examined in the
empirical literature is substantial.

Until recently there had been little theoretical
work which produced easily testable conclusions. A
substantial portion of the work is normative and pre-
scriptive, and much of the descriptive work has concerned itself with the simpler bidding situations of
single-item bidding in one-time-only auctions. (This

is in contrast to the standard empirically observed
situation of multiple-item bidding for heterogeneous
objects in a series of auctions.) Further, the problem of mixing within a single auction items for which
the information levels and the incremental costs of
acquiring information differ markedly for all bidders
is empirically universal, but almost totally ignored,
theoretically. In short, the theoretical literature
has not yet come to grasp with the difficult theoretical issues involved in actual bidding situations,
especially for oil leases.

    In contrast to the theoretical literature, the
empirical literature has been predominantly descriptive, rather than inferential. Even in those situations in which some attempt has been made to test
relevant theoretically derived hypotheses, the difference between the sophistication of the general
theoretical literature and the sophistication of the
theoretical justification for the empirical tests has
been substantial. However, there are some indications
that this current state of affairs will shortly be modi
fied by a more extensive degree of interaction between
the theoretical and empirical work. Theoretical analys
are now beginning to consider more realistic bidding
situations and therefore to generate immediately testable implications. Empirically oriented researchers
are becoming more interested in the use of leasing

data as a tool for the testing of hypotheses generated from the economic theory of bidding and auctions.

In addition, the empirical literature can prove
beneficial to theorists in another important respect.
Careful and structured statistical analysis of actual
bidding situations within a variety of auction con-
texts frequently provides observations on interesting
and unanticipated stabilities in some empirical relationships as well as unanticipated shifts in other
relationships. These observations from historical
data require explanation and thereby stimulate the
development of bidding and auction theory into new
and exciting avenues of research.

The following brief outline and discussion of
the empirical literature follows in part the historical path of the development of the literature. The
first section examines the early investigations into
the distribution of bids within a single auction.
The next section recognizes the effect on the distribution of "low noise" bids, while the third introduces
the problem of "small numbers of observations" in
trying to determine the appropriate distribution.
The fourth section comments on the apparently observed
relationship between the characteristics of bid distributions and the number of bidders. The fifth reports some analysis of potentially great importance;
the comparison of bidding experiments across highly

disparate bidding situations. The sixth section comments on some experiments to examine the properties
of royalty bidding and some of the effects of joint
bidding. The last section, before a final brief summary, discusses the Lohrenz concept of "bidding bias."

I. DISTRIBUTION OF BID AMOUNTS

The early historical development of the statistical analysis of bid distributions used Federal offshore leasing data which began in October 1954.[1] Arps
introduced the idea of lognormality of bids on heuristic grounds. Both Brown and Crawford followed that
notion and between them added the rationalization that
the lognormal distribution was justified by the central
limit effect from the product of independently distributed
random variables; that is, the limiting distribution of the
sum of the logarithms of a large number of independent
random variables is normal. The independent random
variables involved in this process are a firm's estimates of the many factors affecting the value of a
lease. Arps and Crawford used lognormal probability
paper to search for any evidence of lognormality.

---

[1] Arps (1965); Brown (1969); Crawford (1970); Pelto
(1971).

If the distribution is log normal, the plotted points
of the logarithms will lie on a straight line. Arps and
Crawford concluded that the lognormal assumption was
tenable.   Brown proceeded in a more formal and much
more rigorous fashion. He tested the assumption of
lognormality by using the Kolmogorov-Smirnov test
employing a modification for parameter estimation made
by Lilliefors. In the process of accepting the null
hypothesis of lognormality at better than the 5 percent level, Brown verified that logarithmic mean bids
vary by tract and that the variances of the logs vary
by sale, but are homogeneous across tracts within sales.
Finally, sales of drainage tracts were characterized
in the data by the small number of tracts offered,
by bid amounts per acre an order of magnitude greater
than wildcat sales, and bid variances not significantly
different from these for wildcat sales. These results
are interesting in that since drainage sales involve
the maximum anticipated level of informational asymmetry between potential bidders on the estimated values
of the leases, application of a naive bidding theory
with informational asymmetry would lead one to predict much lower bid values for the tracts (even after
allowing for risk reduction) and a smaller percentage
of tracts receiving multiple bids to total tracts
receiving bids. One would also expect, which was
observed, that the percentage of tracts offered which

TABLE 1

Summary of Louisiana Outer Continental Shelf Sales[a]

Date	D = Drainage Sales	Number of Tracts Offered	Number of Tracts on Which Bids Were Made	Number Offered (percent)	Number of Tracts with More than One Bid	Number of Bids (percent)
10/13/54		199	90	45	59	66
7/12/55		171	94	55	65	69
8/11/59	D	38	19	50	13	68
2/24/60		288	125	43	71	57
3/13/62		401	212	53	121	57
3/16/62		380	200	53	133	67
10/ 9/62	D	19	14	74	6	42
4/28/64	D	28	23	82	19	83
TOTAL		1,524	777	51	487	63

TABLE 1 (continued)

Date	Number of Bids Received	Acreage of Leased Tracts (thousands)	Total Bonus from Leased Lands	Millions of Dollars Average Leased Tract Size (acres)	Average per Acre Bonus (dollars)
10/13/54	327	395	116	4,390	294
7/12/55	351	253	100	2,690	396
8/11/59	47	39	88	2,050	2,270
2/24/60	336	464	247	3,710	532
3/13/62	538	951	177	4,490	186
3/16/62	656	927	268	4,640	288
10/ 9 /62	26	16	44	1,140	2,710
4/28/64	69	33	60	1,430	1,850
TOTAL	2,350	3,078	1,109	4,130	361

Source: U.S. Department of the Interior, Bureau of Land Management, Bid Recap of OCS Sales, New Orleans, mimeographed, undated.

[a]Extracted with amendments from Brown (1969), p. 30.

received bids tended to be higher than for wildcat
bids. However, this observation is confounded with
the statistical fact that the drainage sales had
fewer tracts offered relative to wildcat.

Brown, in pursuing the idea that more valuable
tracts would receive more bidders, regressed the number of bidders per tract on the logarithm of the geometric mean of bids on a tract. Although the regression coefficient obtained was very significant, the
statistical procedure is faulty in that the regression
equation used is not identified since the presence
of more bidders leads to a higher expected value for
winning bids. These comments are illustrated in
Table 1.

Pelto was the first to discover that the assumption of lognormality could hold for lease bids only
after some modification.[2] It is also important to
realize that the statistics, the distribution of which
is under discussion, are

$$Y = (b_{max}/b_{ar})n^{-1/2}$$

where b_{max} in the maximum bid for any one tract,
b_{ar} is the arithmetic average of bids on the same
tract, and n is the number of bidders on that tract.

---

[2] Pelto (1971).

Pelto derived the result that $E\{\ln Y\} = 0$ and that
the corresponding variance of $\ln Y$ was 0.078. Pelto
derived the distribution of Y from the assumption
that bids are distributed log normally for two special cases, n = 2 and the limiting case of $n \to \infty$.
In the former situation, the distribution was approximately lognormal, the major difference being in the
tails of the distribution.

Pelto also showed through his analysis that the
average of log bids as well as the variance were increasing functions of n . Indeed, Pelto recognized
that the distribution of bids is a mixed distribution
where the mixing parameter is n , the number of
bidders.

The empirical work undertaken by Pelto employed
lognormal graph paper and statistics from both offshore oil sales and some uranium sales. The lognormal distribution provided a good fit only after the
removal of all bids less than 25 dollars per acre.

II. LOW-NOISE BID

While Pelto in 1971 recognized the need to re-
move very small bids, others were the first to give
a detailed and explicit treatment of the "low-noise bid"
problem.[3] In order to improve the lognormal fit,

---

[3]Pelto (1971).

Dougherty and Lohrenz used the rule that any bid less
than 1/30 of the next highest bid (alternatively less
than 1/30 of the average bid) was to be deleted from
the sample.[4] Deleting low-noise bids improved the
lognormal fit. In 1978, an alternative procedure was
followed to delete low-noise bids and it was also concluded that their omission was important to the acceptance of lognormality.

The main aspect of interest in this discussion
is that the overwhelming majority of low bids were
submitted by a very small number of bidders. For
example, of 169 low bids 147 (87 percent) were submitted by three firms, Speer (83, Domino (12), and
Gulf Coast (52).[5] In the Alaskan sales three-quarters
of the low bids were submitted by one firm, Champion.

III. TESTS FOR DISTRIBUTIONS AND SMALL NUMBERS

Bruckner and Johnson have noted that a major problem with all attempts to date to test for lognormality suffer from small sample sizes.[6] According to the
figures they cite for off-shore lease sales the

---

[4]Dougherty and Lohrenz (1976).

[5]Dougherty and Lohrenz (1976).

[6]Bruckner and Johnson (1978).

distribution of leases by number of bidders is:

Number of Bids	Number of Leases
18	1
17	1
16	6
15	8
14	16

Consequently, because all tests will have low power due to small sample sizes, many null-hypotheses would be accepted at conventional α levels.

In this connection Bruckner and Johnson demonstrate on the basis of the eight leases with 15 bids each that the tests cannot discriminate between the lognormal, beta, log uniform, and even the uniform distributions. (Both chi-square and likelihood ratio tests were used.

In a subsequent paper, Genter and Bruckner devised an ingenious method to overcome the small sample size problem.[7] The procedure capitalizes on the idea of using a part of the sample to estimate the unknown mean value of the specific distribution relevant to each tract and the rest of the data to test the distributional hypothesis after pooling the observations.

If $Y_{ij} = \ln X_{ij}$, $i = 1, 2$, N bids, $j = 1, 2$, N leases; where X_{ij} is the ith bid on the jth

---

[7] Genter and Bruckner (1978).

lease, then, under the null hypothesis, Y_{ij} is distributed as $N(\mu_j, \sigma_j^2)$ for all i. For each lease select at random one of the bids; that is, let $Z_j = Y_{ij}$ for some randomly chosen i. Calculate the sample mean and variance of log bids for each lease sale using the remaining (N bids - 1) observations. Use the calculated sample mean and variance to convert Z_j, $j = 1, 2$, N leases into a "t" statistic with N bids - 2 degrees of freedom under the null hypothesis that bids are distributed lognormally. The derived null hypothesis is that the "t" statistics calculated above are distributed as Student's "t" against the alternative that they are not.

Bruckner and Johnson used ten bid leases with a derived sample size of 42 after eliminating low-noise contamination. The null hypothesis was accepted at α levels better than 0.1. In addition, the authors verified by a sampling experiment that the procedure used at the sample sizes available was able to discriminate between lognormal, beta, loguniform, and uniform distributions.

IV. THE EFFECTS OF VARIATIONS IN THE NUMBER OF BIDDERS

So far in the discussion the dependence of the distribution of bids on the number of bidders has been recognized, but no further consideration has been

given to the matter. As a first, but relatively minor
item, Pelto's conclusion that bid variance increases
slightly in n has not been confirmed by the more detailed analysis of others.[8] In addition, and somewhat
surprisingly, there does not seem to be any evidence
for a time trend in the variance of log bids.

The most important finding is that the lognormal
approximation becomes less useful as n gets bigger,
the lack of fit showing up in the all important tails
of the distribution. The effect was demonstrated by
Lohrenz and Pederson in terms of several different
statistics obtained from on-shore bidding data.[9] The
first implication is that the probability of occurrence
of very large bids is less than would be predicted by
the lognormal distribution. Second, if one plots
against n , the number of bidders, the expected
value of the difference in the logs of the maximum
bid and the average bid, and also plots the observed
sample difference, then the suspected difference is
much greater than that observed. Further, the lack
of fit of the lognormal model gets worse as n gets
bigger. The lack of fit becomes noticeable when seven
bidders or more are involved. Once again, the

---

[8]Dougherty and Lohrenz (1976); Lohrenz and Pederson
(1979a, b).

[9]Lohrenz and Pederson (1979a, b).

implication is that the probability of occurrence
of large bids is less than that predicted by a simple
lognormal distribution model. A third and final statistic obtained from these bidding data is a transfor-
mation of the log difference between the highest and
second highest bids. The difference observed is much
less than predicted by the lognormal model for n = 7 ,
and the difference increases as n increases. Earlier
work by Dougherty and Lohrenz, also gave some indication that as n increases beyond 7 the lognormal
distribution provides a less and less useful approximation to the true, but as yet unknown, distribution.[10]

One might reasonably conclude from this analysis
that for given mean and variance, the actual distribution of bids has less skewness than the lognormal
distribution and, perhaps, a greater level of kurtosis.

V.   COMPARISON OF BIDDING EXPERIENCE

At this time there are available data on a number of bidding situations incorporating a variety
of information about geology, drilling costs, risk,
and climatic conditions, among other facts. Data
are available for off-shore bids made between 1954
and 1977, some on-shore bids between 1972 and 1977,
and bids for Alaska contracts between 1959 and 1974.

---

[10] Dougherty and Lohrenz (1976).

Indeed, bids for Alaskan rights can be separated into
two distinct categories, one with conditions closely
resembling on-shore bidding circumstances, and the
other, on the North Slope, where conditions are similar to the off-shore bids. Detailed discussions of
the Indian on-shore oil lease sales have been made
that provide similar inferences, but the differences
are most enlightening.[11]

In comparing the relatively lower drilling cost
and less risky on-shore leases to off-shore leases,
one notices that the distribution of numbers of bids
is shifted to the right; bidders from firms not in the
top twenty submitted 90 percent of the bids, whereas
among those bidding for off-shore leases, the top eight
firms submitted about two-thirds of the bids. Joint bids
comprised less than 1 percent of the bids which is in
contrast to off-shore bids where, before the ban,
joint bids comprised about 50 percent of the total.

The Alaskan experience can be easily summarized
by saying that the bid distributions for North Slope
tracts were similar to those that were made for offshore tracts and the remainder of the bids for Alaskan
leases were similar to those for on shore leases.

Finally, the Indian lands lease sales which involved some of the least risky areas was characterized

---

[11]Lohrenz (1977); Lohrenz (1978).

by no joint bids, no low-noise bids, but some weak
evidence that the bid variance was less.

VI. SOME COMPARISONS OF BID PROCEDURES

There have been two attempts to utilize bidding
data to test some hypotheses with economic content.
In two off-shore lease sales, Louisiana in 1974 and
Alaska in 1977, a small number of leases were offered
for royalty bids with a given fixed bonus and rental.
There were eight leases receiving 57 bids (average of
7.1 bids per lease) in the former sale and 30 leases
receiving 98 bids (average of 3.3 bids per lease) in
the latter sale. The largest number of bids per lease
was 13. A first tentative conclusion is that there
is no evidence indicating that royalty bidding as opposed to bonus bidding increases significantly the
number of bids per lease. The variance of lease bids
seemed to be homogeneous as in the bonus case. The
main difference discovered in these two minor experiments was that royalty bids appear to be normally
distributed, not lognormally distributed. However,
given the low sample sizes involved, little confidence
can be placed in this result.

Dougherty and Lohrenz made a careful comparison
of joint and solo bids using off-shore data.[12] The

----

[12]Dougherty and Lohrenz (1978).

evidence on numbers of bids and the average value
of bids per lease is mixed; certainly there is no
indication that joint and solo bid distributional
characteristics are strikingly different. However,
there is one clear result: the effect of the ban
on joint bids by major bidders alone only led to an
increase in the number of joint bids between major
and non-major bidders while the number of joint bids
without major bidder participation declined.

VII.   AGGRESSIVE AND CONSERVATIVE BIAS IN BIDDING

Dougherty, Conner, and Lohrenz have defined the related concepts of "aggressive" and "conservative bias"
in bidding.[13] In bidding situations where each bidder has the same preference and draws information
on leases from the same sources, then each bidder's
bid, net of strategy, can be treated as an independent drawing for the same distribution. Consequently,
the expected proportion of bids submitted on leases
less than any particular bidder's bid, say A , is
0.5. Similarly, the probability of winning in bids
against (n-1) other bidders under these circumstances
is n^{-1} .

Lohrenz has raised the question, however, that

---

[13] Dougherty, Conner, and Lohrenz (1979).

if bidders and their bids are identified, then conditional on a given bidder (or even class of bidders)
the expected proportion of bids less than the bids
of bidder A may not equal 0.5, and A may have a
probability of winning not equal to n^{-1} . It is,
of course, to be expected that, if a bidder has a
higher probability of winning, then that probability
gain is paid for by a higher than average value for
the expected difference between the winning high bid
and the average bid or second highest bid; in short,
bidders identified as having higher probabilities of
winning pay for it by expecting to leave more "money
on the table." Bidders with a higher proportion of
bids less than theirs are aggressive, and those with
less are conservative.

Dougherty, Conner, and Lohrenz examined this
issue empirically with off-shore data. The results
indicated that sample estimates of the expected proportion of smaller bids for each identified bidder
varied substantially, but there did not seem to be
any systematic relationship between average amount
of money left on the table and the sample proportion
of bids which were less.

Lohrenz and Pederson made a more detailed and elaborate analysis using on-shore bid data.[14] Once again

[14]Lohrenz and Pederson (1979b).

the identification of specific bidders indicates that
the estimated average values for proportion of bids
less than the bidder's own bid varied substantially
within sales and even after averaging over sales there
were substantial differences. However, caution is
needed in that only active bidders (those who submitted
at least ten bids in a sale) were included.

More interesting, perhaps, is the observation
that solo bidder's bids averaged close of 0.5 as the
proportion of bids less than all solo bidder's bids,
whereas the joint bids proportion averaged slightly
higher. In addition, the average for the small twenty
bidders averaged very close to 0.5 (slightly below),
whereas the top 20 and the top 8 were somewhat greater
than 0.5. Finally, there is some evidence that an
increase in "aggressiveness" is positively correlated
with higher amounts of money left on the table.

VIII.   SUMMARY AND IMPLICATIONS

A very brief synopsis of the major findings of
the empirical literature are mainly negative, but
highly useful notwithstanding. It is by now clear
that the lognormal distribution provides a useful
approximation of bid distributions only for bid situations with less than seven bidders and only after
elimination of low-noise bids. The fact that the bid

distribution is a mixed distribution, with mixing parameter n , has not yet been explored nor has the distribution of n itself been investigated. Low-noise bids seem to provide an obvious example of distribution contamination. One matter to be investigated is whether low-noise bids are purely a function of inexperience on the part of companies submitting bids.

The element of risk in affecting bidding behavior, especially the inducement to engage in joint bids, seems to have received considerable empirical support notwithstanding the small sample sizes involved. This conclusion is most strikingly suggested by the Lohrenz investigation of aggressiveness wherein the estimated proportions indicated that joint bids were more aggressive than solo.

The most pressing need for empirical work in the future is the effort to confront ever more useful theoretical models with tests of the more interesting hypotheses.

REFERENCES

Arps, J. J. (1965). "A Strategy for Sealed Bidding," Journal of Petroleum Technology, Vol. 17, pp. 1033-3<

Brown, K. C. (1969). Bidding for Offshore Oil--Toward an Optimal Strategy. Dallas: Southern Methodist University Press.

Bruckner, L. A. and M. M. Johnson (1978). On the Probability Distribution of Bids on Outer Continental Shelf Oil and Gas Leases, Los Alamos Scientific Laboratory of the University of California under the auspices of the U.S. Department of Energy.

Bruckner, L. A. and M. M. Johnson (1979). "On the Statistical Analysis of Data from Outer Continental Shelf Oil and Gas Leases--Progress Report," Section 5 of the Data Analysis Workshop held August 15, 1979 under the auspices of the U.S. Geological Survey and the Los Alamos Scientific Laboratory.

Crawford, P. B. (1970). "Texas Offshore Bidding Patterns," Journal of Petroleum Technology, Vol. 22, pp. 283-89.

Dougherty, E. L. and J. Lohrenz (1976). "Statistical Analysis of Bids for Federal Offshore Leases," Journal of Petroleum Technology, Vol. 28, pp. 1377-90.

Dougherty, E. L. and J. Lohrenz (1978). "Statistical Analysis for Solo and Joint Bids for Federal Offshore Oil and Gas Leases," Society of Petroleum Engineers, Vol. 18, pp. 87-95.

Dougherty, E. L., F. W. Conner, and J. Lohrenz (1979). "A Study of Aggressive/Conservative Patterns of Bidders and Pre-Sale Evaluations: Federal Oil and Gas Lease Sales," S.P.E. 6807, 52nd Annual Fall Technical Conference of the Society of Petroleum Engineers, Denver, Colorado, October 9-12, 1977.

Genter, F. C. and L. A. Bruckner (1978). Investigation of the Lognormality of Offshore Oil and Gas Lease Bidding Dates: Cramer-von Mises One-Sample Test, Los Alamos Scientific Laboratory of the University of California under the auspices of the U.S. Department of Energy.

Lohrenz, J. (1977). "Sealed Competitive Bonus Bids for Indian Oil and Gas Leases, 1976," ARD Section Report 78-6, Department of Interior.

Lohrenz, J. (1978). "State of Alaska Oil and Gas Lease Bonus Bids: A Statistical Study," ARD Section Report No. 78-38, Department of Interior.

Lohrenz, J. and J. A. Pederson (1979a). "Federal Offshore Oil and Gas Lease Bonus Bids, 1972-1977: Statistical Studies," Applied Research and Analysis Section, Technical Memorandum 79-12, Department of Interior.

Lohrenz, J. and J. A. Pederson (1979b). "Federal Onshore Oil and Gas Lease Bonus Bids, 1972-1977: Statistical Studies," ARD Technical Memorandum 79-11; Department of Interior.

Pelto, R. (1971). "The Statistical Structure of Bidding for Oil and Mineral Rights," Journal of the American Statistical Association, Vol. 66, pp. 456-60.

U.S. Department of the Interior (1978). "Federal Offshore Oil and Gas Lease Royalty Bidding," ARA Section Report No. 78-39.

2

AN EXPERIMENTAL COMPARISON OF ALTERNATIVE RULES FOR COMPETITIVE MARKET EXCHANGE*

Vernon L. Smith

Arlington W. Williams

> In short, the argument that we
> cannot experiment in the behavioral
> sciences because the problems are
> too complex is no more than a blan-
> ket rationalization of our ignorance
> as to what experiments to perform,
> and how to go about performing them
> (Abraham Kaplan, 1964).

1. INTRODUCTION

Double oral auction trading on the New York Stock Exchange, and on most organized stock and commodity exchanges throughout the world, has evolved over more

---

*Research support from the National Science Foundation is gratefully acknowledged.

than two centuries.[1] This evolution has consisted,
in part, of a gradual formulation of rules governing
the mechanics of "floor" trading. Our scientific
curiosity as to why these institutional rules exist
has motivated an interest in studying the effect of
contracting rules on the convergence and efficiency
properties of competitive markets. Does the "specialist book," and the New York Stock Exchange trading
post rule requiring admissible bids and offers to
narrow the bid-ask range, have identifiable affects
on market performance? Our working hypothesis is
that the survival value of a rule is manifest in
measures of improved market performance.

The 21 experiments reported in this chapter use
computerized transformations of the oral double auction that have been programmed by Williams using the
PLATO computer system's TUTOR language. Our interest
in real-time electronic trading institutions is motivated in part by the gradual evolution of both private and government securities markets into systems
based on electronic quotations[2] and in part by the
scientific value of the computer in providing closer
control over the procedures, and recording of data,
in group exchange experiments. Computerized

---

[1]Smith (1976, 1962).

[2]Garbade (1978).

variations on the double-auction are particularly relevant to the continuing debate within the securities industry concerning the design and technological feasibility of implementing an integrated national stock-trading system. (The Cincinnati/NMS pilot project actually tested a fully automated trading system based on the double auction.[3])

Although our primary purpose is to examine questions of institutional design by dissecting certain features of New York Stock Exchange trading, we also examine the effect of subject trading experience on market outcomes. This is important since we want to measure something more than transitory behavior. The first series of PLATO double-auction experiments[4] suggested that alternative bidding rules and subjects' trading experience could significantly affect market behavior. Using inexperienced subjects, PLATO double auctions were much slower to converge toward the competitive equilibrium price than comparable oral double-auctions run "by hand." The implementation of a rule requiring new bids and offers to provide better terms to the other side of the market seemed to improve the convergence properties of the

---

[3] Schorr and Rustin (1978); Crock (1979).

[4] Williams (1980).

computerized mechanism. However, the results appeared
to be similar to the <u>oral</u> double auction when subjects
had participated in a previous computerized double-
auction experiment using different cost and valuation
parameters.

2. THE MECHANISM

In the computerized trading procedure employed
in the experiments reported below, buyers and sellers
enter price quotes by typing in a number on their
keysets and then touching a designated area on their
display screen. Any buyer (seller) can accept a seller's offer (buyer's bid) by touching a box labelled
"ACCEPT." The acceptor must then touch a box labelled
"CONFIRM" at which time the contract is logged in both
the "maker's" and "taker's" private record sheets.
Bids, offers, and subsequent contracts are the only
public information.[5]

Two distinct sets of bidding rules, each having
an optional electronic queuing scheme, are used in
the experiments which follow.

<u>Bidding Rule 1.</u> There is only one (the most recent)
bid or offer displayed on the market at any instant.
A bid or offer remains displayed until it is either

---

[5]Williams (1980) describes this mechanism in detail.

accepted or another bid or offer is made. Any price
quote is rejected if it is entered before the previous quote has been "standing" open to acceptance
in the market for a minimum of three seconds. There
are no rules governing the bid-offer sequence.

This institution represents a thin relatively
unorganized exchange, with features similar to an
over-the-counter telephone market in which a potential buyer or seller has no assurance that successive
quotations will provide better prices. Furthermore,
a price quotation cannot be entered if the telephone
is "busy." Hence, there is a relatively high waiting
cost in gaining access to the market for purposes
of entering a price quotation.

Bidding Rule 2. Price quotes must progress so as
to reduce the bid-ask spread. An outstanding bid
to buy and offer to sell are displayed to the entire
market and are open to acceptance. Any price quote
which does not provide "better" terms is rejected,
and an appropriate explanatory message is sent to
the individual attempting to make the quotation.
When a contract is agreed to, a new auction for one
unit of the commodity begins with no established
bid-ask spread. This corresponds to rules 71 and
72 of the New York Stock Exchange.[6] Until such time

---

[6]Leffler and Loring (1963).

as a contract occurs a potential buyer or seller knows that the terms of trade cannot become less favorable. Under our rule 2 "waiting" incurs the risk that a competitor will make the contract. Under rule 1, to this risk is added the further risk that the subsequent quotation will provide less favorable terms.

Bidding Rule 1Q (Time Queue). Each price quote entered stands displayed to the market for a minimum of three seconds as in rule 1. However, if quotes come in more rapidly than this, they are not rejected but are placed in a queue according to the time of entry (that is, first in, first out). After three seconds the standing quote is automatically replaced by the entry at the front of the queue (no. 1) and the xth queued entry becomes the $(x-1)^{th}$. All participants are given continuously updated information on the current queue length and, if queued, their own position in the queue. As in rule 1, there is no restriction on the bid-ask sequence and only the most recent bid or offer is standing in the market open to acceptance.

This institution is entirely artificial in the sense that it provides a queue (type of "specialist's book") without the bid-ask reduction rule. In studying this procedure we attempt to dissect an observed composite institution.

Bidding Rule 2Q (Rank Queues). Price quotes must

progress so as to reduce the bid-ask spread in rule
2. However, if a bid (offer) is entered which is
not higher (lower) than the currently standing "best"
bid (offer) the entry is placed in a bid queue (offer
queue) rather than being rejected. If queued, the
maker is given the entry's position in a "rank queue"
which continually arrays bids from highest to lowest
(offers from lowest to highest). Subjects may have
only one entry either queued or standing at any point
in time. Queued entries may be withdrawn by pressing a key labelled "-EDIT-." Price quotes standing
as the best in the market cannot be withdrawn. However, the maker may "bump" his own best bid (offer)
with a still better one. Upon the initiation of a
new auction, after a contract has been made, the
lowest queued offer to sell and highest queued bid
to buy are automatically entered as the new (post-
contract) standing bid and offer. This procedure
combines the "specialist's book" with the bid-ask
spread reduction rule which are features of trading
on the New York Stock Exchange. This is the observed
institution that is our primary interest to study
and which is hypothesized to be superior to the test
alternatives mentioned above.

3.   EXPERIMENTAL DESIGN

    The experiments reported in this study use the
structural parameters given in Table 1 which result

TABLE 1

Buyers' Resale Values and Sellers' Costs
as Deviation from P^0

	Unit 1	Unit 2	Unit 3
Buyer 1	+.95	-.10	-.25
Buyer 2	+.70	0	-.05
Buyer 3	+.45	0	-.15
Buyer 4	+.25	+.05	-.20
Seller 1	-.95	+.10	+.25
Seller 2	-.70	0	+.05
Seller 3	-.45	0	+.15
Seller 4	-.25	-.05	+.20

in the market supply and demand arrays shown on the
left of Figure 1.   Trading takes place over a sequence
of at least eight 300 second market periods.   The
competitive equilibrium quantity (Q^0) is seven units
per period if both marginal units are traded.   The
competitive equilibrium price (P^0) is varied by an
arbitrary constant across market replications.   Participants are paid a 10 cent commission per contract
to compensate for subjective transaction costs in
addition to the difference between the selling price

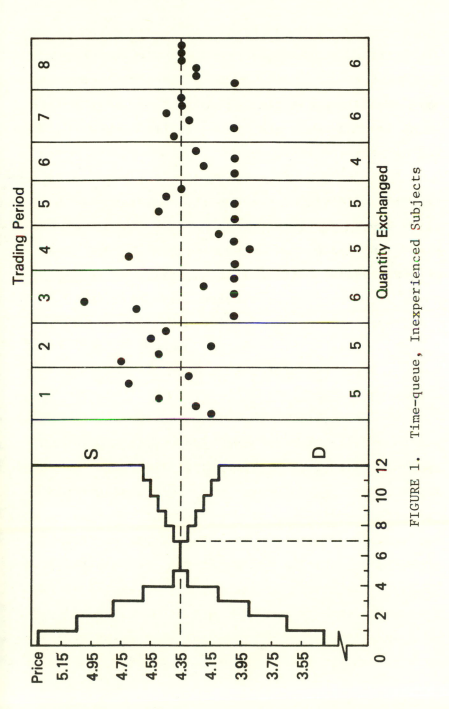

FIGURE 1. Time-queue, Inexperienced Subjects

and the cost (or buyer resale value and purchase price).
In equilibrium, the subjects would earn a total of
$6.20 per trading period. Note that the supply and de-
mand arrais are constructed so that the monetary rewards from exchange are split equally between the buyers
and sellers at P^0.

Subjects were initially recruited from undergrad-
uate and graduate classes at the University of Arizona.
After having participated in any double-auction experiment a subject was considered "experienced." Groups
of experienced subjects were generally recruited by
phone after they had indicated their willingness to
participate in another experiment by leaving their
telephone number. (It may be interesting to note that
the volunteer rate for experienced subjects was very
nearly 100 percent.)

Upon arriving at the PLATO lab each participant
was paid $2 for keeping the appointment and randomly
assigned to a computer terminal. PLATO then was used
to randomize the subjects into individual cost or
valuation conditions, present the instructions at an
individually controlled speed, and then execute the
experiment, strictly enforcing all the institutional
rules of the game. At the end of the experiment subjects were paid in cash the amount of their individual
earnings over the entire experiment. Using the bid-ask
spread reduction rule, electronic queuing, and subjects

trading experience as treatment conditions, the (2×2×2)
eight-celled experimental design, shown in Table 2,
was employed. A total of 21 experiments were conducted

TABLE 2

Number of Experiments
(and Total Number of Periods of Trading)
Classified by Trading Rule Institution
and Subject Experience

	Institution			
Subjects	Rule 1	Rule 1Q	Rule 2	Rule 2Q
Inexperienced	3 (30)	3 (31)	3 (29)	3 (28)
Experienced	2 (19)	2 (19)	2 (20)	3 (25)

with either two or three experiments under each treatment condition (see Table 2).

4.   EXPERIMENTAL RESULTS

The behavior of contract prices over time is
illustrated for four experiments in Figures 1 through
4 in which contract prices are plotted in sequence
for eight trading periods. In the experiment in Figure
1, inexperienced subjects traded under rule 1Q (time
queue) while in Figure 2 inexperienced subjects traded

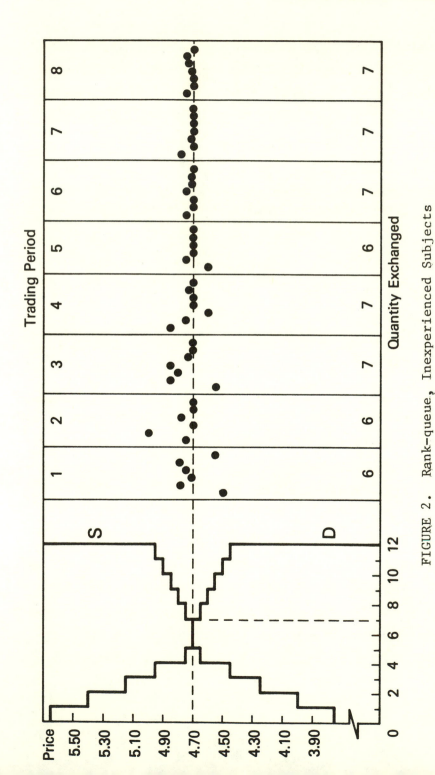

FIGURE 2.   Rank-queue, Inexperienced Subjects

under rule 2Q (rank queues). In Figures 3 and 4 exchange occurred between experienced subjects under
rules 1Q and 2Q. These four experiments illustrate
the range of convergence behavior in the 21 experiments in which experienced subjects using rule 2Q
showed the most rapid convergence to the competitive
equilibrium and inexperienced subjects using rule 1Q
showed the least.

Convergence behavior under each set of trading
rules using inexperienced and experienced subjects
will be summarized for all the experiments in regression form. Letting t = 1, 2, ... be the trading
period, we define

$$\alpha^2(t) = \sum_{k=1}^{Q(t)} (P_k - P^o)^2 / Q(t)$$

which equals the variance in the contract price deviations from the theoretical competitive equilibrium
price in trading period t , where $P_k = P_k(t)$ is
the kth contract price, and $Q(t)$ is the total
number of contracts, in period t . The dependent
variable $\alpha(t)$ provides a measure of price "distance"
from the competitive equilibrium which reflects both
the variance of prices, and the mean deviation of
price from the competitive equilibrium; that is,
$\alpha^2(t) = V(t) + (\overline{P}(t) - P^o)^2$. A market is "close" to

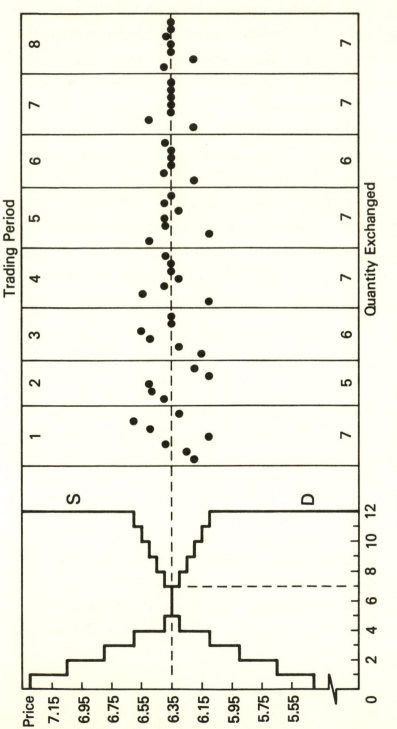

FIGURE 3.   Time-queue, Experienced Subjects

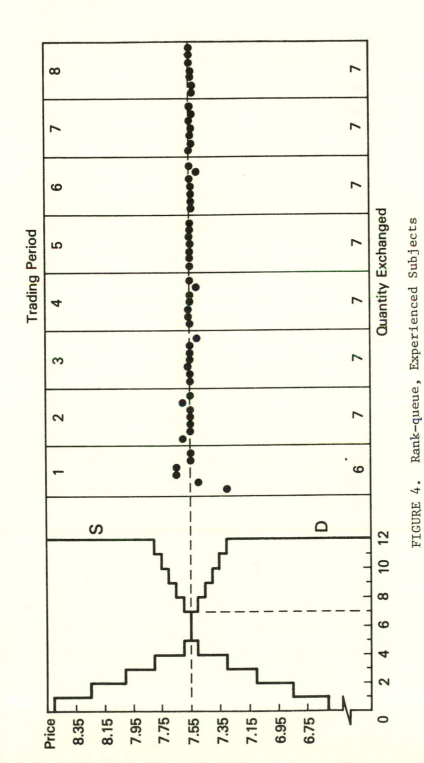

FIGURE 4. Rank-queue, Experienced Subjects

the competitive equilibrium only if the mean price
is near the competitive equilibrium and price variability is low.

Table 3 reports the results, for each trading
institution, of the least squares regression

$$\ell n \ \alpha(t) = a + bt + cX_s$$

where

$$X_s = \begin{cases} 1, \text{ if experienced subjects} \\ 0, \text{ if inexperienced subjects} \end{cases}$$

All four regressions in Table 3 show a significant
exponential convergence rate, with $\alpha(t)$ declining
at a rate varying from 8.7 percent per trading period
under rule 1Q to 20.5 percent per trading period under
rule 2Q. In each institution subject experience has
a large and significant effect on convergence.

The exponential decay functions in Table 3 are
shown in Figures 5a and 5b. In Figure 5a rule 2
prices are closer to the competitive equilibrium than
the rule 1 prices (for $t < 10$), when subjects are
inexperienced. With experienced subjects the price
convergence behavior of the two institutions is practically indistinguishable. It appears that under
rule 1 experienced subjects learn to ignore, that

TABLE 3

Regression Results for Each Trading Institution

Regression Parameter / Institution	a (Constant)	b (Trading Period)	c (Subject Experience)	Adjusted R^2	F for the Regression	Number of Observations
Rule 1	-.817 (-3.42)	-.186 (-5.12)	-1.098 (-5.22)	.51	25.7	49
Rule 2	-1.149 (-7.40)	-.166 (-6.93)	-.875 (-6.35)	.65	45.4	49
Rule 1Q	-1.095 (-8.37)	-.087 (-4.49)	-.736 (-6.35)	.53	28.4	50
Rule 2Q	-1.609 (-7.68)	-.205 (-6.14)	-.872 (-5.01)	.52	28.9	53

All the t-values (shown in parentheses) are significant at $P < .001$.

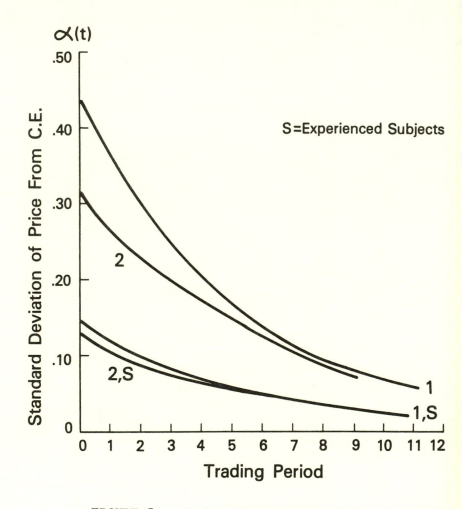

FIGURE 5a.   Price Convergence, Rules 1 and 2

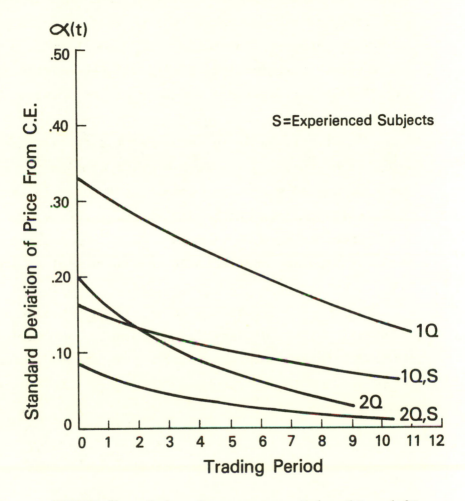

FIGURE 5b.   Price Convergence, Rules 1Q and 2Q

is, they do not accept, bids and offers that fail
to provide better terms. In effect, subjects impose
their own bid-ask reduction rule on their acceptance
behavior. However, the higher R^2 and F values
for the rule 2 regressions (Table 3) suggest that
rule 2 is a more reliable producer of competitive
equilibrium prices than rule 1.

From Figure 5b it is seen that the convergence
behavior of rules 1Q and 2Q are quite distinct even
for experienced subjects. Comparing Figures 5a and
5b rule 1Q provides the least, and rule 2Q the greatest, price convergence behavior. With experienced
subjects trading under rule 2Q conditions prices are
never very far from the competitive equilibrium.

The comparative effect of adding the queuing
condition, or the bid-ask reduction rule, on convergence, while simultaneously correcting for the effect
of subject experience is summarized in the following
regressions:

1. $\ln \alpha(t) = -1.16 - 0.135t + 0.400X_{1Q} - 0.920X_2$
            (-7.67) (-6.46) (3.35) (-7.47)

$$N = 99 \ , \quad R^2 = 0.51 \ , \quad F = 34.4$$

where

$$X_{1Q} = \begin{cases} 1, \text{ if rule 1Q} \\ 0, \text{ if rule 1} \end{cases}$$

2. $\ln \alpha(t) = -0.918 - 0.175t - 0.138X_2 - 0.984X_s$
     $\qquad\qquad$ (-5.99) (-8.11) $\quad$ (-1.13) $\quad$ (-7.88)

$$N = 98 , \quad R^2 = 0.56 , \quad F = 42.9$$

where

$$X_2 = \begin{cases} 1, \text{ if rule 2} \\ 0, \text{ if rule 1} \end{cases}$$

3. $\ln \alpha(t) = -1.05 - 0.184t - 0.658X_{2Q} - 0.867X_s$
     $\qquad\qquad$ (-7.30) (-9.07) $\quad$ (-5.93) $\quad$ (-7.78)

$$N = 102 , \quad R^2 = 0.63 , \quad F = 57.1$$

where

$$X_{2Q} = \begin{cases} 1, \text{ if rule 2Q} \\ 0, \text{ if rule 2} \end{cases}$$

From regression 1, adding the time queue to the unstructured (rule 1) market causes a significant increase in $\alpha(t)$. The time queue was introduced into the mechanism without the bid-ask reduction rule in an effort to reduce the task requirements involved in entering a price quotation into the market. Without this time queue, bids and offers are rejected if they are entered prior to the expiration of the standing time for the current price quotation. The maker must wait until the outstanding quotation "dies" or is accepted before he can enter a quotation. This

procedure proved to be very effort costly for the
subjects as each attempted to enter a new quotation,
but only one could be first. Consequently, the subjects had an incentive to enter more concessionary
quotations under rule 1 than rule 1Q. With the time
queue one is assured that any quotation will work
down the queue and enter the market. This lowers
the opportunity cost of entering less concessionary
quotations. These considerations seem to show up
very strongly in the positive coefficient of the dum-
my variable, X_{1Q} , in regression 1. Further support
is provided by direct examination of the bid and offer
distributions generated by experienced subjects under
the two bidding rules. Table 4 displays central tendency measures and a distribution-free test of the
research hypothesis that price quotations generated
under rule 1Q will tend to be farther from P^o than
those generated under rule 1. The Mann-Whitney unit
normal deviate, Z_u , indicates that time-queue bids
(offers) tend to be lower (higher) than they would
be if there was a queue.

From regression 2, the effect of the bid-ask
reduction rule is to improve convergence, but it is
not statistically significant. (The result is somewhat surprising, given the results of Williams, but
consistent with the small sample of evidence presented
by Smith using oral double auctions. We suspect that

TABLE 4

Comparisons of Rule 1 and Rule 1Q

Quotations as Deviations from P^o

			Bids	Offers
Periods 1 and 2	Rule 1	mean median	-.3765 (-.15)	.2134 (.09)
	Rule 1Q	mean median	-.8606 (-.30)	.3344 (.25)
	Mann-Whitney Z_u		5.313[a]	4.752[a]
	Sample Size	Rule 1 Rule 1Q	(121) (126)	(89) (156)
Periods 8 and 9	Rule 1	mean median	-.129 (-.10)	.1131 (.05)
	Rule 1Q	mean median	-.1484 (-.10)	.1448 (.10)
	Mann-Whitney Z_u		1.324[b]	5.131[a]
	Sample Size	Rule 1 Rule 1Q	(144) (125)	(97) (170)
Periods 1 through 9	Rule 1	mean median	-.2215 (-.14)	.1941 (.05)
	Rule 1Q	mean median	-.3726 (-.15)	.2058 (.10)
	Mann-Whitney Z_u		4.854[a]	8.877[a]
	Sample Size	Rule 1 Rule 1Q	(593) (575)	(422) (754)

[a] Reject H_0, $p = .01$.

[b] Reject H_0, $p = .1$ (direction predicted).

the 2:1 vs. 1:1 rent split may be the cause of the discrepancy.[7]) This is explained, as indicated above, by the apparent behavior of experienced subjects in imposing their own bid-ask reduction rule when this condition is not part of the formal trading rule mechanism. In regression 3, the effect of adding the electronic "specialist's book" or rank queues is to improve convergence significantly. We think this is due to a form of additional price competition "away from the market" as participants modify their queued bids or offers in an attempt to gain a more favorable position within their respective queues.

5. MARKET EFFICIENCY COMPARISONS

Table 5 displays the mean market efficiency per quartile, for each of the bidding rule treatments, using inexperienced and experienced subjects, and where our index of efficiency = 100 (actual earnings ÷ potential earnings), exclusive of commissions. In these calculations the first eight trading periods are divided into quartiles consisting of two pooled trading periods in each quartile. The figures indicate that all four of the bidding schemes studied

---

[7]Williams (1980); Smith (1976).

TABLE 5

Mean Market Efficiency
Experienced Subjects
(Inexperienced Subjects)

	Rule 1	Rule 2	Rule 1Q	Rule 2Q
Quartile 1	84.90	98.18	89.33	99.31
	(86.11)	(83.33)	(93.40)	(86.46)
Quartile 2	98.70	99.74	98.96	99.48
	(96.53)	(95.83)	(98.44)	(97.57)
Quartile 3	99.48	95.06	98.70	99.31
	(92.71)	(97.22)	(98.79)	(99.65)
Quartile 4	99.22	99.22	94.54	99.58
	(99.31)	(97.22)	(98.32)	(99.13)
Overall	97.57	98.05	95.38	99.41
	(93.66)	(93.40)	(97.22)	(95.70)

result in highly efficient markets. See Smith, Williams, Bratton and Vannoni for a comparison of efficiency in the double auction with two versions of a
uniform price sealed bid-offer auction.[8] Using experienced subjects, the rank queue (rule 2Q) is significantly more efficient than the time queue (rule 1Q)
using the Mann-Whitney U-test ($\alpha = .05$) . However,
none of the other three bidding rule comparisons are
significant. Using inexperienced subjects, none of
the four bidding treatments are significant ($\alpha = .05$) .

[8] Smith, Williams, Bratton and Vannoni (1982).

6. SUMMARY

In the context of the supply and demand configuration employed in this study (symmetric exchange surplus, four buyers, four sellers) changes in the double auction's bidding rules have a significant effect on the convergence of contract prices to the competitive equilibrium price. While no significant difference in convergence seems to exist between markets organized under rule 1 compared to rule 2, the introduction of the associated electronic queueing scheme does affect convergence.

The time queue (rule 1Q) acts to destabilize and the rank queue (rule 2Q) acts to stabilize contract prices. We conjecture that by lowering the cost of entering a price quote, the time queue encourages market participants to concede more erratically and slowly in the price bargaining. This increases the risk of waiting for a better quotation, and leads to more erratic contract prices. We further suggest that the rank queue acts to promote additional price competition "away from the market" as participants attempt to gain a favorable position within their respective queues.

The use of subjects with prior experience with the trading mechanism (but not the market parameters) is a powerful treatment variable. Experienced subjects result in a more stable market and appear to be less sensitive to changes in the bidding rules than markets in which inexperienced subjects participate. Market efficiency in the double auction is generally very high. The rank queue combined with experienced subjects yields almost perfectly efficient markets.

We conclude that the rank queue (or "specialist's book"), combined with the rule requiring the bid-ask spread to narrow, provides a trading institution that is superior, in terms of both price stability and market efficiency, to any of the alternative institutions we have studied. Whatever the historical origins of this institution, once established, it appears to have important economic benefits that may help to explain its longevity.

REFERENCES

Crock, S. and R. E. Rustin (1979). "Work on National Stock-Trading System Lags Badly; Some Blame Brokers and SEC," The Wall Street Journal, February 2, p. 32.

Garbade, K. D. (1978). "Electronic Quotation Systems and the Market for Government Securities," F.R.B. N.Y. Quarterly Review, Summer, pp. 13-20.

Kaplan, A. (1964). The Conduct of Inquiry: Methodology for the Behavioral Sciences. Scranton, Pa.: Chandler Publishing Co.

Leffler, G. L. and C. F. Loring (1963). The Stock Market, 3rd edition. New York: The Ronald Press Company.

Schorr, B. and R. E. Rustin (1978). "A Stock-Trading Test Could Presage Future of Securities Industry," The Wall Street Journal, October 3, p. 1.

Smith, V. L. (1962). "An Experimental Study of Competitive Market Behavior," Journal of Political Economy, 70, pp. 111-37.

Smith, V. L. (1976). "Bidding and Auctioning Institutions: Experimental Results," in Y. Amihud (ed.), Bidding and Auctioning for Procurement and Allocation. New York: New York University Press, pp. 43-64.

Smith, V. L. (1980). "Relevance of Laboratory Experiments to Testing Resource Allocation Theory," in Jan Kmenta and James Ramsey (eds.), Evaluation of Econometric Models. New York: Academic Press, pp. 345-377.

Smith, V. L., A. W. Williams, W. K. Bratton, and M. G. Vannoni (1982). "Competitive Market Institutions: Double Auctions versus Sealed Bid-Offer Auctions," American Economic Review, Vol. 72, pp. 58-77.

Williams, A. W. (1980). "Computerized Double Auction Markets: Some Initial Experimental Results," Journal of Business, Vol. 53, pp. 235-58.

3

FEDERAL MINERAL-LEASE BIDDING DATA BASES AND THE REAL WORLD*

John Lohrenz

Ray A. Waller

I. INTRODUCTION

Table 1 summarizes the status of the several federal mineral-lease data bases for which data is public.

By far the most common method for offering

---

*Russell G. Wayland and Hillary A. Oden were early proponents of data bases. Others who contributed measurably include Robert H. Lawton, M. Risser, Kenneth A. Douglas, Robert S. Martin, Frankie W. Conner, R. Gordon Peterson, Joan L. Keiper, Michael H. Seeb, and Joyce Gore. Still others include John L. Sibert, Lawrence A. Bruckner, Myrle M. Johnson, and Anthony F. Montoya.

TABLE 1

Federal Mineral-Lease Bidding Data Bases: Summary of Status

	Data Base	Leases in Data Base	Time Period Covered	Includes Production Data
LPR-5 & -10	Federal Offshore Oil & Gas	Receiving any bids	1954-1978	Yes
LPR-19[a]	Federal Offshore Oil & Gas	Issued	1957-1976	Yes
LPR-17.3[b]	Federal Offshore Oil & Gas (Gulf of Mexico only)	Receiving any bids	1974-1976	Yes
LPR-18	Federal Onshore Oil & Gas	Offered	Mid-1972 1977	No
	Indian Oil & Gas	Offered	1976-1977	No
	State of Alaska Oil & Gas	Offered	1959-1974	No
	Federal Geothermal	Offered	1974-1977	None
LPR-20	Federal Coal	Issued	1965-1978	Yes

[a] LPR-19 includes all the data types included in LPR-5 and -10 plus individual well and platform data.

[b] LPR-17.3 includes the data element of LPR-5 and -10 plus geographical coordinate data for generating annotated, color and/or grid coded maps.

Federal leasing has been sealed bonus bidding wherein
the bidder offering the highest "front end" cash bonus
may be awarded the lease subject to a predefined schedule of royalty assessed to any subsequent production.
The data base for bonus bidding includes the bid amounts
and their ownership. More recently, some leases have
been offered under a sealed royalty bidding system wherein
the bidder offering the highest royalty may be awarded
the lease subject to a present bonus. In this case, all
royalty bids and their ownership are included in the
data bases. Actually, the Outer Continental Shelf Lands
Act Amendments of 1978 provides for offering leases
using a profit sharing or working interest bidding procedure as well as the bonus and royalty bidding alternatives already used.

It is the data base users who are the object of
this chapter. While there are many users, they are
varied. From the many users, we have some observations
of interest to other users. In Section II, we classify the three kinds of users as empiricists, mechanists, and theorists. The bidding data base users
would <u>like</u> to have stems from considering what bidders
might desire in an ideal bidding data base (Section
III). In Section IV, on the laws of data bases applied
to mineral-lease bidding data, users are regarded as
managers of the data bases. Finally, an unsurprising
prediction about the future of these federal mineral-

lease data bases is proposed in Section V.

II. THE THREE KINDS OF USERS

Users of these federal mineral-lease bidding
data are classified as empiricists, mechanists, or
theorists. Any such classification oversimplifies,
but it can be useful. Empiricists use the data base
simply as a source of data for observing frequencies
and correlations among variables. The scattergram
is a basic tool.[1] Other tools are useful for exploratory correlation searches on multidimensional data.[2]
The disadvantage of the empiricists' product is that
no correlation proves that a mechanism exists between
correlated variables. The use of a correlation for
prediction may imply hidden as well as explicit assumptions. Therefore, defense of any empirical correlation is difficult. For example, Lohrenz and Oden
presented histograms showing that leases with higher
bonuses per acre tended to return a higher royalty
per acre from production. Not so, said one declaimer.
The lower bonus leases were leases the bidders thought
were gas leases which had, the declaimer avowed, a

---

[1] Applied Research and Development Section Report No.
77-30 (1977).

[2] Bruckner and Mills (1979); Bruckner and Montoya (1979)

[3] Lohrenz and Oden (1973).

product of lower value than the higher bonus leases
the bidders thought were oil leases. One might think
to check that conjecture by dividing the population
into leases and bidders thought were gas and oil leases.
However, those data were and are unavailable. So,
the declaimer could not be answered from the data.

Mechanists start by presuming some mechanism (or
model). Providing the data required to test the mechanism are in a data base, mechanists use data bases
to validate that the data fit the mechanism. A favor-
ite example of mechanists-at-large in mineral lease
bidding is the work that assumes that bonus bids on
leases are drawn from a random lognormal distribution.
As Crawford pointed out, the mechanism purported to
prevail if bids are lognormally distributed is that
bids are computed in a multiplicative process in a
manner that, in concert with the central limit theorem,
causes bids to be lognormally distributed. And that
presumed mechanism is the springboard for mechanists
"measuring" the lognormal distribution.[4] However,
theorists know that the fit of data, is hardly conclu-
sive evidence that the presumed mechanism is in force.
In particular, the fact that data fit one mechanism
does not preclude the same data fitting other mechanisms. The antipathy of theorists to mechanists

_____

[4]Crawford (1970).

assuming that the lognormal distribution applies to bidding data has been expressed.[5]

Theorists use the data to seek a theory which describes how individual bidders bid. Further that theory should be sufficiently robust to predict how individual bidders would bid under alternatives for offering the leases.

Arguments among empiricists, mechanists, and theorists using the federal mineral lease bidding data bases are common. They suggest something akin to the Heisenberg uncertainty principle. That is, the closer one is to an exact measure, the more difficult the actual measurement. Thus the theorists' goal to correlate past bids from theory and predict future bids under different alternative bidding situations is unattainable from available data.

How might the theorists' goal be attained? What bidding data base is needed (and can it be obtained)? These questions introduces the next section.

III. AN IDEAL BIDDING DATA BASE

An ideal data base which permits examination of bidding theories requires salient data on actual bids.

---

[5]Brown (1969); Dougherty and Lohrenz (1976); Dougherty and Lohrenz (1977).

[6]Stark and Rothkopf (1979).

To understand the data for an ideal data base imagine
a peculiar kind of poker game in which someone (perhaps a government), offering to sell an object by
competitive bidding, invites participants to gamble.

Imagine a table of poker players at five-card
draw with two hands dealt. The first hand dealt to
you, before any drawing, is a pair of deuces, and
the other hand is three jacks. For this pseudo-poker
to better resemble bidding for mineral leases with
the huge uncertainties involved, we should have only
a (flawed) estimate that you have a pair of deuces
in one hand and three jacks in the other.[7] Further,
any knowledge beyond historical biases and variances
between actual results and estimates is unlikely.

Of course, three jacks, if you really have them,
is a better hand than two deuces (if you have them).
But, the three jacks are not competing against the
two deuces; each must compete against a different
set of hands. Nonetheless, the three jacks are more
valuable in the sense that every poker player would
prefer to have three jacks over two deuces ceteris
paribus. Assume that you are as prudent a poker player
as mineral lease bidders are prudent. How would you
bid the three jacks? The two deuces?

In poker, just as in mineral lease bidding, you

---

[7]Bruckner and Johnson (1978).

know the potential outcomes. A draw could make your
hand more powerful. You can win "big" with a relatively weak hand and lose "big" with a relatively
strong hand. The probabilities do not favor that
outcome, but the probabilities are positive. It is
not evident whether or not the three jacks or two
deuces should be bid upon. First, your bid depends
upon your perception of the hand you hold and its
prospects. Second, your bid is affected by your perception of what your competing players think they
hold. In particular you may bet a weaker hand (say,
two deuces) more aggressively than a stronger hand
(say, three jacks). A third effect suggests that
"One of the first goals of a society is to make its
inhabitants feel safe."[8] The societal goal is also
a goal of prudent poker players and mineral-lease
bidders. While both would like to win as much as
possible, they do not want to worry about having to
leave the game. A bidder once confided the conster-
nation of his organization's board of directors after
discovering they had spent a distressingly large portion of their current liquidity in one federal offshore
oil and gas sale. This followed the board's decision
to be aggressive in that sale. That would certainly
be analogous to poker players with "hot" hands bidding

---

[8]Slater (1976).

high, then worrying about their dwindling chips.
Fourth, your bid is affected by your memory of history.
Because of this memory, you would conceivably play two
poker situations differently, although they have exactly the same "optimum" bid based on everything else
you know. Fifth, being a prudent player does not
mean that other players concur. For example you might
enjoy poker for the comaraderie at least as long as
you do not lose too much. Perhaps you bid aggressively.
Or perhaps, conservatively. Probably every player
has bid at some time to imply something untrue. The
point is that poker players, like mineral-lease bidders, can have different measures of success. One
bidder's rational behavior may be another bidder's
idea of irrational behavior.

An example of disagreement over what constitutes
rational bidding is a bidder who bids very high on
leases with a kind of corporate ego tweaked by another
bidder's well-publicized exploration successes. That
high bidding appeared eminently reasonable to the bidder, no doubt. Some other bidders thought the bids
foolish and the impetus for them more foolish.

In summary, we have identified five considerations
affecting a poker player's bid or a minimal lease bid.
These are:

For the Poker Player

1. The hand you think is being held and the expectation of what that hand may become.

2. The hands you think the competing players are holding and what they might become.

3. How large or small the stack of chips you have before you is.

4. Things that have happened before in this kind of game with these players.

5. The things you want out of the game.

For the Mineral Bidder

1. The estimate of what the lease contains and what value might come from it.

2. What you think competing bidders think about the lease and what they might do.

3. How what you bid and what happens might affect your cash flow.

4. The previous history of bidding on leases.

5. The things you hope to get done by bidding.

All of these considerations would affect how you bid in a poker game and for mineral leases being offered.

To complete the poker analogy to mineral-lease bidding we should consider a mineral-lease bidder as a participant at a number of simultaneous tables of poker. The poker player playing at a number of tables may, in fact, seek entry to additional poker tables and to leave others. Obviously, such intentions affect the player's bids. A mineral-lease bidder once

attributed his organization's aggressive bidding to
the expectation of certain expropriation payments.
That would be like a poker player bidding higher on
one table because he expects to be told to lease
another.

Unlike poker, where a player on many tables
could transfer winnings from one table to another,
and, at any time, compute a single number of the
value of his holdings on all tables, mineral-lease
bidding does not allow such simple machinations.
That is one breakdown in the poker game analogy.

Mineral-lease bidders, as poker players playing
simultaneously at different tables, may have strong
physical relationships between tables; that is, there
may be a physical benefit to be playing at a specific
set of tables such that a loss threatened on one table
calls into question the safety of more than just the
table in question. A mineral lease bidder who has
favorable contracts to deliver finished products to
a certain region that is threatened by inadequate
supplies may be more aggressive in a bidding game
for leases that could alleviate the threat.

If considerations that affect poker players'
bids also affect mineral lease bidders' bids, it is
not surprising that bids may appear to arise by some
random distribution even if no bid is random. (This

appears also to be the reason why it is difficult to
discriminate among statistical distributions to find
a "best" model describing the bids.)[9]

Let us return now to the question at the start
of this section. What are the data we would need to
have an ideal data base to seek the bidding theorists'
goal of modeling bidders' bids in such a way that we
can predict future bidders' bids? Consistent with
the five considerations of our poker player and mineral-lease bidder, we need each bidder's estimate
of the value of the lease in question, each bidder's
estimate of his competitor's thoughts and tactics,
each bidder's liquidity that would be affected by
the bidding, each bidder's recorded history of successes and failures on leases of the type in question,
and each bidder's stated goal or function which is
being optimized. In addition, we need for each bidder the status of all other business enterprises of
the bidders. Further, all of these data would have
to be available in some fully structured quantitative
format. We do not, of course, have all of these data
in our current inventory of federal mineral-lease data
bases. We do not want to jump to a conclusion that
it would be completely impossible to get such a data
base, but it certainly would be difficult and costly.

---

[9]Bruckner and Johnson (1978).

What bidding theorists along with empiricists
and mechanists should renew, we think, from noting
the gap between the ideal and actual data bases is
a sense of humility. The federal mineral-lease bidding data bases contain, at best, only a modicum of
the relevant data. Further, theorists, mechanists,
and empiricists are fallible in modeling and predict-
ing bids.

IV.   THE LAWS OF DATA BASES APPLIED TO MINERAL
LEASE BIDDING DATA

At the outset we noted that this chapter is intended for users of federal mineral-lease bidding
data bases. In Sections II and III, we have addressed
people who use the data. We now shall address those
users who manage data bases.

We first state three laws applicable to all data
bases--not just mineral-lease bidding data bases.
They are exactly analogous to and, in fact, drawn
from the three laws of thermodynamics. Like those
laws, these data-base laws state constraints, limits,
and unavoidable burdens. Also, as for the laws of
thermodynamics, there is no proof of them but there
are also no creditable violations. By the first law,
one cannot get information based on data that is not
accessible in a data base. According to the second

law, when there is questionable or apparently erroneous data in a data base, the only way the apparent
problem can be resolved and, if necessary, corrected
is by doing work outside the data base and applying
results of that work to the data base. The third
law, states that the only data base which does not
have questionable or apparently erroneous data is a
data base that is not being used. The law of both
data bases and thermodynamics have an aura of simplicity that mask an always abortive attempt to commit
exactly what the laws prohibit. A few tales about
users (and prospective users) of the federal mineral-
lease bidding data bases as related to the three laws
follow.

Tale No. 1: Data Doesn't Have a Family Name. One
potential user asked us, "Why don't you have any environmental data in your data base?" As it happens,
we did have a user who used the federal offshore oil
and gas data base-production data to look for correlations between the amount of production and spills
as part of a study on that environmental problem.
Nonetheless, another potential user expressed the
opinion that the data in the data base "were not re-
sponsive to environmental concerns." These potential
users, of course, did not have a fundamental understand
ing of what data bases are. Data are not classed by

hue and color of any one person's particular application.   There is no such thing as environmental data
per se just as there is no such thing as anti-environ-
mental data per se.   Rather, there are data covering
the meterology and pollution, among other conditions
which relate to environmental questions and policies.
To this point, the first law notes there is only data
without qualification which one can use to mold some
kind of information which may be related to the environment or which is not, which is generally based on a
nontechnical value judgment.   Data cannot be politi-
cized; information can.

        We seek comprehensive sets of data to add to the
federal mineral-lease bidding data bases.   However, in
adding data we must compare the value to users to the
cost of adding the data rather than the "brand name"
of the information the added data would supposedly
provide.   No data is categorized by its intended use
in any particular application.   Data does not belong
to any particular application, family of applications,
or family--which motivates the title of this tale.

Tale No. 2: Data That's Not. We are frequently asked
why we do not have or get reserve data in our oil and
gas data bases.   Reserves, in that context, mean the
reserves which will be recovered at a future date.
The answer is simple.   We do not have future recoverable reserves in the data bases because future

recoverable reserves are <u>not</u> observable data. They
are all estimates about which there is no agreement
except that all estimators agree they are flawed and
subject to huge uncertainties. The most meaningful
and interesting studies using the data base assume
observable data. As an example, the bonus a bidder
offered is observable data.

Users must understand the differences between
observed data and estimates. That is, we must not
try to get information based on data that is not observed.

Tale No. 3: <u>Seek What You Will Define</u>. The single
type of application that has attracted the most use
and users of the federal mineral-lease bidding data
bases has dealt with the broad question of <u>competition</u>.
As one user put it, "We want to use the data base to
determine if there has been competition or not." That
is a clear, simple, and laudable intent. But, is it
a technically complete and realistic intent? We think
not. Perhaps this is why that, when it is necessary
to be tactful with users, we have memorized the stock
riposte to that intent, "Please recognize that it
is unlikely that you will be able to use the data
bases to get a definitive answer to what you seek."
When we can, we ask the user what is meant by competition. Sometimes the user responds with a definition

that can be directly generated from the data in the
data base. Concentration ratios are a specific example.[10] However, any single measure of competition,
be it concentration ratios or something else, is an
incomplete and flawed measure. But, at least, these
can be computed from the data and, hopefully, will
be used properly with their burdens to meaningful
interpretation realized.

Many users, however, somehow remain incredulous.
Just like the medieval "thinker" who thought the laws
of thermodynamics making perpetual motion machines
impossible were some kind of conspiracy to hide their
availability, so the assessment that the question of
competition is unanswerable from the data is viewed
by some as a kind of obstruction erected to hide the
answer.

We have tried—with occasional success—surrepti-
tiously to instruct these users in the first law by
asking, "What would you expect from the data if there
were no competition?" Or, the converse, "If there
were competition?" Sometimes, there is a realization
that there is no such think as no competition and no
such thing as total competition. Anyone's definition
of competition implies that an amount deemed adequate,
of desirable competitive activities is present. What

---

[10]Applied Research and Analysis Section Report No.
79-4 (1978b).

the desirable activities are and the amount deemed
adequate are policy value judgments about the technical assessments cannot be made unless the activities are quantitatively defined. When the activities
are quantitatively defined in such a way that the
data allow their evaluation, the data base can be
of assistance. The apolitical data base cannot, however, itself serve to promote or defend the policy
inherent in any specific definition of what constitute
desirable kinds and amounts of competition.

Tale No. 4: The Action Is in the Kitchen, but Few
Want to Go in There. Users, naturally, see the data
bases as a source, hopefully, of answers to their
questions. What users often fail to see is the expense
of time, money, and effort that must be expended to
build and maintain a data base. Building and maintaining the federal mineral-lease bidding data bases
has cost, to date, almost $10 million. These are
not huge data bases, but the costs of getting the
source data, putting it in the data base, and checking the data base to find and correct the more egre-
gious errors are high. In our case, the $10 million
approximation does not include reports, many times
of use in themselves, which were generated in the
process of checking the data bases.

        Users are not the only ones who sometimes exhibit

a proclivity to ignore the process of what gets them
the data they use in the data base. Systems designers
have been guilty as well. In early efforts to compu-
terize these data bases, the systems designers spent
much time and money selecting the hardware and soft-
ware systems which would optimally process the data
they had not seen for users who were not able to tell
them what they wanted! When the systems designers
sent the people to assemble the data for their data
base, the predictable wail arose, "Your data doesn't
fit our system."

Whether you are a systems designer or a user,
you cannot avoid the question of how the data got
there. Some might seek the goal, as the systems designers of the previous paragraph did, of designing
the data base so its maintenance is transparent to
users. But the goal is a delusion. You cannot divorce
the proper use of a data base from knowing how the
data got in the data base.

Indeed, the corollary to Murphy's law applied
to building and maintaining data bases is that the
source data for your data base is always in worse
shape than you thought it was. Source data for a
data base often are nonexistent when one eventually
seeks it. The second law prevails. Data does not
come from the real world to the data base and spon-
taneously find its appropriate notch. And the second

law requires a lot of time and money.

Tale No. 5:   Thank Goodness for Little Complaints.
There have been many complaints about apparent errors
in the data base. For example, early in the life of
the data bases, we found that almost 100 percent of
the royalty due to one federal offshore oil and gas
lease sale came from one lease of many producing.
The reason was due to a shifted keypunched field which
credited a lease with a $10 million royalty in one
year when the lease actually had none. (Another lease
actually had $34,331 royalty that year, but showed
up in the data base with $3433.) The data-base system
has all kinds of safeguards to prevent these kinds
of errors, but somehow the errors occurred. In each
case, we found the error because it led to an observable oddity. Further, correcting the error was possible by tracking it through the data system. The
potential for technical foolishness hidden in data is
enhanced in many situations, by what may be called
the "interest and error in the extremes principle."
So many times, the user is interested in extreme values
(such as the highest bid, or highest production) in
the data base. Further, errors in a data base frequent
most affect extreme values of computations for a data
base.

   We now mention one array of errors discovered in

the LPR-19 data base involving well completions to
illustrate one of the more troublesome facets of a
data-base manager's plight. The LPR-19 data base
included individual well data without completion data
originally. We decided to add completion data subsequently. After we added completion data, we found
something peculiar. The data showed that, overall,
completed wells clearly tended to be the earlier wells
drilled on a lease. While that could happen sometimes,
that was not an expectation given the usual scenario
of exploration drilling. You can imagine the conster-
nation when we discovered that when adding the completion data, the addition had been made without regard
to which particular well in a lease had been completed.
If a lease with 21 wells had 17 completions, then the
first 17 wells were taken as completed of the 21 in
drilling data sequence. Those who handled the data
said, "You did not tell us completion data were for
individual wells." The reply was, "We didn't think
it necessary to specify that completions apply to
particular wells." After more mutual reproach, we
started over with adding the completion data. The
second law applied again.

Especially for competition studies, one would
like to be able to consistently identify bidding organizations. Just like a bettor at a race track examining the past record of a particular horse, one

would like to examine the past record of a particular
bidder. Users try to do this, and we try to help them
with codes in the data base, but the results are never
wholly satisfactory. There are basically two reasons.
The first is mergers, purchases--whole or partial, and
other corporate arrangements which leave the decisions
as to who was really a distinct bidding organization
separate from all others murky. The second is joint
bidding and some of the joint-bidding situations have
been described which cloud the definition of a distinct
individual bidder.[11] Now, what users would like to
have is not just a current list of distinct, individual
bidders, but one for any arbitrary time. (We are
seeking to add assignments to the data bases in order
to facilitate this.) However, it is clear there will
always be ambivalences and arbitrariness in any definition of distinct, individual bidders.

Some users see "mistakes" in how the data in the
data base are arranged. For example, when more than
one owner participates in a joint bid, the tape and
card formats of the data bases include the bid value
only for all owners. For some users and their applications, it would be more efficient to repeat the bid
value for each owner. But for other users, that would
be a redundancy and would require reprogramming of

---

[11]Dougherty, Johnson, Bruckner, and Lohrenz (1981).

their applications. As data-base operators, we see
the plethora of user applications and know that no
single data-base format can be optimum for all or
even most applications. Conceivably, one could do
a census of applications and arrive at some optimum
format for all, but we think that hardly justified
given the constantly changing mix of applications
and our inability to predict the future applications.

    As every data-base manager knows, the cycle that
keeps a data base alive is new applications leading
to new specifications for the data in the data base
leading to more new applications and so on. The best,
indeed, the necessary evidence that runs the cycle
is, users' complaints. Without them the data base
would be "dead."

V. THE END IS NOT NEAR

    Students sometimes remember the three laws of
thermodynamics as: (1) You cannot win. (2) You cannot break even. (3) You cannot get out of the game.
    In Sections II and III, we have shown that, at
best, any data base is that subset of the real world
needed to find the solution to your question. Further,
we have not captured the requisite data to do that in
the federal mineral-lease bidding data bases. In the
games between our data bases and the real world on

the real world "court," we have lost, so far.   Immediate prospects for winning there are not good either.

In Section IV, we recounted some of the games we
played against the real world on our data bases' court.
The real world has been winning there, too.

But unlike the won-loss record of competing teams,
you do not count data-base wins and losses, but only
consider that you could and did keep playing the game.

It is, after all, the purpose of these data bases
to obsolete themselves. So we, too, consider the pros-
pect of having obsolete data bases of federal mineral-
lease bidding data on our hands. But, the end does
not appear to be near and, until that dismal end, we
shall, no doubt, lose many more bouts with the real
world.

REFERENCES

Applied Research and Analysis Section Report No. 78-30
    (1978a). "User Documentation for the LPR-20 (Coal)
    Data Base." Cons. Div., U.S. Geol. Surv., Denver,
    June 19.

Applied Research and Analysis Section Report No. 79-4
    (1978b). "Federal Offshore Oil and Gas Lease Con-
    centration Ratios (Update through CY77)." Cons.
    Div., U.S. Geol. Surv., Denver, October 16.

Applied Research and Analysis Section Technical Memo
    79-20 (1979). "LPR-5/-10 Data Base Documentation."
    Cons. Div., U.S. Geol. Surv., Denver, February 23.

Applied Research and Development Section Report No.
  77-30 (1977). "Scattergrams of Bidding Data for
  Federal Offshore Oil and Gas Leases." Cons. Div.,
  U.S. Geol. Surv., Denver, September 26.

Brown, K. C. (1969). Bidding for Offshore Oil, Toward
  an Optimal Strategy. Dallas: Southern Methodist
  University Press.

Bruckner, L. A. and M. M. Johnson (1978). "On the
  Probability Distribution of Bids on Outer Continental
  Shelf Oil and Gas Leases," LA-7190-MS, Los Alamos
  Scientific Laboratory.

Bruckner, L. A. and C. F. Mills (1979). "The Inter-
  active Use of Computer Drawn Faces to Study Multidimensional Data," LS-7752-MS, Los Alamos Scientific
  Laboratory.

Bruckner, L. A. and A. F. Montoya (1979). "The Use
  of an Oil Truck Figure to Represent Companies Involved in Offshore Oil Leasing," LA-7653-MS, Los
  Alamos Scientific Laboratory.

Crawford, P. B. (1970). "Texas Offshore Bidding Patterns," Journal of Petroleum Technology, pp. 283-89.

Dougherty, E. L., M. M. Johnson, L. A. Bruckner, and
  J. Lohrenz (1981). The Economics of Exploration
  for Energy Resources, edited by J. B. Ramsey.
  Greenwich, Ct.: JAI Press, Inc., pp. 227-40.

Dougherty, E. L. and J. Lohrenz (1976). "Statistical
  Analyses of Bids for Federal Offshore Leases," Journal of Petroleum Technology, pp. 1377-1390.

Dougherty, E. L. and J. Lohrenz (1977). "Money Left on the Table in Sealed, Competitive Bidding: Federal Offshore Oil and Gas Lease Bids," Proc. SPE Petroleum Economics and Evaluation Symp., Dallas, February 21-22, pp. 291-300.

Lohrenz, J., D. A. Dunham, and H. Tomlinson (1979). "A Study of Factors Affecting Profit for Different Federal Offshore Oil and Gas Lease Bidders," SPE 7714, Proceedings of the SPE-AIME Symp. Petroleum Economics and Evaluation, Dallas, February 11-13, pp. 43-52.

Lohrenz, J. and H. A. Oden (1973). "Bidding and Production Relationships for Federal OCS Leases: Statistical Studies of Wildcat Leases, Gulf of Mexico, 1962 and Prior Sales," SPE 4498, preprint of paper presented by the 48th Annual Fall Meeting of the SPE, Las Vegas, September 30 – October 3.

Peterson, R. G., L. L. Fulton and G. S. Koontz (1976). "LPR-18 Lease Production and Revenue," General Services Administration, Denver, 1976.

Public Law 95-372, S.9, The Outer Continental Shelf Lands Act Amendments of 1978, September 18, 1978.

Sibert, J. L., R. Phillips, and J. Lohrenz (1978). "A Data Base Management System for Spatial Display of Federal Offshore Oil and Gas Lease Data," LA-UR 77-2031, Los Alamos Scientific Laboratory.

Slater, P. (1976). The Pursuit of Loneliness. Boston: Beacon Press.

Stark, R. M. (1979). "Competitive Bidding and Estimating: Some Contemporary Issues," Paper presented at the University of Sussex, Third International Conference on Operational Research, Bowness-on-Windermere, April 3-6.

Stark, R. M. and M. H. Rothkopf (1979). "Competitive Bidding: A Comprehensive Bibliography," Operations Research, Vol. 27, pp. 364-390.

Systems Analysis and Design Section Report No. 77-17 (1977). "Documentation of Computer Programs for the Study, 'The Internal Rate of Return on 1954-1962 OCS Oil and Gas Lease Sales and an Appraisal of the Effectiveness of the Bonus Bidding Procedures' (Grant No. 14-08-0001-G-265)," Cons. Div., U.S. Geol. Surv., March 4.

Waller, R. A., E. A. Monash, and J. Lohrenz (1977). "Some Computerized Graphic Technical Applications for Federal Mineral Lease Management Support," LA-UR-77-583, Los Alamos Scientific Laboratory.

4

ON COMPETITIVE BIDDING APPLIED[*]

Robert Wilson

I shall first describe the simplest model of
competitive bidding and then indicate some of its
applications.

1. THE SIMPLE MODEL

Suppose that each of a number of firms has access to public information implying the value V
of the item is lognormally distributed with mean M
and varilog v_0 (variance of the value's natural

[*]This work was supported by Office of Naval Research
Grant No. ONR-N00014-79-C-0685 at the Center for Research on Organizational Efficiency at Stanford University.

logarithm). Independently, each firm observes privately an unbiased estimator S that is lognormal with mean V and varilog v_1. The "proportions" of public and private information are $f_i = v_2/v_i$ where $f_0 + f_1 = 1$ determines v_2. Combining these sources, the firm's assessment of the value is lognormal with median $M^{f_0}S^{f_1}$ and varilog v_2. The conditional distribution of this median is lognormal with median $M^{f_0}V^{f_1}e^{-.5v_2}$ and varilog f_1v_2. Consequently, if one entertains the hypothesis that competitors' bids have a conditional distribution that is lognormal with median $AM^{f_0}V^{f_1}e^{-.5v_2}$ and varilog $v_3 \geq f_1v_2$, the conditional probability $P(B,V)$ that a bid B will win over one such competitor is given by the normal distribution function evaluated at the argument

$$s_3^{-1}[.5v_2 + \ln(B/AM^{f_0}V^{f_1})]$$

where $s_i^2 = v_i$. Further, if the number of competitors has a Poisson distribution with mean N, then the conditional probability of winning is $P_N(B,V) = e^{-N[1-P(B,V)]}$, the probability of winning is $P(B) = E\{P_N(B,V)\}$, and the expected revenue is $R(B) = E\{VP_N(B,V)\}$, from which one must subtract the expected bid cost $BP(B)$. Maximizing the expected profit $R(B) - BP(B)$, one finds that the optimal bid satisfies

$$B = \frac{NR*(B)}{s_3 P(B) + NP*(B)}$$

where

$$P*(B) = E\{P_N(B,V)Z(B,V)\} ,$$

$$R*(B) = E\{VP_N(B,V)Z(B,V)\} ,$$

and $Z(B,V)$ is the normal density at the same argument as $P(B,V)$.

The relevant question, of course, is how to assess the median bid factor A used by competitors. If one supposes that it is the same as ours, namely $B = AM^{f_0} S^{f_1}$, then substitution in the previous formula yields

$$A = \frac{NR*}{s_3 P + NP*} .$$

Here, one applies the observation that $x = \ln(V/M^{f_0} S^{f_1})/s_2$ is a standard normal variate, so that

$$R^* = E\{e^{s_2 x} P_N(x) Z(x)\}$$

$$P^* = E\{P_N(x) Z(x)\}$$

$$P = E\{P_N(x)\}$$

and P(x) and Z(x) are the normal distribution
and density functions evaluated at the argument

$$s_3^{-1} [.5 v_2 + f_0 f_1 \ \ell n(S/M) - f_1 s_2 x] \ .$$

We notice that if the proportion of public informa-
tion is negligible, so that $f_0 \overset{\sim}{\sim} 0$, then in fact
the bid factor A is invariant (independent of the
firm's private estimate S). All the expectations
can be computed with ample accuracy, using the seven-
point quadrature based on the Hermite orthogonal poly-
polynomials, on a hand calculator.

2.   APPLICATIONS

This model, with many (seemingly endless) practical "bells and whistles," has been used to analyze
bids prepared for OCS leases. It includes the evidence compiled by the USGS that bids are apparently
lognormally distributed, with the varilog v_3 usually
about unity and that the number of bidders is appar-

ently Poisson within certain classes of leases. It
is specifically adapted to account for the effects
of adverse selection (winner's curse, or other names);
for example, the expected profit conditional on winning, $R(B)/P(B)$, is ordinarily far less than the
initial assessment.

It is well suited to provide the kind of information desired by management: probability of winning,
expected profit, expected "money left on the table,"
the discount for adverse selection, the "equilibrium"
bid factor, etc. A single program on the TI 59 hand
calculator provides all of this information (and much
more). In practice, of course, the direct judgment
of managers is the deciding factor in preparing bids
but along the way the calculator on the desktop is
a handy aid to examine the consequences of various
assumptions and assessments. Frankly, I attribute
part of the consistent excess of v_3 over $f_1 v_2$
observed in practice to the idiosyncracies of managers
and accountants, among others; the remainder is due
to variations among firms' estimates of N , discount
rates, price schedules, taxes, exploration costs,
and procedures among other considerations. None is
presumed to be subject to adverse selection.

The postmortem has an immediate focus: comparing actual and predicted frequencies of winning (or
more generally, rank orders), money left on the table,

etc. A more substantive exercise is to correct one's
original median assessment of the value by the rank
order of one's bid (or more generally, based on all
the bids using the "equilibrium" bid factor), and
then to compare this posterior assessment with the
winning bid to estimate the profit obtained by the
winners. For example, the posterior mean conditional
on rank k of n , assuming bids reflect the ordering of private estimates, is

$$\frac{E\{VP(B,V)^{n-k}[1 - P(B,V)]^{k-1}\}}{E\{P(B,V)^{n-k}[1 - P(B,V)]^{k-1}\}}$$

where the expectation is conditioned on one's privately
observed estimate S . This exercise enables one to
appraise the extent to which competitors appreciate
the effects of adverse selection--which is the crucial
determinant of whether it is profitable to bid on
OCS leases in the first place.

PART FIVE

METHODS AND PROBLEMS IN
PROCUREMENT ESTIMATION AND BIDDING

1140
U.S.

1

BIDDING ON NEW SHIP CONSTRUCTION

Peter DeMayo

INTRODUCTION

United States naval shipbuilding contracting
is usually considered to be one of the most chal-
lenging of the contractual arrangements. A naval
ship is more than a weapon system. It is composed
of several offensive and defensive systems, as well
as providing a place of work and residence for the
officers and men who operate it for extensive periods
of time. It is more a construction effort, than one
of manufacture, typical of other weapon systems.

The production lead time for constructing a
naval ship is four to six years and is a labor-
intensive operation. For example, a single nuclear

attack submarine requires five to six million man
hours to construct. In terms of cost, the material/
labor split is about 35/65. The Navy buys its ships
under a contract that has two distinct phases. Phase
one is the production planning and material acquisition phase. This phase takes about one-third of the
total contract performance (about two years for a
submarine). At this point, about two-thirds of the
material has been bought but only about 20 percent
of the total man hours have been expended. Phase
two is the production phase which covers the remaining two-thirds of construction and involves the efforts
of the various construction trades and associated
engineering support. In the construction of an attack
submarine approximately 4 1/2 million man hours will
be expended over the four-year phase-two period.

To place naval shipbuilding in context the following represents an overview of navy procurement ex-
tracted from the Survey of Contracting Statistics
(NAVMAT P-422), September 1978.

In FY 1978 the Navy spent some $21.8 billion
on military equipment, supplies, and services. Approximately 2.3 million contracts were awarded. In
terms of relative emphasis the dollar amounts are:

        Sea $9.1 billion
        Air $4.7 billion
        Supply $4.5 billion

One way of looking at Navy procurement is to focus
on the high dollar value contracts. In FY 1978, 555
contracts or less than 1 percent of the total accounted
for $12/6 billion (58 percent) of the total dollars.
In terms of type of contract the following is a breakdown:

Firm Fixed Price	$8.2 billion
Fixed-Price Incentive	$3.8 billion
Cost Type	$6.6 billion

For the purpose of this presentation the focus
is on the fixed-price incentive (FPI) contract. While
some of the mature Navy airframe programs use the
firm fixed-price contract for production, it is the
current Navy policy to use the fixed-price incentive
contract for shipbuilding.

General information on incentive contracts appears
in the Appendix. The following are some of the key
characteristics of the FPI contract. This type of contract is also diagramed in Figure 1. The target cost
is a negotiated figure which should represent the most
realistic cost outcome. Cost sharing is a government
specified figure which represents the government and
contract share of costs over a calculated range of
possible cost outcomes. (For example, an 80/20 share
line means government bears 80 percent of cost changes
and the contractor 20 percent.) Point of total assumption is that point in an FPI contract where it converts

FIGURE 1.

FIXED-PRICE INCENTIVE PROFIT MATRIX

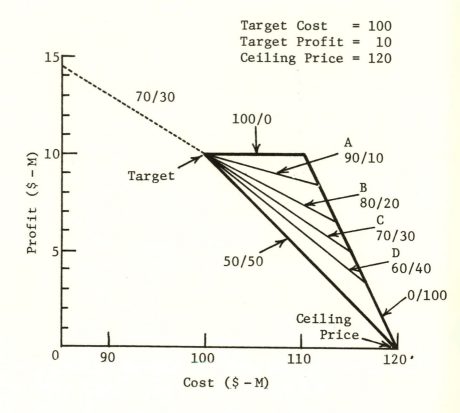

Target Cost = 100
Target Profit = 10
Ceiling Price = 120

to an FFP contract and where the contractor absorbs
all costs (0/100 share). The ceiling price defines
the maximum government liability expressed as a percentage of target cost. Government specifies this
figure.

COMPETITION FOR SHIPBUILDING

Many of the studies of the defense market place
have focused on the aerospace industry. In that arena
competition generally revolves around development or
at best limited production with the winner virtually
assured of several years of annual production contracts
on a sole source basis.

Shipbuilding represents a different situation.
First there are some types of ships which can only
be built at one shipyard. As a result all nuclear
carriers are built at Newport News and all ballistic
missile submarines are built at the Electric Boat
Co., located in Groton, Connecticut.

A second category of ships are combatants (such
as destroyers) and support ships (repair ships, oilers)
which are built at a variety of shipyards throughout
the United States. For example, the FFG-7 program
has three active producers, and a recent award for a
cable laying ship had three active competitors. Finally there are nuclear attack submarines which can be

built at two shipyards: Newport News and Electric Boat
Co. The remainder of this discussion will focus on the
SSN 688 class nuclear attack submarine which has been in
production since 1970. Table 1 portrays the history of
the SSN 688 program.

TABLE 1

SSN 688 Contract History

Date	Number of Ships	Share Ratio	Ceiling Price	Contractor
02/70	1	70/30	125	Newport News
01/71	7	70/30	116	Electric Boat
01/71	4	70/30	111	Newport News
10/73	11	85/15 (3%) 70/30	123	Electric Boat
08/75	5	95/5 (11%) 85/15	133	Newport News
09/77	3	80/20	135	Newport News
04/79	2	80/20	135	Electric Boat

The implications for competition in shipbuilding
are different than they are in aerospace. Properly
managed, the Navy can maintain a competitive environment as it has done in the SSN 688 program. Each
SSN 688 submarine represents a business base of about
$140 million. (Note that the balance of this chapter
will deal in dollar figures in terms of 1978 dollars.)
Contract awards are important to Navy shipbuilders

from both a profitability and survival standpoint.
For example, the annual sales volume at Electric Boat
Co. is about $900 million. However, they are doing
this level of business under only three contracts.
Therefore, in shipbuilding the opportunities are few.

PRICING AND BIDDING ON NAVY SHIPBUILDING

The Navy offers its shipbuilding contracts on a
negotiated basis using an instrument called the request for proposal (RFP). There are numerous terms
and conditions associated with the negotiation of the
contract. However, the prices of the ships themselves
predominate and are the primary factors in making an
award decision. As indicated earlier the Navy typically specifies the sharing arrangement and the ceiling price as well as type of contract. The contractors
bid target cost and profit and the most economical delivery date. The evaluation process goes through
several phases of negotiation leading to a best and
final offer which preceeds the award of the contract.

Cost growth due to inflation is handled in a
special way in shipbuilding contracts. The contract
is priced in base-year dollars. An escalation provision covers cost growth in material and labor throughout the production period. The amount of reimburse-
ment is based on BLS incides which are established

in the contract, The estimate in most recent SSN
688 competition was that escalation would increase
cost by about one-third. As a matter of policy the
risk of this cost growth is fully absorbed by the
Navy.

The contractor must then put together his pricing proposal based on his estimates of material and
man hours to complete a five to six year task. In
doing this the contractor typically relies on a variety of weight accounts upon which he maintains a
historical data base. This is important, because,
while the contractor must construct the ship to several thousand detail design drawings, he determines his
prices and bids based on established weight accounts.
Most of the folklore of shipbuilding problems have
centered around the thousands of changes that many
contend the Navy makes in its contracts. The facts
are that there is considerable turmoil in the early
stages of a shipbuilding program as the detailed design drawings are produced and modified as a result
of early construction experience. Therefore it takes
about three to four years to "shake down" the design
of a new class of ships. This reality must or should
be accommodated in the early contracts for a new class
of ships. However, a stage is finally reached when
the design of a ship is determined and relatively few
changes are made to the detail drawings required to

build a ship.   In the case of the SSN 688 program
the phase of extensive design changes was from 1970
through 1974.   Since 1975 the SSN 688 design has been
relatively unchanged and represents little or no cost
risk to either the Navy or the contractor.

A PERCEPTION OF THE BIDDING STRATEGY
ON THE 1979 SSN 688 COMPETITION

The most recent SSN 688 competition for two submarines was held in 1979.   This fifth production contract was awarded about nine years after the start
of the SSN 688 program.   The design package was well
understood by both the Navy and the two competing
contractors: Electric Boat Co. and Newport News.
There was also a great deal of information on cost
and constructions available to both the Navy and the
contractor.

Referring back to Table 1 it is clear that the
Navy has not significantly modified the incentive
structures in the various SSN 688 contracts.   In fact
it might be concluded that the incentive terms in the
latest contract are more liberal than those in the
earlier contracts.   After nine years of experience
both contractors should have a good assessment of
the risks of constructing the SSN 688 submarine.
They should be able to manage to a much narrower

range of cost outcomes than might be expected in the
early stages of the program. Incentive contract theory
would dictate that more cost risk be shifted to the
contractor in these later contracts.

The competition for the 1979 contract was extremely
close. Based on the target cost evaluation criteria,
Electric Boat Co. was declared the winner. The results
of the competition yielded a lower contract cost figure
than had been anticipated by the Navy. However, the
award decision has also been a source of concern to
navy officials. The problem relates to the cost sharing above target cost, which is primarily borne by the
navy. Even though Electric Boat Co. won the contract
based on a target cost the Navy would ultimately pay
any final cost figure up to the ceiling price. In
other words, if Electric Boat Co. managed this contract at a cost higher than target, it might frustrate
the perceived advantages of competition. If they
come in close to PTA they would earn a profit of more
than 7 percent with the Navy paying 80 percent of
all costs over target. Based on the liberal sharing
arrangements set out by the Navy that there was an
opportunity for the winning contractor to be the high
cost producer. An analysis of the cost history indicated that Electric Boat Co. might have difficulty in
adhering to the target cost figure. However, they
confirmed the bid they submitted as realistic and

achievable.

The facts described above represent one of the
realities of incentive contracts. While published
literature on incentive contracts provides some general guidance on allocation of cost risk on an equitable basis, there is no known source of information
that deals with sensitivity analysis aspects of sharing arrangements to assist in award decisions. However, the 1979 experience exemplifies the need for
changes in the Navy strategy to enable competitive
contracts to be awarded more successfully.

THE NEED FOR A REVISED STRATEGY FOR SSN 688 BIDDING

The Navy planned a competition in 1980 for three
additional SSN 688 submarines. There was a desire
to benefit from the lessons learned in the 1979 competition, achieve the lowest competitive price and frustrate an attempt at gaming. (Gaming as used in this
context refers to a bid at one cost point with the
full intention of managing at a higher cost point.
Senior navy officials referred to that as "gaming.")

Some type of fixed-price incentive contract was
planned for the FY 1980 buy. The appropriate structuring arrangements were considered. It was decided
that one way to deal with the potential of gaming
would be to tighten up the share lines and reduce

the target to ceiling spread. The possible impact
of this is shown in Figure 2. The 1979 actual incentive structure is plotted along with a hypothetical situation using a 60/40 share line and a 120
percent ceiling price. The unanswered question was
what the impact of this change would be on the bidding strategies of the two competing contractors.
Since the prevailing view was that Newport News tends
to bid on the basis of managing to target cost, the
impact on its bidding pattern should be minimal. The
key question thus was whether the proposed structure
would motivate Electric Boat Co. to both bid and manage to a cost figure that is close to target. The
view in the Navy was that the tighter incentive features would at least increase the cost risk to Electric Boat Co. if it is pursuing gaming policy. If
the bidding patterns in the 1980 buy could reflect
this approach, then the Navy might feel more comfort-
able with the benefits of competition.

POSTSCRIPT

For a number of reasons the Navy did not execute
the FY 1980 buy of SSN 688 submarines until August
1981. That contract, for three submarines, was negotiated with Newport News. Electric Boat Co. was excluded from the competition. Some changes were noted

FIGURE 2.

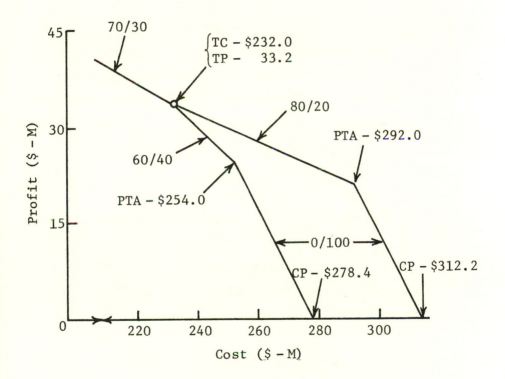

in the incentive features of that contract. The share line was 50/50 with ceiling price at 130 percent of target cost. At PTA, the contractor would earn only a 4.3 percent profit compared to profit of around 7 percent in previous SSN 688 contracts.

The Navy is currently (1981) negotiating a sole source contract with Electric Boat Co. and intends to use similar incentive arrangements. The Naval Sea Systems Command is also in the process of requiring tighter incentive arrangements in mature ship programs. In particular a 50/50 sharing arrangement will probably be adopted. This policy will be contained in the Ship Acquisition Policy Manual (NAVSEA Instruction 5000.4).

However, the ultimate test of the tighter incentive arrangements will be in a competitive situation. There is the possibility that the Navy will be able to test this out in subsequent buys of the SSN 688. That would allow for continued research into this very complex and important subject.

APPENDIX: INCENTIVE CONTRACTS BACKGROUND

1. The use of incentive contracts goes back to the early 1960s under the sponsorship of both DOD and NASA. Most of the appropriate policy and procedure are contained in the Joint DOD/NASA Incentive

Contracting Guide, October 1969.

2.   The simple objective for most incentive contracts is to motivate the contractor to earn more
compensation by achieving better performance and controlling cost.   As such the incentive contract is a
communication device between the government and the
contractor.   Structuring an incentive, particularly
over a multiphased program, is intended to be an iter-
ative exercise.

3.   The production of most DOD weapon systems
is under fixed-price incentive (FPI) contracts.   While
there is a lot of thought given to the transition
from cost-type development and early production contracts to FPI production contracts, almost no thought
is given to a transition to a firm fixed price (FFP)
on downstream production.

4.   There are several factors that must be considered in structuring an incentive contract.   These
evolve around the issues of cost, technical, and schedule uncertainty.   A fallout of these issues are a
range of possible cost outcomes on a given contract.
These ranges involve both contractor and government
estimates.   When the band of possible cost outcomes
is narrow, the implication is a high degree of certainty
in achieving technical and schedule alternatives and
in realizing cost objectives.   Under these conditions
a fairly tight FPI contract would be called for. (The

FFP alternative also should be considered.) Conversely when the range of cost outcomes is fairly broad more liberal cost sharing arrangements are called for in either an FPI or CPIF contract.

5. Cost sharing is an integral part of incentive contracts. The range of incentive effectiveness (RIE) is a term which refers to the range of cost sharing which occurs, expressed in terms of cost dollars. In an FPI contract cost sharing stops at the point of total assumption (PTA), which is the point where a contract converts to a FFP. At that point, referred to as the 0/100 share line; the contractor assumes all of the cost risk.

6. Target cost is a primary reference point in FPI contracts. While there are a range of possible cost outcomes, target cost is intended to be the most probable cost outcome. Target cost is a subject of negotiation, along with target profit. In each con- tract an assessment needs to be made on the expected deviation from target cost to actual cost. When con- fidence in cost estimates are high, it is reasonable to expect target cost is an achievable figure. It follows that the contract should be structured to motivate the contractor to manage to target. The incentive to achieve this motivation is realized pro- fit percentages over various cost outcomes.

7. The ceiling price is a final reference point

which needs to be understood. This represents the
maximum liability to the government and is expressed
as a percentage of target cost. Generally speaking
wide target-to-ceiling spreads are called for on complex, risky contracts, and a narrower spread on those
requirements which contain a lesser degree of risk.
On FPI contracts the ceiling price is reached where
the 0/100 share line crosses the cost axis.

   8. By referring to Figure 1 the reader can see
the various FPI reference points illustrated. Note
that PTA is that point where the selected sharing
arrangements (for example, 70/30) intersects the 0/100
share line.

   9. The preceding intends to indicate that several factors must be considered in the structuring
of an FPI contract. It is not enough to focus on just
the share lines or the ceiling price. Rather the
focus must reflect a trade-off between the risks of
the instant contract, the motivational goals expected
of the contractor and expected value of different
arrangements to the government.

   10. The Navy approach in FPI contracts is to
specify the sharing arrangements and the ceiling price
in the request for proposal (RFP). The contractor is
required to propose target costs and target profits,
which are subjects of negotiation.

2

COMPETITIVE BIDDING FOR DEFENSE CONTRACTS
William F. Samuelson

1. INTRODUCTION

The dominant features in the government procurement of major programs and systems in the area of defense are the degree of technological sophistication required and the accompanying risk experienced in research, development, and production.

The strict technological requirements and the accompanying risk and uncertainty in the production and development of major weapon systems have been described in detail.[1] Without exception, the theoretical models of system acquisition take procurement

---

[1] Peck and Scherer (1962); Scherer (1964a); Fox (1974).

uncertainty as the fundamental economic fact in the government's contracting problem. Procurement risk poses many problems for the government buyers and potential contractors alike. The following questions arise: How should the Department of Defense select firms to undertake its procurement contracts? Given the degree of uncertainty in the development and production of defense programs, how can the government design bidding and contracting arrangements to promote efficient firm selection while providing a degree of insurance against risks to the contractor selected?

Our investigation focuses exclusively on competitive procurements, that is, those in which two or more firms compete for the contract award. Typically, firms vie for the contract by submitting proposals that outline technical and design features of the system, the firm's management capabilities, and a complete set of cost estimates for the program. At the same time, the government selection authority negotiates contract terms with each firm prior to selection. Thus, the source selection procedure is one of extensive review. On the basis of technical merit, the program cost estimate, and the terms of the negotiated contract, the government buyer selects a firm for the procurement.

I shall present a formal model of optimal

contractor selection and examine ways in which the
government can utilize competitive bidding procedures to promote efficient contract awards. Specifically, firms compete for the contract award by
submitting bids which specify the contractual terms
they are willing to accept. The bidding procedure
that is modelled is, more or less, an idealized version of the competitive negotiations between the
government buyer and the firms during source selection. The analysis emphasizes that these bids are
an important source of information about the procurement capabilities of the competing firms. (Of course,
direct scrutiny of technical designs and cost estimates is a separate, important source of information.)
The government's task then is, first, to institute
bidding procedures which transmit the maximum amount
of accurate information about firm capabilities; second,
to extract correctly this information from the bids
(this is an inference problem); and third, to employ
this information to solve its selection problem.

The different types of contractual arrangements
currently employed in defense procurement can illustrate the nature of the government selection problem
when the cost of a defense program is highly uncertain. Suppose a number of firms are competing for
a procurement that is to be awarded under an incentive
contract. Under such a contract, the winning firm

earns a profit

$$\Pi(c) = \Pi_T + b(c_T - c) \tag{1}$$

where c is the ultimate cost of the program (a random variable at the time of signing), b is the firm's
cost sharing rate, Π_T is its target profit, and
c_T is its target cost. This formulation departs
slightly from the contract forms, fixed-price incentive and cost-plus incentive, used in actual practice.
Besides administrative and accounting differences,
the types differ from one another (and from the linear incentive contract in our model) in their sharing
of costs for large overruns and underruns. For details
see The Incentive Contracting Guide (1969). Under the
terms of eq. (1), if the actual program cost matches
the target cost $(c = c_T)$, then the firm earns target profit Π_T . For positive sharing rates, the firm shares in
cost overruns and underruns. Typically, the government
establishes a uniform sharing rate (to hold for all
firms), and each firm submits a cost and profit target. The government writes a cost-plus contract when
b = 0 . Regardless of the ultimate cost of the program, the firm is guaranteed a profit Π_T , and the
government bears all cost risk. At the opposite extreme, the government writes a fixed price contract

when b = 1 . Now it is the firm that bears all of
the cost risk. Its profit is reduced dollar for dollar with program cost increases.

The cost-plus contract (frequently used by the
Defense Department in the 1970s for programs of research and development) is a response to the fact
of procurement risk. Assuming that the firm is risk
averse and that the government buyer is risk neutral
(due to the size of the financial assets it commands
and its ability to pool risks), the cost-plus contract
represents an optimal risk-sharing arrangement. It
should be evident, however, that as a means of selecting a firm the employment of this contract is inefficient. Each firm's submission of a target cost conveys no information about its likely procurement cost.
Note that when b = 0 , the firm earns profit
$\Pi(c) = \Pi_T$ irrespective of the target cost submitted.
Since the firm is not held responsible (made to pay)
for cost overruns, the government obtains no information from the target cost submission. Recognizing
this fact, the government has only the (guaranteed)
profit target submissions as a basis for the contract
award.

At the opposite extreme, the fixed-price contract requires the firm to bear full responsibility
for cost. The implication is that the firm's profit target will include a risk premium as compensation for bearing this cost uncertainty. In terms
of risk sharing, this contractual arrangement is

suboptimal. The fixed-price contract, however, offers a selection advantage. Under this contract, the target cost and profit submissions fully reflect the firm's mean production cost and profit requirement (the latter including a risk premium). Scrutiny of eq. (1) indicates that the firm must submit a target cost equal to its mean production cost in order to earn an expected profit equal to its target Π_T. In short, under a fixed price contract the firm submitting the lowest total price bid, $\Pi_T + c_T$, is identified as the lowest total cost contractor.

To sum up, because the cost-plus contract provides complete insurance against cost risk for the winning firm, the target cost and profit bids represent a poor basis for identifying the competitor with the lowest expected total cost. The fixed-price contract offers superior selection performance at the cost of a risk premium charged to the government by the winning firm. To determine an optimal-incentive contract, the government must trade-off the insurance and selection benefits of different degrees of cost sharing.

The discussion is organized as follows. Section 2 outlines the assumptions of the basic model and formulates the government's selection problem. Section 3 presents a simple example to illustrate the main results, while Section 4 provides a summary and concluding remarks.

2.   THE BASIC MODEL

This section provides a normative model of source
selection in competitive procurements.   The essential
details of the source selection process (as modelled)
are summarized in the stylized decision tree below.

Source selection begins with the government's
decision to solicit proposals from competing firms.
Rounds of review (focusing on technical merit, management capabilities, and firm cost estimates) follow.
In our formulation, this review is strictly for the
purpose of information acquisition.   The branches
emanating from point   B   indicate the possible information results the authority may obtain from this
stage.   Ideally, the output of this review would be
joint probability assessments of the capabilities
and costs of competing firms.   As a practical matter,
assessment takes the form of numerical scores for a
number of evaluation categories.

Following this review, the selection authority
establishes the ground rules for the evaluation of
contract offers and selection of the winning contractor.   (This stage is indicated in the tree by the
decision branches emanating from point   C .)   Two of
the myriad of procedures have already been noted.
At one extreme, the government specifies a fixed
price contract and awards the program to the firm

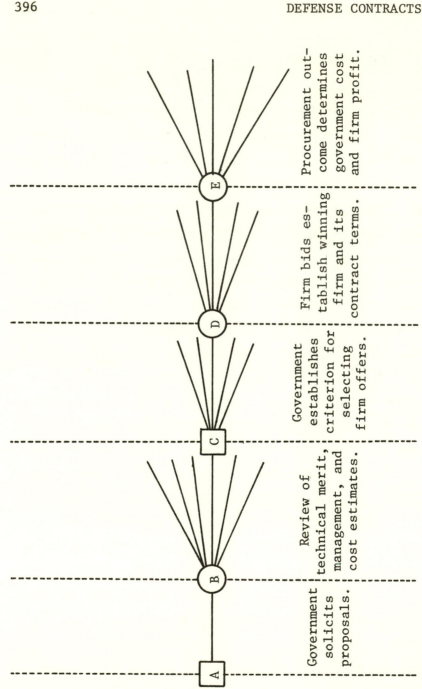

submitting the lowest price.   At the other, the government awards the contract on a cost plus basis
to the firm requiring the lowest guaranteed profit
fee.   More generally, each firm is free to submit
the terms of an incentive contract that it is willing to accept.   (Possible bids of the competing firms
are indicated by the branches emanating from point
D .)   The government applies its selection criterion
to determine its preferred contract (and contractor)
of these submissions.   The precise details of the
selection procedure are outlined below.

   The signing of the procurement contract (point
E)   marks the end of the source selection process.
Of course, the ultimate cost of the procurement to
the government and the profit of the firm are determined only at the completion of the program (when
production cost c is known).

   This formulation suggests certain features of
the contracting setting which have direct implications for the study of competitive bidding.   First,
in any source selection competition, firms bid for
the right to enter into a contractual arrangement
with the buyer.   Given the degree of risk in defense
procurements, these contract terms typically call
for some degree of risk sharing between buyer and
contractor.   As a result, the payoffs to both the
contractor and the buyer are uncertain at the time

of contract signing and are only resolved at the completion (or termination) of the procurement. The
government leasing of oil tracts by competitive bid
shares this feature of "post signing" uncertainty.
The classic auction model, in which a good is sold
to the bidder submitting the highest fixed price,
does not.

Second, the fact that firms bid for a contract
provides for certain generalizations of the classic
auction model. Since contract clauses must be written for a variety of contingencies, multiple parameters are required to specify the complete terms of
the contract. Thus, we can anticipate each firm submitting a multicomponent bid specifying the contract
terms it is willing to accept should it be awarded
the contract. (Indeed, each firm might submit multiple bids indicating a whole set of acceptable
terms.) From the set of submissions, the buyer will
select the contract terms (and the firm offering
those terms) that it judges to be most attractive.

With this overview of the elements of source
selection in hand, we can proceed to describe the
assumptions of the basic model. The government buyer
must award the procurement contract to one of n
potential contractors. It is assumed that all parties possess von Neumann-Morgenstern utility functions which depend on income alone. Each of the

firms is risk averse and the government is risk neutral.   Thus, the government's objective is to complete
the program at minimum expected cost.

Though procurement uncertainty ranges over a number of dimensions, including system performance, time
of completion, and ultimate dollar cost, this model
considers only the last of these--variability in program cost.   The intention is to consider in as simple
a manner as possible the implications of procurement
risk (in the cost dimension) for the conduct of bidding and contractual arrangements of defense procurement.   Uncertainty in the single dimension of cost
is sufficient to bring out the main points of analysis.   While the formulation of trade-offs between
the multiple attributes, performance, time of delivery, and cost, is an important issue for the
economic efficiency of procurement, we abstract from
this problem in the present discussion.

An initial assumption outlines the characteristics of competing firms.

A.1.   The production cost of the ith firm, c_i ,
is a random variable distributed according to the
cumulative distribution function, $F_i(c_i)$, known
only to the firm itself.   The firm's mean production
cost is denoted by m_i .   Each firm claims an opportunity cost for the use of its productive resources.

This cost, denoted by Y_i , is known with certainty
by the firm but is not known by the government or
any other competitor. A firm has no control over
its production or opportunity costs—that is, firm
i cannot influence $F_i(c_i)$ or Y_i .

This assumption underscores the point that only the
firm itself knows its opportunity cost and distribution of production cost. It is this informational
asymmetry which is the key point of the proposed contracting and selection model. If it were true that
the government possessed complete knowledge of each
firm's characteristics, the selection authority could
achieve a "first best" contracting solution by selecting the firm promising the lowest total procurement
cost $m_i + Y_i$ and offering that firm a cost-plus
contract. Lacking this "perfect" information, the
government's assessment of the firm's cost characteristics is based upon information obtained in its
review of cost estimates and upon what it can infer
from the firm's offer of contractual terms.

The firm's opportunity cost Y_i represents the
certainty equivalent profit that the firm can earn
by employing its resources in their next best use
(in production for the private sector or in other
public procurements). The sum of opportunity and
production cost constitutes the total cost of production of the firm. Once again, partial knowledge

concerning the opportunity costs of the firms may be
possessed by the government.

The presence of cost variability after the signing
of the contract and the fact that firm decisions can
influence cost introduce the possibility of "moral
hazard." A firm that pays only a small share of cost
overruns has a diminished economic incentive to hold
down costs. Under a cost-plus contract, the firm
has no incentive. Thus, moral hazard is a separate,
and important, argument in favor of contracts carrying larger firm sharing rates. By assuming that the
contractor has no influence over the probability distribution of production cost, we deliberately abstract
from the moral hazard issue in order to focus squarely
on the selection benefits of incentive contracts.

We have emphasized that the government's information about firms comes from two separate sources
--the review process and the submission of competitive bids by firms. Whether one source is more or
less valuable than the other depends upon the specific circumstances of the procurement. Clearly, competitive bids will carry relatively little weight
to affect the decision on which firm will be awarded
a contract if the process of proposal review succeeds
in singling out an efficient firm. In this case the
government may confidently view an aggressive bid
from a competing firm as "unrealistically low" (or

as an attempt at a "buy in" strategy). However, the case for competitive bidding is strongest when the government recognizes that firms may differ greatly with respect to capabilities but cannot, on the basis of proposal review, identify the firm with the lowest expected cost. (Indeed, critics of the review process question the government authority's ability to assess the accuracy of submitted cost estimates and make projections of contractor costs.) Consistent with our emphasis on the role of competitive bidding in contracting, it is this latter case that we have implicitly in mind in the ensuing analysis.

The following assumptions outline the government' information about the firms and its contracting and selection procedure.

A.2. Based on its proposal review, the government formulates a joint probability distribution for the cost characteristics of competing firms. These characteristics include mean production cost, m_i , and opportunity cost, Y_i , for $i = 1, ..., n$.

A.3. The government employs a linear incentive contract which specifies the firm's contingent profit as

$$\Pi(c) = a - bc \tag{2}$$

In turn, the government's contingent procurement cost is

$$T(c) = a + (1-b)c \qquad (3)$$

Given this contract form, each firm competes for the award by submitting an offer, $O_i = (a_i, b_i)$, that it is willing to accept. As before, b is the firm's cost sharing rate; the parameter a is termed the firm's profit fee. The government then employs the preannounced selection functions, $S_i = S_i(a_i, b_i)$, to "score" each firm's offer. By convention, the firm with the lowest selection score is awarded the contract. The winning firm signs a contract at the terms that it bid.

The linear contract form has been employed in a number of investigations of defense contracting. Some have used the form to analyze aspects of the moral hazard problem in contracting.[2] Others have based a number of results on it concerning the bidding strategies of competing firms.[3] Still others have relied upon the form to study the effectiveness of incentive contracts.[4] Only McCall and Canes

---

[2] Scherer (1964b); Cummins (1977); Williamson (1967).

[3] Baran (1972); Holt (1977).

[4] Cross (1968); Fisher (1966).

consider the role of the linear contract in the government's contractor selection problem.[5]

The specification of the linear incentive contract in eq. (2) is equivalent to the standard
parameterization used by DOD. This is evident since
eq. (1) can be rewritten $\pi(c) = [\Pi_T + bc_T] - bc$.
It follows that the forms are equivalent provided
$a = \Pi_T + bc_T$. Indeed, since the firm's profit (and
the government's cost) depends only on the sum
$a = \Pi_T + bc_T$, it is incorrect to assign separate
importance to the values of Π_T and c_T submitted.
Our parameterization avoids such potential problems
by removing a redundant parameter.

In actual practice, there is considerable
confusion about the role of the cost target in contract negotiations. For instance, the Incentive
Contracting Guide (1969) at times interprets the
target as an actual cost estimate, for example, as
the mode or the mean of the firm's cost distribution.
This confuses two separate sources of information.
One source is the proposal view ("should cost" estimates and the like) and the other is the collection
of bids submitted by firms.

The provision for different selection functions
for firms stems from the fact that the government

---

[5]McCall (1970); Canes (1975).

will likely formulate different probabilistic cost
assessments of firms based on proposal review. The
use of different selection functions recognizes that
firms may enter the bidding competition on different
footing. In the example of Section 3, the government
possesses symmetric information about firms. In this
case, a common selection function, $S_i(a_i, b_i)$
$= S(a_i, b_i)$, is optimal.

A final assumption describes the typical firm's
bidding behavior.

A.4. Each firm makes a truthful bid; that is firm
i makes offers $O_i = (a_i, b_i)$ which satisfy

$$u_i(Y_i) = Eu_i(a_i - b_i c_i) \tag{4}$$

where u_i denotes the firm's von Neumann-Morgenstern
utility function. The set of such bids is termed the
firm's offer curve. Equivalently, bids on the firm's
offer curve satisfy

$$a_i = Y_i + b_i m_i + R_i(b_i) \tag{5}$$

where $R_i(b_i)$ denotes the firm's risk premium under
sharing rate b_i . Each firm submits a bid on its
offer curve which maximizes its probability of selec-
tion--that is, an offer which minimizes $S_i(a_i, b_i)$.

This assumption defines the firm's offer curve as
the set of minimally acceptable bids--those that
leave the firm indifferent to winning the award or
pursuing its next best alternative. The equivalent
condition in eq. (5) reflects the fact that the
firm's profit fee must cover its opportunity cost,
its expected share of production cost, and an added
risk premium as compensation for profit variability
stemming from uncertain cost. This risk premium is
zero under a cost-plus contract (b = 0) and increases with the sharing rate.

While one would expect a utility maximizing
firm to adopt a bidding strategy which permits it
to earn a profit above its opportunity cost, two
different arguments can be made in defense of the
truthful bidding assumption. First, under a "uniform" contract where the government sets a common
sharing rate for all firms, Y_i can simply be rein-
terpreted to include a provision for profit above
the return available from the firm's next best alternative. From the government's point of view, the
only relevant fact is that the firms differ with
respect to the fixed profit required of the contract.
Whether these differences stem from alternative opportunities or from differences in bidding behavior
is immaterial.

Second, the government can insure truthful bidding by offering the winning firm the privilege of
recontracting at terms corresponding to those of the
second lowest scoring firm. If S_1 is the selection
score of the winning firm and S_2 that of the run-
nerup, then the winner is allowed to recontract at
any terms, $O' = (a', b')$, provided $S_1(a', b')$
$\leq S_2$. Under this recontracting option (which is
the analogue of a "second bid" auction) the dominant
strategy of each firm is to submit the bid on its
offer curve which minimizes its selection score S_i .

With these four assumptions, the government's
optimal selection problem can be simply stated:

Subject to the conditions for selection described in Assumption A.3 and for firm bidding behavior in Assumption A.4, the government seeks selection functions $S_i(a_i, b_i)$ to minimize

$$E[T(c_1)] = a_1 + (1 - b_1)Ec_1 \tag{6}$$

where $O_1 = (a_1, b_1)$ and c_1 are the contract terms
and program cost respectively of the winning firm,
and where expectations are taken with respect to the
probability distribution described in Assumption A.2.
After substituting eq. (5) into eq. (6), the government's expected procurement cost can be rewritten as

$$E[T(c_1)] = Y_1 + m_1 + R_1(b_1) \tag{7}$$

indicating that the government's expected outlay must cover the firm's opportunity and production costs as well as its risk premium when $b_i > 0$.

3. A SIMPLE EXAMPLE

The following example provides an illustration of the government's selection problem. Suppose that the "typical" firm competing for the contract in question is one of two types. An "efficient" firm has a mean production cost of $95 million and demands an opportunity profit of $7 million. An "inefficient" firm has a mean production cost of $105 million and an opportunity profit of $5 million. Its opportunity cost is lower than its rival's due to less attractive opportunities in the private sector. Both types of firms charge the same risk premium, $R_i(b) = R(b)$ for all i . To keep things simple, suppose that only two firms compete for the award. Each firm's type is drawn independently of the other, and each type is equally likely.

Clearly, a "first best" solution would have the government select the efficient firm (if one is competing) and offer it a cost-plus contract. (If it faces a pair of inefficient firms, the government should also employ a cost-plus contract.) Given the distribution of firm types, the government would hire

an efficient firm (expected cost of $102) with prob-
ability 3/4 and an inefficient firm (expected cost
of $110) with probability 1/4. The government's ex-
pected cost ex ante, therefore, is $104.

Of course, the first best solution is impossible
for the government to implement. Instead, we note
a quartet of second best-selection options available
to the government. The contingent outcomes under
each of these options are listed in Table 1 below.

TABLE 1[a]

a)

	Firm II Type	
Firm I Type	(7,95)	(5,105)
(7,95)	102	110
(5,105)	110	110

b)

	Firm II Type	
Firm I Type	(7,95)	(5,105)
(7,95)	102	107
(5,105)	107	112

c)

	Firm II Type	
Firm I Type	(7,95)	(5,105)
(7,95)	102+R	102+R
(5,105)	102+R	110+R

d)

	Firm II Type	
Firm I Type	(7,95)	(5,105)
(7,95)	102+R	102+R
(5,105)	102+R	110

[a]The government's ex ante expected cost of each procedure is found by averaging the four table elements.

Under selection rule a, the government issues a cost-plus contract and choose the firm making the lowest profit fee bid.   This rule is implemented by specifying

$$S(5,0) < S(7,0) < S(0_i)$$

where $0_i \neq (5,0)$ or $(7,0)$.   This can aptly be called a case of "misordered selection" since awarding the contract on the basis of lowest profit fee results in the selection of the high cost firm.   More generally, selection is misordered if the winning firm (subscripted 1) is not the lowest cost contractor, that is, if a second firm exists such that $T_2 < T_1$ but $a_2 > a_1$.   Since $T_i = Y_i + m_i + R_i(b)$ and $a_i = Y_i + bm_i + R_i(b)$,   from eqs. (7) and (5), selection is misordered if and only if

$$[m_1 - m_2] + [R_1(b) - R_2(b)] > [Y_2 - Y_1] > b[m_1 - m_2]$$
$$+ [R_1(b) - R_2(b)]$$

Since the inefficient firm is selected (if one is competing), the government's expected cost _ex ante_ is \$108.   (See Table 1a.)

Under rule b, the government issues a cost-plus contract and chooses a firm at random by assigning $S(5,0) = S(7,0)$.   Since a firm of either type submits the offer $0_i = (7,0)$,   the government's expected cost <u>ex</u> <u>ante</u> is $107.

In this case, rule b offers a lower expected procurement cost <u>ex</u> <u>ante</u> than rule a. However, the relative cost of rule b versus rule a depends directly on the distribution of firm types. For instance, it is easy to check that if it is virtually certain that a pair of inefficient firms are competing for the award, the government should hold these firms to a $5 million profit fee by using rule a. This illustrates an interesting result. Suppose that rule a is optimal. Then a profit offer of $7 million immediately marks the bidder as an efficient firm. Nonetheless, the government's precommitment to selection on the basis of least profit fee denies it the option to choose what it knows to be the low cost firm. Here is a counterexample to the common-sense proposition that an optimal selection procedure should never award the contract to a firm whose offer marks it as more costly than some other competitor. (Indeed, special cases can be constructed in which rule a dominates rules b, c, and d.)

Under rule c, the government issues a uniform incentive contract with $b = .2 + \varepsilon$ (where ε is in the positive neighborhood of zero) and chooses the lowest profit fee offered. This is the smallest sharing rate that distinguishes efficient and inefficient firms. When $b = .2$, both types submit the profit fee

$26 + R(.2)$. For $b > .2$, the efficient firm submits the lower profit offer and is selected. Since
an efficient firm is selected (if one is competing),
the government's expected cost ex ante is $104 + R(.2)$.

     Finally, under rule d, the government issues a
"signalling" contract by assigning

$$S(26 + 96\varepsilon + R(.2 + \varepsilon, \ .2 + \varepsilon)) \ < \ S(5,0) \ < \ S(0_i)$$

for all other offers 0_i . As in rule c, an efficient
firm is awarded the contract if one is competing.
However, if two inefficient firms compete, the government issues cost-plus contracts, thereby saving the
payment of a risk premium. An inefficient firm is
not forced, as in rule c, to submit a sharing rate
of 20 percent. The signalling contract implies an
expected cost ex ante of $104 + (3/4)R(.2)$ and dominates the uniform incentive contract of the third
rule.

     The signalling contract is less costly than the
cost-plus contract of a, provided $R(.2) < (16/3)$.
When firms of different types compete for the award,
the signalling contract offers superior selection.
However, this benefit is obtained at a cost in the
form of the risk premium charged by the efficient
firm under an incentive contract. For sufficiently
high risk premiums (due to severe program risks

and/or highly risk-averse firms), a signalling contract may be suboptimal.

Features of this simple example find interesting parallels in the Navy's recent experience in awarding ship-building contracts. First, the degree of incentive in an incentive contract should be tailored to the riskiness of the particular program. For instance, the 1979 SSN 688 submarine competition marked the fifth production contract in a program initiated nine years earlier. The competitors could be expected to manage to a much narrower range of cost outcomes than in the earlier stages of the program and, therefore, could bear a greater share of the cost risk (without requiring a substantial risk premium). In a high risk development program, on the other hand, the balance shifts in favor of incentive contracts with low sharing rates or cost-plus contracts.

The closeness of the submarine competition also underscores the potential selection benefits of increases in contractual incentives. The Navy awarded the contract to Electric Boat Co. despite suspicions that the shipyard could not meet its target cost. Since the Navy held an 80 percent cost share, there was the danger that a significant cost overrun would reverse the shipyard's apparent cost advantage. The

navy's situation is similar to that portrayed in our
example. At a low sharing rate an inefficient firm
eager for the contract award may submit a low cost
target (or profit target for that matter) and land
the contract. The lessons of our example suggest a
possible solution. What's called for is an increase
in the firm's cost share (perhaps up to 40 percent)
and a reduction in the spread between the target cost
and the cost ceiling. In our terms, an increase in
the sharing rate (provided it is large enough) elimi-
nates the problem of misordered selection while adding little in the way of a risk premium.

4. CONCLUDING REMARKS

What are the implications of the proposed contracting model for procurement and source selection
as presently practiced by the Department of Defense?
First, though the information content of firm bids
has been emphasized, this is not to deny the potential value of proposal review. A logical approach
should assimilate both kinds of information. From
the proposal review, the government should first develop probability distributions for each firm's char-
acteristics--most importantly, its expected production
cost, but also its opportunity cost (and possibly its
risk premium). On the basis of submitted bids, these

distributions can then be revised (in the standard
Bayesian fashion), a set of expected costs computed,
and the least-cost firm awarded the contract.

   For instance, if the government assessed a tight
probability distribution for the mean production cost
of a firm, then its submission of an unexpectedly low
cost target might have a very small effect on the
revised probability distribution. Instead, the impact would occur in the revision of the firm's opportunity cost. Based upon the revised estimates--dif-
ferent for each contractor--the government could
logically choose a competing firm as the least-cost
producer.

   Second, the model suggests a general trade-off
between the insurance and selection benefits of incentive contracts. The Department of Defense has
long recognized that incentives should be tailored
to the degree of risk in the procurement but too often
sees this choice as all or nothing--a cost plus contract or a fixed-price contract. In the past, the
department has emphasized the merits of incentive
contracts in motivating firms to hold down costs but
has not explicitly recognized the benefits of high
sharing rates in contractor selection. This is in
contrast to an important result of the present model:
Under weak assumptions about the contracting environment (the existence of a continuum of firm types and

bidding which is "well-behaved"), neither a cost-plus
contract nor a fixed-price contract is optimal. Specifically, one can show that the marginal cost due to
a greater risk premium of increasing the sharing rate
is zero at $b = 0$, while the marginal selection
benefit (that is, the reduction in cost due to more
accurate firm selection) is zero at $b = 1$. Elsewhere, marginal benefits and costs are positive.
Consequently, the least cost, uniform incentive contract must have a sharing rate in the open interval
$(0,1)$.

The trade-off extends to procurements in which
multiple objectives are present. When contract outcomes range over a number of dimensions, such as system performance and delivery time as well as cost,
the government should write a contract with multiple
incentives. Under a multiple incentive contract the
firm's contingent profit might take the form

$$\Pi(c,g,t) = \alpha - \beta c - \psi g - \gamma t \qquad\qquad (8)$$

where g is a measure of technical performance and
t denotes time of delivery. Despite the additional
complexity, the selection problem is much the same
as it was in the single attribute setting. Firms sub-
mit multicomponent offers $0_i = (\alpha, \beta, \psi, \gamma)$ which form
the basis of the contract award. The government

evaluates offers by means of a selection function
$S(\alpha,\beta,\psi,\gamma)$. For each objective, the larger the incentive element in the contract, the greater the
authority's ability to discriminate among firms.
Under a signalling contract, the government can make
important inferences about the firm's capabilities
from the penalties (and rewards) it offers for deviations in performance.

Most important, the model suggests that the Department of Defense could reduce procurement costs
by employing signalling contracts. Instead of specifying a uniform sharing rate for all firms, the
government should solicit unrestricted offers. Indeed,
the result that emerged in the comparison of the third
and fourth rules in the example can be generalized.
Given any uniform incentive contract with $b > 0$,
there exists a signalling contract that dominates it.
The government should allow a firm to signal its low
expected production cost via a high sharing rate bid.
Other things (the profit fee) being equal, the government should favor a high sharing rate not only because
this reduces directly its own cost, but also on account
of the low mean production cost such as bid signals.
To sum up, competitive bidding under signalling contracts offer the selection authority a flexible and
efficient means of procurement.

REFERENCES

Baran, D. P. (1972). "Incentive Contracts and Competitive Bidding," American Economic Review, Vol.
62, pp. 284-94.

Canes, M. (1975). "The Simple Economics of Incentive
Contracting: Note," American Economic Review, Vol.
65, pp. 478-83.

Cross, J. G. (1968). "A Reappraisal of Cost Incentives in Defense Contracts," Western Economic Journal, Vol. 6, pp. 205-25.

Cummins, J. M. (1977). "Incentive Contracting for
National Defense: A Problem of Optimal Risk Sharing," The Bell Journal of Economics, Vol. 8, pp.
168-85.

Fisher, I. N. (1966). "Cost Incentives and Contract
Outcomes: An Empirical Analysis," The Rand Corporation, Report RM-5120.

Fox, J. R. (1974). Arming America: How the U.S. Buys
Weapons, Division of Research, Harvard Business
School, Boston.

Holt, C. A. (1977). Bidding for Contracts, doctoral
dissertation, Carnegie-Mellon University, Pittsburgh,
Pa.

McCall, J. J. (1970). "The Simple Economics of Incentive Contracting," American Economic Review, Vol. 60,
pp. 837-46.

Peck, M. J. and F. M. Scherer (1962). The Weapons
Acquisition Process: An Economic Analysis, Division
of Research, Harvard Business School, Boston.

Scherer, F. M. (1964a). "The Theory of Contractual Incentives for Cost Reduction," _Quarterly Journal of Economics_, Vol. 78, pp. 257-80.

Scherer, F. M. (1964b). _The Weapons Acquisition Process: Economic Incentives_, Division of Research, Harvard Business School, Boston.

Department of Defense and NASA (1969). _The Incentive Contracting Guide_. Washington, D.C.: U.S. Government Printing Office.

Williamson, O. E. (1967). "The Economics of Defense Contracting: Incentives and Performances," in R. McKean (ed.), _Issues in Defense Economics_. New York: Columbia University Press.

3

EVALUATION OF COMPETITIVE ALTERNATIVES FOR WEAPON SYSTEM PRODUCTION

Charles H. Smith

This paper describes a model for analyzing alternatives concerning competition in the production phase of a weapons system. The model applies to the production of systems for which high costs of introducing and sustaining competition offset the effect of competitive forces. The model includes the effects of learning, capacity constraints, and costs of layaway, reactivation, start-up, direct production, etc. The strategies available include sole-source, full competition, or limited competition. A numerical example is presented, and the applicability of the model is discussed. Nonprice aspects of the competition decision are not treated in this report.

421

INTRODUCTION

One of the many significant decisions faced when
acquiring a major weapon system concerns the issue
of competition. Should the production phase of the
system acquisition be competitive, and, if so, what
form should the competition take? For some systems
the difference between a right and a wrong decision
on these questions means $100 million or more. In
this paper an approach is presented that provides
insight into the scope and impact of the competition
decision. The methodology arose from the attempt
to apply previous empirical findings in the context
of a specific missile system project. The available
data were an insufficient guide to decision-making,
and it was necessary to construct a model to serve as
a decision framework for the data.

I shall attempt to convey three principal ideas.
First, a useful model for analyzing competition questions has been developed. Second, the constraints
on the practical use of the model are not severe.
Third, the model points to areas requiring improved
empirical findings.

Basically, the model considers the long-term
cost effects of different competitive choices for
a system given a stream of annual production requirements. The model formalizes cost trade-offs existing

between competitive forces of the marketplace and
cost increases from sources such as establishment
of more production facilities. Traditionally, naive
rules of thumb have been applied in determining the
competition decision. Sometimes, with little justification, reductions of fixed percentages of total
cost have been assumed to result from competition.

Recently researches have begun to examine these
trade-offs. Empirical studies estimating the reduction in unit costs attained from introducing a competitive environment have been reported by Burt and
Boyett, Lovett and Norton, and Daly et al.[1] These
studies suggest that 10-40 percent reductions in recurring costs per unit may typically result when
competition is introduced into a sole source supplier
situation. The empirical data tends to be highly
variable. Special circumstances of a given acquisition situation may dramatically alter the savings
expected. Yet these studies provide some guidance
for the necessarily judgmental estimate of the effect
of competitive intensity on unit costs.

Reduction in unit recurring costs is not sufficient to justify competition, however. Systems are
often acquired over multiple-contract award periods,

---

[1]Burt and Boyett (1979); Lovett and Norton (1978);
Daly et al. (1979).

and maintaining a competitive environment over several
contract periods has its own expenses. Thus, in general, the decision is not limited to a choice between
a sole source and a single buy-out competition for
all remaining production. One may, therefore, need
to consider the competitive environment that will
exist when a future contract is awarded.

Nonprice aspects can be quite important in making the competition decision. For example, a split
award using two producers may be desired to increase
reserve capacity. Since the model developed here
does not treat nonprice considerations, it should
be considered as only one part of a full decision
analysis.

METHODOLOGY

Model Description. The setting of concern to us is
the production of large quantities of complex items
such as tanks or missiles. Because the end items
are so specialized and complex, substantial costs
will typically be incurred by introducing competition. For example, additional tooling and learning
may be required. Also the quantity to be purchased
is typically large enough that production requirements can extend over more than one contract performance period.

For such systems the learning curve exerts an
important influence on expected system costs. For
these systems the original producer is usually the
system developer. While production output is still
low, a second source can be educated (by the use of
small buys) in order to reach a level of competitive-
ness with the original producer.

The preceding tends to justify a major limitation of the present model which is that only two
producers are considered. It is assumed that if a
second source is used, it will be ready at the beginning of the first period of time considered by
the model. Finally, if the potential second source
is not maintained, then awards for all future time
periods will be sole source.

The competitive production alternatives treated
by the model are stated below.

1. Sole source. The system developer becomes
the sole source producer. Alternatively, periods
of competition are held, but eventually one firm becomes sole source for buys in subsequent periods.

2. Buy out. A second source is developed.
After the second source has demonstrated its capability, a buy-out competition results in the award
of all current period requirements to the lowest
offeror from the two sources.

3. Split-award. A second source is developed,

but both producers are retained by making split awards.
The government retains the right to award the lowest
cost producer with a larger percentage of the buy.

4. <u>Layaway</u>. One of the sources is not used
during a contract period, but the equipment is maintained so that the potential for a second source continues.

Again note that in the model the choice made in
one contract period affects the possible choices in
subsequent periods. For example, a buy out in period
one precludes the possibility of a split-award in
period two unless the second source is placed on layaway during period one.

Several other features reflected in the model
are now stated. It is likely that the primary competitive decision will be needed prior to the identification of both of the potential sources. Therefore, it is assumed that both of the potential producers are equal in terms of efficiency and capacity.
Production output rates that are above or below
specified values result in increased unit costs.
The lines also have maximum and minimum output levels
within which production must lie. A key assumption
of the model is that the intensity of competition
surrounding a particular acquisition affects the unit
price. Unit price level for an award is affected
by the number of available sources and the price

level set by the degree of competitive intensity in
the prior period. In the case of split awards the
competitive intensity is affected by the minimum award
percentage expected by the contractors. The learning
curve is incorporated in the model to deal with the
accumulation of contractor experience. Since the production awards considered will typically be large,
concern for securing work in the future time periods
is assumed to have negligible impact on current period
contract price behavior. That is, the contractors
are assumed to "bid honestly" rather than "buying in"
with an unjustifiably low bid. Finally, it is assumed
that multi-year awards can be made.

The general mathematical statement of the model
equation and constraints is quite complex and is summarized in the appendix. Let it suffice to say that
the total costs for a contract award period are a
summation of product costs (fixed and variable), and
costs of layaway, maintenance, and reactivation of
lines (if appropriate). All costs represent costs
to the government and therefore include the contractors' fees. As indicated above, product costs are
dependent on the degree of competition present during
the precontract award phases. The notational complexity arises from the specific forms of the various
cost functions needed to make them compatible with
the several features described earlier. The optimum

sequence of competitive or noncompetitive alternatives minimizes the total discounted cost over the
entire time interval for which production requirements exist. A computer program has been written
to solve the problem described above by a dynamic
programming approach.

The model is applied below to a numerical example.
The example also can be used to show the optimum
choice of an acquisition strategy can change with
alterations in the requirements flow. In applying
the model it is necessary to estimate the values for
several parameters. These parameters include the
initial costs for establishing the required number
of producers, the minimum and maximum annual production rates attainable by a single producer, the cost
penalties for annual production outside of an efficient range, the discount rate, the estimated unit
variable cost under full competition, and the learning curve slope.

In addition to these parameters it is necessary
to estimate a penalty factor (expressed as a percentage of the fully competitive unit costs) for various
deviations from a fully competitive situation. For
example, we might estimate 15 percent as the penalty
factor for a sole source following another noncompetitive period but only 10 percent for a sole source
showing a residual effect from a prior competition.

A projected production requirements stream is
displayed in Table 1.   This situation was analyzed

TABLE 1

Requirements Stream

Contract Period	Year	Output Units/Year
1	1	18000
1	2	18000
2	1	18000
2	2	18000
3	1	18000
3	2	18000
4	1	18000
4	2	18000
5	1	14000
5	2	10000
Total		168000

using parameter values considered plausible for a
hypothetical missile system.   The recommended strategy was successive buy-out competition for each contract award.   Some of the alternatives and their
percentage deviation from the optimum are displayed
in Table 2.

TABLE 2

Initial Decision	Cost Above Minimum (in percent)	Optimum Sequence
BO	Minimum	BO-BO-BO-BO-BO
SS	13	SS-SS-SS-SS-SS
SA	2	SA-BO-BO-BO-BO

where BO = buy out,
       SS = sole source,
       SA = 75 - 25 percent split award.

   The requirements from Table 1 were then increased
by 28 percent in each of the first eight years. Under
such projected requirements growth the preferred initial strategy becomes a split award. In fact the model
predicts a 60%-40% split award in the first period
will be optimal. The projected percentage split is
important because it impacts the cumulative experience
gained by the contractors. In this case the presence
of increasing cost penalties as maximum capacity is
approached has overcome the benefits of the greater
competitive force present in a buy-out situation.

Applicability. Several important questions can be
raised regarding the applicability of the model. It
is my claim that the limitations to practical use
of the model are not severe.

   Parameter estimation is an important consideratio

Indeed a large number of parameter estimates are required. It is felt, however, that the project management office and the developing contractor will be
able to provide increasingly reliable data as the
required decision time approaches. Further, sensitivity analysis is necessary anyway and will often
show that the optimal decision is relatively stable
to sizable changes in most of the parameters.

A given situation may require changes to the
basic model formulation. Some changes, such as a
change in the objective cost function, ought to be
easy to implement. This is possible because the basic
structure of the solution algorithm is not altered.

Some possible changes, however, have a fundamental impact on the model. An example of such a change
would be an expansion to accommodate more than two
producers.

A complex model needs some justification of its
complexity. Two points are made in this regard.
First, the decision considered here is made only
once per applicable system, but the impact of the
decision is quite substantial. Therefore, the decision is worthy of detailed analysis. Secondly,
the empirical work performed so far reveals a great
variability in the response to competition. This
variability suggests that the analyst must seek additional insight by examining the details of the

particular system being studied.

The greatest limitation to the use of the model
is the need to estimate a competitive intensity penalty factor. It is here that the decision maker must
balance current empirical results with personal judgment. At the present time empirical research can
only suggest a rough average value for the effect of
competition on unit costs. Yet the decisions must
be made, and the factors identified do influence the
correct decision.

Thus there remains a real need to better define
and quantify the mechanism by which competition exerts
its influence on weapon system costs. It is recommend
that future work focus on this empirical documentation
of the effect of competition. For example, does competition exert its influence by altering the learning
curve slope, or does it work through a one time "squee
ing-out" of a fixed percentage of unit costs?

APPENDIX

Model Summary. In order to describe the model mathematically the following notation is used:
  j = index for the production facilities (contrac-
        tors) in use.
  n = index for the time periods (contract award
        periods) in the planning horizon.

N = the number of time periods in the planning horizon.

x_n = variable representing the number of producers with a contract award in period n .

$y_{j,n}$ = variable proportion of the total production requirement for period n awarded to producer j .

y_n = variable denoting $\max_j \{y_{j,n}\}$.

z_n = variable denoting the number of producers available for awards at the beginning of period n .

m = minimum production rate for a producer.

M = maximum production rate for a producer.

$I(z_1)$ = initial costs incurred in order to establish z_1 producers at the beginning of period 1.

Q_n = maximum cumulative production quantity attributable to a single producer through period n . (Depends on production history prior to period n . Used to account for improvements in cost due to experience.)

$D_n(x_n, y_n, z_n, y_{n-1}, z_{n-1}, Q_{n-1})$ = function measuring the standard product costs incurred in period n using x_n producers with y_n maximum percentage to a single producer; with a competitive

environment described by y_{n-1} , and z_{n-1} ;
and with experience level measured by Q_{n-1} .

$P_n(x_n, \{y_{j,n}\}, z_n, y_{n-1}, z_{n-1}, Q_{n-1})$ = function measuring penalty product costs incurred in period n due to production volume outside the efficient capacity region.

$V_n(w)$ = costs incurred to reactivate w facilities.

$L_n(w)$ = costs incurred to layaway w facilities.

R_n = production requirement in period n .

Then the general problem can be stated as follows

$$\underset{\{(x_n,y_n,z_n):1\leq n\leq N\}}{\text{Minimize}} \quad I(z_1) + \sum_{n=1}^{N} [D_n + P_n$$

$$+ V_n(\max(x_{n+1} - x_n, \ 0)) + L_n(\max(z_{n+1} - x_n, \ 0)$$

where we require

$$z_{N+1} = z_N = x_N = x_{N+1}$$

$$x_n \leq z_{n+1} \leq z_n \quad \text{for} \quad 1 \leq n \leq N-1$$

$$m \leq y_{j,n} R_n \leq M \quad \text{for} \quad 1 \leq j \leq x_n \ , \ 1 \leq n \leq N, \ R_n > 0$$

$$x_n, \ z_n \in \{0,1,2\} \quad \text{for} \quad 1 \leq n \leq N$$

$$x_n = 0 \quad \text{if and only if} \quad R_n = 0 \quad \text{for} \quad 1 \leq n \leq N$$

$$\sum_{j=1}^{x_n} y_{j,n} = 1 \quad \text{for} \quad x_n > 0$$

$$Q_n = \sum_{i=1}^{n} y_i R_i \quad \text{for} \quad 1 \leq n \leq N$$

and

$$x_0 = y_0 = z_0 = Q_0 = 0$$

In order to define the model, specific cost forms must be specified for D_n, P_n, L_n and V_n. The complete specification of these functions in a manner consistent with the assumptions of the report requires further notation and is not presented here.

REFERENCES

Burt, D. N. and J. E. Boyett, Jr. (1979). "Reduction in Selling Price after the Introduction of Competition," Journal of Marketing Research, Vol. 16, pp. 275-79.

Lovett, E. T. and M. G. Norton (1978). "Determining and Forecasting Savings from Competing Previously Sole Source/Noncompetitive Contracts," Army Procurement Research Office, APRO 709-3, Fort Lee, Va.

Daly, G. G., H. P. Gates, and J. A. Schuttinga (1979). "The Effect of Price Competition on Weapon System Acquisition Costs," Institute for Defense Analyses, IDA Paper P-1435, Arlington, Va.

4

A METHOD FOR ESTIMATING THE COST OF CHANGES FOR NAVY SHIPBUILDING PROGRAMS[*]

Colin P. Hammon

David R. Graham

INTRODUCTION

Changes to a ship during a construction program can disrupt work and increase costs by more than the costs of the work explicitly attributable to the change. In the 1960s and 1970s changes were the focus of controversy in several claims against the Navy. Changes were the central issue in these claims because the

[*]This chapter is based on work done by the authors while they were at the Center for Naval Analyses. No endorsement of the conclusions of recommendations by the U.S. Navy should be inferred. The essential content was presented at the Ninth Annual DOD/FAI Acquisition Cost Symposium, Annapolis, Maryland, June 1980.

true cost of changes was uncertain, but perhaps more
importantly, changes were often the shipbuilders'
only legal basis for claims to recoup cost overruns
regardless of why the overrun occurred. Consequently
the Navy's Shipbuilding Procurement Process Study,
which is aimed at reducing the potential for shipbuilding claims, recommends that changes be fully
priced as the work is done.[1] Present methods of pricing changes either do not allow for the full cost of
changes, including disruption costs, or they rely
on complicated subjective judgments. One method for
handling changes is for the Navy and the contractor
to agree, in advance, on a system for fully pricing
change costs that is fair and binding. This would
make it clear how much changes would cost the Navy
and would provide a framework for deciding who is
responsible for all costs.

    This study presents a statistical method for
estimating the total man-hour costs of changes, which
is the most significant element of uncertainty in
establishing the costs of changes. The method is
objective in the sense that once the variables of
the equation are determined, the results depend only
on what is observed in a given yard for a particular
period of time. The cost estimates depend on observed

----

[1]Assistant Secretary of the Navy (1978).

values of the variables independent of value judgments
concerning the past or future.

The model yields estimates of the total man-hour
costs of changes. These consist of three components.
The first, the hardcore cost, is the contractor's estimate of the net cost in labor hours needed to accom-
plish the tasks specified by the change. Hardcore
costs are audited and may be negotiated downward but
they generally are not disputed. In this study, hardcore costs serve as a measure of the size of a change.
The second and third components are direct disruption
and indirect disruption. Direct disruption costs include local program disruption costs that are directly
correlated with hardcore changes. Indirect disruption costs are the added man-hour costs that are incurred if the contractor responds to a change by
adding workers or increasing overtime.

Only costs that are statistically related to
changes are included in direct and indirect disruption.
Changes and disruption due to changes are only part
of the reason why ships cost more than the contractor's
original estimate. The model is also used to estimate
the independent effect on efficiency of shipyard manning, labor turnover, and labor skills.

The role of changes and disruption in past shipbuilding claims, and how this study supports recent

efforts to avoid claims is described first. The second
section describes how the total cost of changes is
estimated. Applications of the statistical cost model
to the FF 1052 and DD 963 programs are reported in
the third section. In the fourth section, we summarize
the findings and briefly outline how a change-pricing
system based on a statistical cost equation could be
put into practice.

CHANGE PRICING AND THE NAVY'S CLAIMS PROBLEM

In the 1960s, the Department of Defense adopted
procurement policies designed to increase suppliers'
incentives to hold down costs. Fixed-price or cost-
sharing contracts became standard policy for all Naval
shipbuilding. In theory, these contracts limited the
Navy's responsibility for cost growth. In practice,
when the Navy made design and specification changes,
it became potentially liable for cost overruns just
as under a cost-plus contract. The difference was
that under the new policies the contractor had to
file a claim to get additional compensation. This
is the fundamental reason why changes led to claims
in the late 1960s and 1970s. Although hard-core change
remained at about the same fraction of total man hours
in these decades as they had been in the 1950s, claims

became a substantial part of shipbuilding costs.

Of course, these policies alone are not sufficient to explain claims. Claims would not have been incurred without overruns, and inflation combined with limited cost escalation coverage contributed to overruns. Changes also contributed to overruns, but more importantly, changes provided the necessary legal justification for claims. When contractors had overruns, the changes were blamed. Virtually every shipbuilding program completed in this period resulted in a claim.

The Ship Procurement Process Study sought ways to avoid future claims.[2] Many of its recommendations reversed the policies of the 1960s, and returned more responsibility for costs to the Navy. The study initiatives may have reduced the severity of claims. They have not eliminated changes or later claims against unpriced changes.[3] The fee the contractor earns on cost-plus and incentive contracts depends on how well cost and schedule targets are met, so changes still lead to disputes over how targets should be adjusted when changes are made.

---

[2] Assistant Secretary of the Navy (1978).

[3] Interview with Assistant Secretary of the Navy (1981).

To reduce claims the Navy needs a better way
to handle changes within the context of the basic
contract. One way is for the contractor and the
Navy to agree on a method for pricing the full cost
of changes. To be acceptable in the long run, however, such payments must be realistic and fair to
both sides. Thus, we believe that successful full
pricing requires a method for estimating the total
cost of changes which is accurate and based on actual
costs. Full change pricing, based on such a method,
could essentially eliminate the risk of claims.

ESTIMATING THE TOTAL COST OF CHANGES

The Navy is legally responsible for hardcore
change and disruption costs under the doctrine of
"equitable adjustment." However, there is no clearly
established method of calculating the amount of the
equitable adjustment. The problem is one of identifying all relevant costs. In recent cases the courts
have ruled that the contractor is entitled to "being
made whole." This implies that he is entitled to
the recovery of reasonable costs based on his position
as a result of the change and his industrial practices.
This is in contrast to the criterion of "fair market
value" which implies payment commensurate with the

industry costs at large. At the same time the contractor is obliged to mitigate unreasonable costs
such as failure to obtain the best available price
for material.[4]

The hardcore costs of changes can be estimated
using accepted industrial standards. These costs
are associated with specific identifiable tasks that
are added or deleted by the change. However, disruption cannot be tied to specific change related tasks.
Part of direct disruption costs result because changes
may have a compounding effect on efficiency over a
number of ship systems, cost centers, or programs.
Indirect disruption results because the contractor
responds to changes by altering the schedule, work
force or the amount of overtime worked, which also
has an effect that is not localized to a particular
change. It would be impossible through established
accounting procedures to objectively identify these
disruption costs with a specific change. The total
cost of changes is estimated here by showing how the
man-hour cost of a ship varies as the number of hardcore change hours varies across ships of a given kind.

The Model. Theoretical analyses of the ship-building
process identified the major variables that, in

---

[4]U.S. Navy Sea Systems Command (1979).

principle, explain the total man-hour costs.[5]   A general ship-building cost equation would require variables describing the ship, shipyard facilities, other
work in the yard, the work force, contract terms,
Navy and shipyard management, and program changes
and delays.   The focus here is on the more manageable
task of describing the total man-hour cost of changes
for a specific ship-building program.

The following variables are included in the cost
equations: learning (productivity increases as more
ships of a kind are built); a measure of changes in
each ship; manning levels of the program and other
programs in the yard; variables that describe the
work force (skills, experience, overtime).

Changes present a difficult measurement problem.
A change has many dimensions, including the number
of hardcore man hours, hardcore material costs, the
trades affected, the compartment or ship systems affected, and whether it is implemented early or late
in the construction process.   Conceptually, one can
describe all the variables perfectly.   There are practical limitations, however, and the equation will be
more easily understood if the number of variables can
be kept tractable.   Thus, only hardcore change hours
are used to measure the size of a change.   However,

---

[5]Hammon and Graham (1980).

hardcore changes appear to serve very well to measure
the effect of a change on total man-hour costs.

The cost equation for the empirical analysis
is presented in (1). The average man hours used
per unit of output is the dependent variable. The
independent variables are either totals (such as
total hardcore change hours) or averages (such as
the average number of workers, the average experience
level of the workers, or the average skill level of
the labor force). Each ship is a unit of observation.
The observation period is defined either in terms of
a fixed amount of output (for example, completion of
the ship) or in terms of a fixed period of time (for
example, one year).

$$\ln(MH/Q) = A + a \ln M + b \ln H + c \ln EX + d \ln SK$$
$$+ e \ln N + f \ln HC + g \ln MO + h \ln D + u$$

(1)

where: $\ln$ denotes the natural logarithm

MH = man hours applied to a ship

Q = output (physical completion)

M = number of workers

H = average hours per work day

EX = experience of work force

SK = skill level of work force

> N = ship construction sequence (related to
>   learning; the improvement in efficiency
>   for the construction of each subsequent
>   ship)
>
> HC = hardcore change hours
>
> MO = man hours applied to other programs
>
> A = intercept term
>
> D = delay in ship delivery
>
> u = statistical error term

a,b,...,h = coefficients (man hour elasticities)

The coefficient of each variable shows how total man hours change for given output when the value of one variable changes, and all the other variables remain the same. Thus, these coefficients show the quantitative relationship between man hours and each of the explanatory variables.

Calculating the Cost of Changes. The coefficient of hardcore change hours in eq. 1 shows the percentage increase in total man hours for a 1 percent increase in hardcore change hours, when all the other right-hand variables are held constant. Direct disruption costs are calculated from this coefficient as hours per change hour. Since the implied increases in man hours for each hour of hardcore change work includes the hardcore hour, it must be subtracted from the total man hours go up by say $2\frac{1}{2}$ hours, one hour is hardcore, and the additional $1\frac{1}{2}$ hours is direct disruption.

The indirect cost of changes equals the costs due to increases in the work force, or in overtime that are, in turn, due to changes. The equations include these variables, so the costs of such adjustments are not included in the direct disruption cost. To estimate the indirect cost of changes, the effect of changes on manning and overtime must first be estimated. The effect of these variables on man hour costs are then calculated. For example, if changes cause manning to increase by ten percent, the indirect disruption cost equals the estimated man-hour cost associated with this increase in manning. The sum of direct and indirect costs equals total disruption. The total unit cost of changes equals the sum of total disruption plus the hardcore costs.

EMPIRICAL ANALYSIS OF TWO SHIPBUILDING PROGRAMS

The methodology described above was applied to the Avondale FF 1052 and Ingalls DD 963 ship-building programs. These programs were chosen because of the availability of data, and because each involved a substantial number of ships. The Avondale yard built 27 of the FF-1052 class frigates between 1966 and 1974.

These ships involved a substantial amount of change
work and Navy-induced delay. Ingalls built 30 of the
DD-963 class destroyers between 1972 and 1980. This
program had relatively few changes. However, compli-
cations associated with startup of a new yard and
stretch-out of the Navy LHA program resulted in more
work in the yard during the DD-963 program than had
been planned.

Several versions of the statistical equation
were estimated for each program. The findings were
generally consistent across these different equations.
Thus, a representative subset of findings are reported
here. The equations explained more than 90 percent
of the variation in the natural logarithm of production man hours across data points for each program.
When the Ingalls data were divided into seven labor
departments, the equations typically explained between
60 and 70 percent of the variation.

Calculated unit costs of changes varied depending
on certain ship-yard labor characteristics and the
magnitude of changes relative to total work on the
ship. When calculated at the sample means of these
variables, the unit cost of changes for all production
labor was estimated to be about 3.5 hours for the
FF 1052 program and 2.5 hours for the DD 963 program.
The DD 963 program unit costs ranged from a low of

1.4 hours for the sheet metal department to a high
of 4.4 hours for the paint department.

The Units of Analysis. The units of analysis are
described in Table 1. The data were observed for
each of 24 ships of the FF 1052 program. A total
of 56 annual observations of 26 different ships were
used for the DD 963 analysis. Seven labor departments
were analyzed individually as well as total operations
man hours for the DD 963. The basic methodology is
the same in both cases.

Variables. The equations include variables for hardcore change hours along with manning, labor skills
and experience, ship construction sequence number,
and sometimes, overtime and delay. These variables
appear in Table 2. Interactions of changes with manning and turnover were also considered. Including
these variables with changes allows prediction of the
effect of changes on man hours for different levels
of manning or turnover. It should be emphasized that
the unit of observation is not an individual change.
Total hardcore hours for all the changes implemented
in the observation period were used to explain man
hours in the period. However, over the many changes
included in each observation, the individual differences tend to average out, and hardcore man hours
are a good measure for the overall impact of changes.

TABLE 1

Units of Analysis for the
Avondale FF 1052 and Ingalls DD 963 Programs

	Avondale FF 1052	Ingalls DD 963
Observation units	Each ship	Annual observations on each ship, fiscal years 1975-1978
Sample size	24 ships[a]	56 observations on 26 ships
Man hours variables	Total production man hours	Total man hours for operations[b]
		Departments: hull manufacturing services pipe outside machinists sheetmetal paint electrical

[a]Data were not complete for the last three ships (HN 25-27) of the program.

[b]Ingalls' total operations include nearly the same number of crafts as did Avondale's total production.

TABLE 2

Variables Used to Explain Man Hours

	Avondale FF 1052	Ingalls DD 963
Learning	Sequence number of ship	Sequence number of ship
Manning	Average full-time-equivalent workers on each ship	Yard workers (payroll) LHA program labor (equivalent men) Submarine overhaul labor (equivalent men)
Labor skills and experience	Labor turnover rate (annual)	Journeymen/total labor percentage Labor turnover rate (quarterly)
Overtime		Overtime hours
Changes	Negotiated change hours plus Navy claims team estimate of unnegotiated hardcore hours	Estimated production work added change hours
Delay	Total delay in ship delivery	Change in estimated completion date during period (days)
Construction output	The total ship	Man hours earned in period adjusted for changes in plan
Interaction variables	Changes × turnover	Changes × manning Changes × turnover

<u>Estimates of the Regression Equations</u>. The findings
demonstrate the importance of learning, changes, manning, and labor skills and experience in explaining
man hours. The regression estimates for total production man hours for the FF 1052 and DD 963 programs
are presented in Table 3. Across from each explanatory variable is its coefficient (elasticity). The
elasticity of man hours with respect to a given variable is the percentage change in production hours
that would result from a 1 percent increase in the
explanatory variable when other explanatory variables
are held constant.

The FF 1052 Program. The equation explained
99 percent of the variation in the natural logarithm
of man hours used to build the 24 FF 1052's. All
variables were significant at the 0.95 level and each
has the sign predicted by the theoretical analysis.

The learning coefficient shows that when the
number of completed ships is doubled, the cost of
the last ship in the second group is 18 percent below the cost of the last ship in the first group.
This translates into a learning rate of 88 percent,
slightly better than the learning bid by Avondale.
(Learning rate is the cumulative average cost of 2x
units expressed as a percentage of the average cost
of x units.)[6] Note that the greater the learning

---

[6]Pegel (1976).

TABLE 3

Findings for Equations Explaining
Total Production Man Hours
for FF 1052 and DD 963 Programs

	Man-hour elasticities	
Explanatory Variable	FF 1052	DD 963
Learning	−.182	−.361
Changes	.285[a]	.053[b]
Yard manning		.439[b]
Ship manning	.248	
Yard manning × change interaction		.519
Yard turnover	.667[a]	
Turnover × change interaction	.953	
Submarine program manning		.407
LHA program manning		.184
Delay	.143	

[a]Computed at sample mean values of changes and turn-over.

[b]Computed at sample mean values of changes and man-ning.

rate the lower the efficiency gains for subsequent units.

Increasing ship manning led to increased man-hour requirements. Each increase of 1 percent in ship manning is predicted to increase man-hour requirements by about 1/4 of 1 percent.

The coefficient for hardcore changes depends importantly on labor turnover. Changes are more costly when they are made during periods when turnover is high. The turnover-hardcore change interaction coefficient of .953 implies that a 1 percent increase in turnover increases the man-hour cost of a change by nearly 1 percent. The reported change and turnover elasticities are computed for the sample mean values of turnover and changes.

Delay was a very important determinant of man-hours in the FF 1052 program. This is not surprising. This program was marked by many delays due to late delivery of plans, specifications, and equipment. The delay coefficient shows that every 1 percent increase in ship delay increases the man-hour cost of the ship by .143 percent. This figure implies that a one-month increase in delay increased man-hour costs by 51 man months (8200 man hours).

The DD 963 Program. Equation 1 explained about 94 percent of the variation in the natural logarithm

of total operations man hours across the 56 observations on the DD program. The estimated learning coefficient is -.361. This implies a learning rate of
78 percent when other factors are held constant. Litton was not able to get its high-efficiency assembly
line production process into operation as quickly as
planned. The earlier LHA program was also in the
yard longer than intended, which to some extent limited
the availability of facilities for the DD program and
forced the use of more workers in the yard than intended.
This learning therefore partly reflects the breaking-
in of the new yard, a move to the planned production
process, and diminishing influence of the LHA.

A significant interaction effect was found between
hardcore change hours and yard manning. The coefficient
implies that a 1 percent increase in manning increases
the cost of changes by .519 percent. The elasticities
of manning and changes shown in Table 3 are computed
at the sample mean values of changes and manning.

Manning dominated all other labor variables in
explaining man hours in this program. This variable
is a proxy for labor quality. As manning was increased,
it became more difficult to hire the desired number
of quality workers. The other labor variables (overtime, turnover, and the percent of the work force
that were journeymen) were insignificant when the

manning variable was included in Table 3. These variables are highly correlated with manning, and although
they are important determinants of man-hour costs,
the data do not allow us to isolate their independent
effect on costs. Each of these variables is significant for total operations labor and some of the individual production departments when manning is excluded.

Yard manning, submarine program manning, and LHA
program manning must be interpreted together. These
three variables represent two interdependent effects.
One is the effect of total yard manning on productivity. The other is the effect of programs competing
for facilities and labor quantity and quality.

When total yard manning goes up, holding submarine and LHA manning constant, the added workers
by definition go to the DD 963 program. Thus, the
yard manning coefficient shows that a 1 percent increase in DD 963 manning, holding the other programs
constant, increases man-hour requirements by .439
percent. The submarine and LHA variables show the effect
of adding men to these programs while holding total
yard manning constant. Both effects are positive.
An increase of 1 percent in submarine workers at the
expense of the DD 963 program increases DD man-hour
requirements by .407 percent. An increase of 1 percent in LHA workers increases DD man-hour requirements

by .184 percent.

Since yard overmanning due to the delay of the LHA is considered to have been a major factor in Ingalls' production problems, manning of the LHA was expected to be a significant variable in explaining DD 963 man hours. The significance of the submarine program variable is somewhat surprising. The submarine work is physically separated from the other programs, and the submarines never accounted for more than 8 percent of the yard's operations labor work force. However, some observers conjecture that the submarines were sometimes given the most highly skilled workers at the expense of the other programs. In addition, the time pressures of the overall work might also have diverted a disproportionate amount of management attention to this work.

The DD 963 Program by Labor Department. Table 4 summarizes the qualitative findings for seven Ingalls' production departments. The basic specification is the same as used for the overall analysis. This includes the manning-change interaction term as well as any additional variables that are significant. Across from each variable are the findings for each of the seven departments. With the exception of delay and ship sequence number, all of the variables are measured separately for each of the labor departments.

A plus sign or minus sign shows the direction of effect when the variable is significant in explaining
department man hours. A blank indicates the variable
was not significant for the base case estimates.

Learning is the only variable that is significant across all departments. The hardcore change
hours variable is significant for all departments
but one. Either the turnover-change or manning-
change interaction variable was significant in every
case. These qualitative findings are consistent with
the findings for total operations man hours.
Nevertheless, the findings indicate considerable differences among labor departments.

The yard manning variables show the effect of
building up manning of the DD 963 program while holding constant the manning levels of the other two programs. This means man hours fell (efficiency rose)
as more men were added to the hull, outside machinist,
paint, and sheet metal departments. We conclude that
these departments were generally manned below their
optimum levels. This is consistent with the manning
history of these crafts.

For the basic specification, turnover is significant for three departments (outside machinist, paint,
and sheet metal). Three departments (pipe, paint,
and electrical) have significant turnover-change interaction. Pipe, machinist, and electrical departments

typically require highly skilled workers which were
chronically in short supply. This could explain why
turnover is more of a problem for those departments.

The number of journeymen and overtime were significant in a few cases. However, the number of
journeymen was never significant when included in
the same equation with yard manning. For most departments, this variable closely followed yard manning;
when the yard was building up, journeymen fell as a
share of the total work force. Thus, the effect of
this variable can not be distinguished from the effect
of yard manning.

Overtime was significant for two departments.
It was anticipated that overtime increases man-hour
costs. This is the finding for the hull department.
However, man-hour requirements were reduced by the
use of overtime in manufacturing services. The manufacturing services department performs support functions for the other departments and includes carpenters
and launch pontoon personnel. These workers play a
key role in events such as a launch where timing is
critical. One interpretation consistent with the
findings is that adherence to a schedule and proper
sequence are particularly important contributors to
efficiency for manufacturing services. Thus, the use
of overtime is an efficient use of man hours.

TABLE 4

Qualitative Findings for Equations Explaining Man Hours
for Major Ingalls' Labor Departments

Explanatory Variable	Hull	Manufacturing Services	Ingalls' Labor Departments				
			Pipe[a]	Outside Machinists	Paint[a]	Sheet Metal[a]	Electric
Learning	−	−	−	−	−	−	−
Changes	+	+	+		+	+	+
Yard manning	−	+		−	−	−	+
Manning-change interaction	+	+			+	+	+
Turnover				+	+	+	
Overtime	+	−					
Submarine program			+	+	+		
LHA program	+					+	+
Delay			−				

[a]The manning-change estimates represent the base case, and all the findings in the table apply to that case. However, for these shops the turnover-change interaction is significant and yields greater explanatory power than the base equation.

The delay variable did not significantly explain
total operations man hours. However, delay is significant for two labor departments. Sheet metal department man-hour requirements were greater as the delay
increased, but pipe department man-hour requirements
declined. The negative delay coefficient suggests
that the original ship delivery schedule requires
the pipe department to work at a faster than efficient
rate. Thus, efficiency rose when a ship was delayed.

The Man-Hour Cost of Changes. In this section the
estimated coefficients of the cost equations are used
to estimate the total cost of changes. The sensitivity of the cost of changes to varying levels of manning and turnover is also explained.

The FF 1052 Program. The direct disruption cost
is sensitive to the level of turnover. Direct disruption varies between .81 and 2.67 when turnover
is varied 10 percent below and 10 percent above the
mean value of 60 percent. At the mean of turnover,
direct disruption is 1.78 hours per hardcore change
hour.

Some delay was caused by changes and is therefore
related directly to hardcore changes. To identify
the indirect disruption cost of delay due to changes,
the equation shown in Table 3 was estimated with delay omitted. Using this estimate of the change

elasticity the indirect disruption cost of delay was calculated as 0.5 man hours per hardcore change hour.

Omitting manning from the estimating equation resulted in a serious misspecification. Therefore the indirect effect of this variable was estimated differently. On average, change hours accounted for $10\frac{1}{4}$ percent of total hours. These additional hours could have been put in partly by hiring more workers and partly by delaying the program. It is assumed that 10 percent more men were hired. Turnover was not positively related to ship manning for this program so it was assumed that turnover was not affected.

These findings for manning imply that a 10 percent increase in manning increases total man-hour costs by about $2\frac{1}{2}$ percent. This is roughly 1/4 hour of indirect disruption for each hour of hardcore change work. The total cost of one hardcore change hour is shown in Table 5.

TABLE 5

Estimated Total Cost of One Hardcore Change Hour
for the FF 1052 Program at Mean Values

1.00	Hardcore change hour
1.78	Direct disruption costs
.50	Indirect cost of delays due to changes
.25	Indirect cost of 10 percent added ship manning
3.53	Total

Table 5 shows that total disruption equals 2.5 hours
per hardcore change hour.

   The DD 963 Program.   The total unit cost of changes
is shown in Table 6.   These estimates are calculated
at the sample average values of manning and turnover.
No indirect costs of changes were found for this program.   Therefore, the total unit cost of changes
reported in Table 6 is the same as the direct unit
cost.

   For total DD 963 operations, direct disruption
is $2.48 - 1 = 1.48$ man hours per hardcore hour of
change work.   The direct disruption costs of changes
varies considerably among labor departments.   However,
the pattern of the findings is consistent with the
expected pattern of direct disruption costs for the
various departments.   The pipe, paint, and electrical departments, crafts which are expected to be more
susceptible to disruption because of the nature of
their work, have greater estimated direct disruption
costs.

   Delay is not a significant variable in the equation explaining total hours.   Delay is closely correlated with changes.   Thus, any delay costs are
included directly in the change coefficient.   Delay
is significant only for the pipe and sheet metal departments.   The pipe department was chronically under-

TABLE 6

Estimated Total Cost of One Hardcore Hour
of Change for the DD 963 Program
at Mean Values of Manning and Turnover
(Fiscal Years 1975-1978)

	Hardcore Hour	Direct Disruption Cost	Total Cost for Each Hour of Hardcore Change Work
Total production	1	1.48	2.48
Hull	1	0.75	1.75
Manufacturing services	1	1.26	2.26
Pipe	1	2.12	3.12
Outside machinists	1	0.94	1.94
Paint	1	3.36	4.36
Sheet metal	1	0.39	1.39
Electrical	1	2.93	3.93

manned and delay of the ship reduces manning and man-
hour costs for the pipe department. It is not surprising to find that delays attributed to changes also
reduce costs. Thus, the direct unit cost of delay
is negative. The sheet metal cost is positive, and
about the same magnitude as for pipe.

   The indirect disruption costs of changes were
negligible for this program. There are two reasons
for this. First, DD 963 program changes represented
a small fraction of the total work in the Litton yard,
so work force adjustments due to changes were minimal.
Indeed, manning coefficients were negative for the
hull, outside machinist, paint, and sheet metal departments. This implies that the net effect of a labor
force buildup due to changes would be to reduce man
hours. The available evidence indicates that these
negative coefficients reflect Ingalls' difficulties
in hiring and retaining workers at some times in the
program. Thus, the size of the work force was determined mainly by hiring and retention problems
and did not respond to changes. Second, overtime is
significant in the cost equation for only two crafts:
the hull department and manufacturing services. However, the correlations between overtime and changes
are negative and small for these crafts. Thus, we
conclude that although overtime is significant there

are no appreciable overtime costs due to changes for
these crafts. Moreover, this variable is not in the
equation explaining total operations man hours, so
that any cost of overtime correlated with changes is
already included in the coefficient of the change
variable.

SUMMARY

The statistical model explained more than 90
percent of the variation in the natural logarithm
of total man hours per unit of output for both the
FF 1052 and DD 963 programs. In every instance statistically significant estimates for the major variables were obtained, and these estimates were uniformly
in agreement with theoretical expectations. Moreover,
the magnitudes of the estimates are plausible and
differences in the estimates across programs are consistent with the known differences across programs
as well as across Ingalls' labor departments.

The analysis shows that: (1) learning was an
important cost determinant for both programs. For
the FF 1052 program actual learning when other sources
of inefficiency are controlled for was only slightly
better than bid. The very steep learning curves for
the DD 963 program reflect substantial start-up costs

as the new yard was being broken in. (2) Changes
affect production man hours significantly. Total
disruption was 2.5 hours per hardcore change hour
for the FF 1052 program and 1.5 hours per hardcore
change hour for the DD 963 program. This is consistent with the fact that substantially more changes
were made in the FF 1052 program. In the DD 963
program, changes were more disruptive for the highly
skilled shipboard crafts, which is also a plausible
relationship. (3) Increased manning and labor turnover increase production man hours significantly.
(4) The cost of changes depends on the values of
these manpower variables. (5) Delay significantly
affected production man hours independently of changes
in the FF 1052 program, but not in the DD 963 program.
This reflects the importance of delays due to bottle-
necks in missing plans, specifications, and equipment
for the FF 1052. In contrast delay was generally
not the result of such problems as missing plans or
equipment in the DD 963 programs; rather the contractor
responded to changes by delaying the program as evidenced by the high correlation between changes and delay. (6) Competing programs (LHA and submarine over-
hauls) had a measurable impact on DD 963 operations
labor. This was also true for five of the seven individual departments. It is particularly noteworthy

that the same basic model worked so well for these
two different programs. These findings justify confidence in the model and in the estimates of disruption derived from the model.

A System for Pricing Changes. A system to price changes
would require three basic steps. (1) At the outset of the program, the Navy and the contractor would
agree on a price equation. This equation would be
estimated for a comparable ship type and shipyard
in order to establish benchmark disruption factors.
(2) These cost estimates would then be used to price
changes for an agreed-to period. Finally, (3) at
stipulated intervals the equation would be reesti-
mated, and the disruption factors would be adjusted
as necessary. The adjustment period for a pricing
system could be as short as three months or as long
as the entire contract period. It would be possible
to include more complete measures of changes and other
variables in future applications. Variables thought
to be important determinants of inefficiency, such as
personnel transfers, absenteeism, out-of-station work,
rejected work, and work interruptions could easily
be included directly in the estimating equation. The
cost equation would be made more accurate and flexible as the frequency of updating, the detail of the
analysis, and the number of variables considered were

increased.   Of course, it would also be more costly.
Further experience will be necessary to determine
the most cost-effective combination of frequency,
detail, and variables.

The cost equation measures the contractor's
actual cost of performing change work.   This could
create a problem because any system for pricing
changes, including the one outlined here, may offer
incentives to increase the price above that which
is equitable.   First, any such system gives the contractor incentives to negotiate higher hardcore costs
than is warranted.   Second, contractors could try to
"game the system" by making early changes appear very
costly, and thereby obtaining inflated prices for
later changes.

Contractors always have incentives to ask for
more.   In the pricing system envisioned, here the
hardcore costs of changes would be set in the same
way as they are today.   Thus, overstating hardcore
costs would be no more and no less a problem than it
is today.   Although the potential for inflating the
cost of changes would continue to present a significant problem and deserves further consideration, the
potential for inflating the cost of changes would be
far more limited than it has been in the past.   By
taking into account the many sources of cost increases,

other than changes, the model greatly limits the
potential for overstating the cost of changes.

The issues raised in this brief discussion will
best be resolved with practical experience in using
a change pricing system. The best way to gain this
experience is by further experimentation with the
method using data from an ongoing program.

The results show that even the simple model used
in this analysis is a powerful tool for explaining
man-hour costs. A model estimated for an on-going
program, in which better data could be made available
for measuring changes, manning, skills, and yard characteristics, could be expected to work even better.
We therefore believe this model holds great promise
as a means for pricing changes in future shipbuilding
programs.

REFERENCES

Assistant Secretary of the Navy (M,RA&L) (1978).
  "Naval Ship Procurement Process Study," Department
  of the Navy, Washington, D.C.

Hammon, C. and D. Graham (1980). "Disruption Costs
  in Navy Shipbuilding Programs," Center for Naval
  Analyses, Alexandria, Virginia, Study Report CNS
  1149/April.

Pegel, C. C. (1976). "Start Up or Learning Curves, Some New Approaches," Decision Sciences, Vol. 7, No. 4, pp. 705-13.

Interview with Assistant Secretary of the Navy (Shipbuilding and Logistics) George A. Sawyer, October, 1981.

U.S. Naval Sea Systems Command (1979). U.S. Navy Shipbuilding Claims Manual.

5

APPLICATION OF THE CONCEPTUAL MODEL
FOR SETTING DESIGN-TO-COST GOALS:
THE FFG-7

Michael G. Sovereign

INTRODUCTION

A model for the cost (quality-quantity) trade
off implicit in the design of a commodity was developed several years ago.[1] In economics, commodities
are a primitive (or a "given") while for engineering
economics the problems are of design of commodities
or systems. Engineers perform cost-quantity trade
offs to determine the design of a new system. For
example, for a new aircraft, "Is it better to have
one large aircraft or many smaller ones?" In the
design of military systems the problem is usually

---

[1]Sovereign (1975).

stated as:

> Given a mission requirement and a
> fixed budget, what is the optimal
> number and design (quality) of sys-
> tems to be obtained?

This important problem has received considerable attention in recent years because of the phenomenal increase
in the unit cost of military systems. Some observers
attribute this to "military inefficiency" or "waste."
However, it is also true for commercial systems. The
cost of a 747 aircraft is about one thousand times
that of a DC-3, but no one would argue that DC-3's
are more economical for United Airlines today.

I will review a conceptual model[2] and report
on a recent study of naval ships that provides its
first empirical quantification. The empirical results
are consistent with the model or observed decision
making in this specific case.

THE CONCEPTUAL MODEL

The driving forces in the quality-quantity trade off
are threefold as shown in Figure 1 and described below.
The first is the cost of performance of one unit (one system) as a function of the quality. In design, this
is called a cost-estimating relationship (CER). The

_____

[2] Sovereign (1975).

explanatory variables for cost per unit are either
physical characteristics or performance characteristics. This distinction is similar to the difference between intermediate products and final outputs.
If the variables are of the performance type (speed,
payload), it is a performance CER. CERs of this
type are not as widely available as physical characteristic CERs based on weight, size, or number of
parts, but they are not unusual in the design process.
The second driver is the cost per unit versus quantity produced, for a constant quality. This is a
well-known function known as the learning curve and
is usually assumed to be loglinear. The third relationship is the total force effectiveness or performance as a function of quantity and unit effectiveness. This is usually determined from a model of
the mission or from empirical data. A simple example
is that effectiveness of a billion dollars worth of anti-
tank missiles is equal to the probability of kill per missile times the number of missiles that can be purchased
for the billion dollars.

The relationships described above must be solved
simultaneously in order to produce the optimal design
and quantity. A general set of functional forms for
the model are given in Figure 1 to illustrate solutions. The performance CER is nonlinear because the
marginal cost of increased performance rises with

FIGURE 1

Conceptual Model for the
Quality versus Quantity Trade Off II

1. Performance CER $\qquad$ $Y = \frac{1}{a}X^e + b$, $e \geq 1$

2. Learning Curve (unit) $\qquad$ $B^0 = Z^c \frac{Y}{c}$

3. Force Effectiveness $\qquad$ $F = Z^d X$, $0 \leq d$

where

$\qquad$ Y = cost per unit

$\qquad$ X = unit performance

$\qquad$ Z = quantity

$\qquad$ F = force effectiveness

$\qquad$ B^0 = given budget

a, b, c, d, e constants

given technology. For example, the cost of speed
rises faster than linearly with Mach number. The
learning curve assumed here is the standard unit
learning curve:

$$c = h+1$$

$$h \equiv \text{learning curve parameter}$$

$$h = \frac{\log S}{\log 2}$$

$$S = \text{learning curve slope as a decimal}$$

If quantity is doubled, the unit cost drops to S
of the cost before the doubling of quantity.

In this formulation of the problem, the budget,
B^0, is assumed known. The force effectiveness equation is assumed to be a simple product of quantity
and <u>unit</u> performance with quantity modified by exponent d to allow for saturation or synergy. If d
is greater than one there is saturation, that is,
each additional unit contributes less effectiveness
than the previous one. If d is greater than one
there is a synergistic effect.

In order to illustrate simultaneous solution
of the three relationships we take a particularly
simple case as shown in Figure 2. Here we assume
that unit cost is proportional to unit effectiveness,

FIGURE 2

CONCEPTUAL MODEL FOR THE
QUALITY VERSUS QUANTITY TRADEOFF III

Four-Quadrant Graphical Solution: Case I

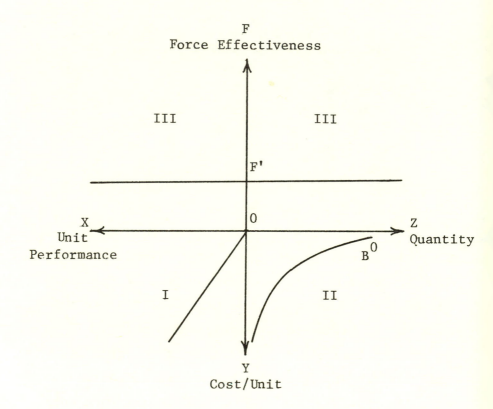

I	Proportional Performance	$Y = \frac{1}{a}X$
II	No Learning with Fixed Budget	$B^0 = ZY$
III	Multiplicative Force Effectiveness	$F = ZX$

Infinite Number of Optimal Solutions!

that there is no learning and that force effectiveness has neither synergy nor saturation but is simply
the product of quantity and unit effectiveness. This
would seem to be a reasonable first approximation.
We then attempt a simultaneous solution. A method
of simultaneous solution used in economics is to set
up a four-quadrant graph with the four variables to
be solved represented as increasing from their mutual
origin. Then Quadrant I contains the CER, Quadrant
II contains the learning curve represented as a fixed
budget or hyperbola in this special case of no learning. Quadrants III and IV represent the force effectiveness and quantity. The horizontal line at F'
is the solution constructed by starting at any point
on the horizontal axis, dropping down to the curve
below, passing horizontally to the other curve and
then vertically to the other portion of the horizontal
axis. This establishes a pair of related unit effectiveness and quantity that can be obtained for the
given budget. The product of this pair is force effectiveness and is plotted above both of the points
on the axis. Interestingly enough, the plotting of
these points constructs the horizontal line at F' ,
its height determined simply by constants a and
B^0 . In other words, there are an infinite number
of equally good solutions to this simple problem.
Intuitively, the quantity-versus-quality trade off

is <u>not</u> <u>interesting</u> if there is no learning, if unit
performance is proportional to cost and if force effectiveness is the product of unit effectiveness and
quantity! Any combination has equal force effectiveness. Since these assumptions are often not a bad
first approximation, it is now obvious why some people
have ignored the question in decision making. Unfortunately, this also makes it clear that when there
<u>is</u> a trade off of interest, the solutions will depend
upon detailed knowledge of rather technical nature
for each of the three driving relationships. It simply
isn't possible to say that either "numbers do not
matter" or "only technology counts" as often appears
in the popular press. The three relationships must
be known before the answer can be obtained. This
question is under current discussion in defense cir-
cles, particularly concerning aircraft and tanks.

This model has been solved for many more interesting cases than the simple one shown in Figure 2,
as shown in Table 1.[3] Depending upon the combination
of assumptions concerning the shapes and parameters
of the learning curve, the performance CER and force
effectiveness curves, it may be optimal to buy only
one <u>very</u> fancy system, <u>or</u> a very large number of
very simple systems (there is a practical limit on

[3]Sovereign (1975).

TABLE 1

Results of Design-to-Cost Cases

One	Many	Optimum Number	Appendix Case Number	Force Effectiveness	Learning	CER
			1	CON	NO	PRO
X			2	SAT	NO	PRO
X			5	CON	NO	FIX
X			17	SAT	NO	FIX
If $b < c$	$b > c$		6	SAT	YES	PRO
$b < \dfrac{1}{e}$	$b > \dfrac{1}{e}$		15	SAT	NO	INC
$b < \dfrac{c}{e}$	$b > \dfrac{c}{e}$		9	SAT	YES	INC
$c > b$		If $b > c$, $\left(\dfrac{B(b-c)}{bf}\right)^{1/c}$	13	SAT	YES	INC
		$\left(\dfrac{cB(1-c)}{f}\right)^{1/c}$	8	CON	YES	FIX
		$\dfrac{B(1-b)}{bf}$	11	SYN	NO	FIX
		$\left(\dfrac{B(b-c)}{bf}\right)^{1/c}$	12	SYN	YES	FIX
	X		4	CON	YES	PRO
	X		7	CON	NO	INC
	X		10	CON	YES	INC
	X		3	SYN	NO	PRO
	X		17	SYN	YES	PRO
	X		14	SYN	NO	PRO
	X		16	SYN	YES	INC

TABLE 1 (continued)

CON ≡ Constant effectiveness/unit, given unit per-
        formance.
SAT ≡ Saturation occurs in free effectiveness,
        $b < 1$.
SYN ≡ Synergy occurs in free effectiveness, $b > 1$.
PRO ≡ Cost/unit proportional to performance.
FIX ≡ Cost/unit pro with fixed cost (nonzero inter-
        cept).
INC ≡ Cost/unit increases more rapidly than perform-
        ance.

b   is the exponent in the force effectiveness equa-
    tion.
c   is the learning curve parameter, $c \leq 1$.
e   is the exponent reflecting increasing marginal
    cost of performance, $e \geq 1$.

Source: Rodrigues (1978).

how simple an aircraft can be). Under certain conditions there may be an optimal answer between one
complex system and very many simple ones. This is
intuitively possible as discussed below.

THE FFG-7 DECISION

My research was started on the hypothesis that
the combination of the three phenomena discussed
above must produce the optimum shown to Congress by
Vice Admiral Price in defending the size of the most
recent U.S. destroyer-size ship, the FFG-7 class.
This ship has been attacked by Admiral Rickover and
others as "not good enough" even at $50 million each
in 1972 dollars, approximately ten to 20 times as
much as World War II destroyers, which were much
smaller. Admiral Price's defense to Congress included the curve shown as Figure 3 which shows an
optimum in force effectiveness at the size of the
FFG-7 with a given budget for these type of ships.
Here quality can be roughly represented by size or
displacement because the displacement is the effective
limit on the weight of weapons, men, and propulsion
equipment that can be put on board the ship.

Although the model developed above proves that
such an optimum can exist, it was impossible, despite considerable research, to find any explicit

Fixed Budget Buy

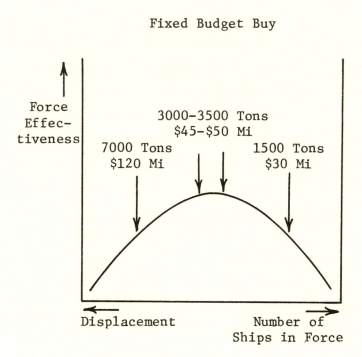

FIGURE 3

Vice Admiral Price's Congressional Curve

identification of the force effectiveness relationship that would be needed to produce Admiral Price's
curve in Navy records. The cost relationships and
learning curves are well known, but the force effectiveness was apparently done on the basis of the
admiral's experience and intuition. But certainly
it should be possible to measure such effects by
either detailed simulation of alternative battle
formations or perhaps by some more simple quantification of the force effectiveness such as was mentioned for missiles, the product of probability of
kill times number of ships.

   Commander Jose A. T. C. Rodrigues of the Portu-
guese navy performed such a quantification, and was
able to derive a curve quantitatively similar to that
of Admiral Price's by a series of steps using empirical engineering analysis consistent with his
academic background.[4] He built both a simple and
a more complex model of destroyer effectiveness.
With these models he evaluated existing designs of
destroyers built by the United States for their unit
effectiveness. With the known cost and learning
curve relationships for these historical ships and
the force effectiveness relationships, he was able
to plot a simultaneous solution curve similar to the

---

[4]Rodrigues (1978).

one that Admiral Price showed Congress. It showed
an optimal value for the same approximate size as
the FFG-7.

For the simple model, Rodrigues found in the
literature a performance CER for escort ships which
was produced by the Navy's Center for Naval Analysis.[5]
They found that the cost of a ship could be satisfac-
torily related statistically to an additive index
of the on-board sonar, guns, surface missile systems,
anti-submarine rockets, and helicopters as shown in
Figure 4. (Helicopters are an alternative means of
delivering antisubmarine torpedoes.) With this measure of unit performance and with the simple assumption
that force effectiveness is just the product of the
CNA index times the number of ships that can be bought
for a fixed budget, the plots shown as Figure 5 were
obtained. The curve on the left has been adjusted
for the cost of differences in speed of the ship.
Although neither of the curves has as definite an
optimum as we might desire, they do confirm that the
most recent designs are competitive in that they have
approximately the same force effectiveness for a
given budget.

Rodrigues then proceeded to build his own more
complex models of the force effectiveness from his

---

[5]Wilson (1972).

FIGURE 4

SHIP PERFORMANCE INDEX

(ESCOMO MODEL OF CENTER FOR NAVAL ANALYSES)

$$\text{INDEX} = 2 \cdot \text{SONAR I} + \frac{\text{GUN I}}{5} + \text{SMS I} + \text{ASROC I} + \text{HELO I}$$

where   SONAR I $= \dfrac{\text{MAX RANGE}}{\text{FREQUENCY}}$

GUN I $=$ RANGE $\times$ BORE $\times$ NUMBER COMPONENTS

SMS I $=$ RANGE $\times$ NUMBER COMPONENTS
$\begin{pmatrix} \text{SURFACE} \\ \text{MISSILE} \\ \text{SYSTEMS} \end{pmatrix}$

ASROC I $=$ 10

HELO I $=$ 5 $\times$ NUMBER HELOS

CER

$$\text{COST/SHIP} = 18.02 + .1936 \text{ I} \quad R^2 = .95$$

(ADJUSTED FOR 30 KNOTS)

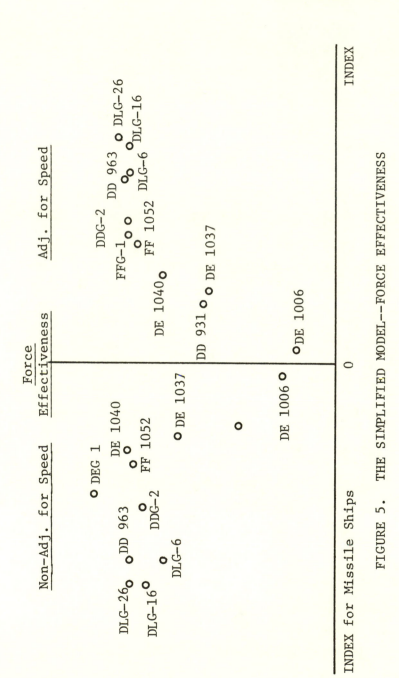

FIGURE 5.   THE SIMPLIFIED MODEL--FORCE EFFECTIVENESS

own background, believing that the simplicity of the
CNA model of ship effectiveness might be disguising
some of the conceptual model's power.

A major problem in naval ship design is that
modern escort ships have both an antiaircraft and
an antisubmarine mission. (They are typically not
designed to fight other surface ships.) Thus Rodrigues was forced to measure both of these capabilities. Because it is difficult to see how to combine
these effectiveness measures, he plotted the force
effectiveness measures separately as well as combining them as a simple product to get an overall curve.
These curves were similar in showing optimum at
roughly the same point, as will be shown later after
those effectiveness models are briefly described.

ASW is highly dependent on search capability
as well as the weapons measured in the CNA model.
For this reason, Commander Rodrigues treated the complex
model for ASW effectiveness by establishing two measures, one involving the sonar detection range and
the other a modification of the CNA weapons effectiveness model. These were then combined as a product.
The sonar detection range was not directly input to
the computation however. Commander Rodrigues felt
that the contribution of the sonar range enters operational effectiveness in terms of how large a convoy-
screening circle can be formed by the number of ships

which could be purchased. The ships are spaced as
a function of their sonar range. Thus an effective
radius of a convoy was calculated to be multiplied
by the weapons effectiveness.

This calculation results in a plot such as shown
in Figures 6 and 7. These figures show that for ASW
effectiveness alone, the recent large multipurpose
ships such as DD 963 and DLG 26 class are almost as
nonoptimal as the older class of destroyers DD 931
and DE 1006. The single-purpose ASW frigates DE 1037,
DE 1040 and FF 1052 classes do comparatively well.
However, the former ships also have guns and missiles
and should do better at AAW.

For gun effectiveness, a measure "weight of broad-
side" was calculated.[6] This is a product of the weight
of the shell fired times firing rate and is appropriate for the "curtain of steel" approach to AAW of
World War II.

For missiles, both range and rate of fire are
important. The area under the curve of range versus
rate of fire was computed. Rate of fire decreases
with range because of the limited number of fire control channels must be devoted to the missile for the
entire flyout period. This product was then multiplied by a function of the warhead weight to adjust

---

[6]Washburn (1976).

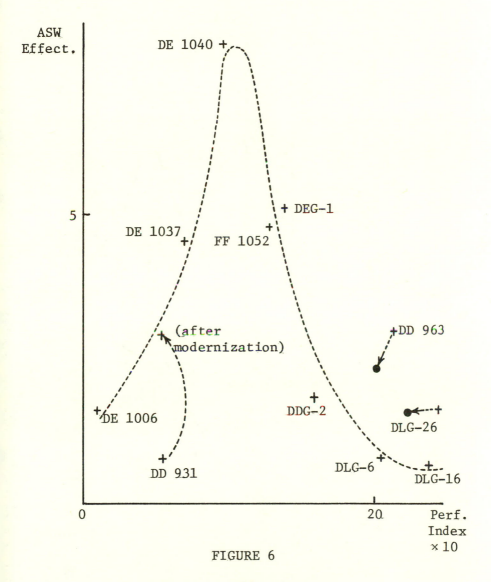

FIGURE 6

ASW Force Effectiveness

Source: Rodrigues (1978).

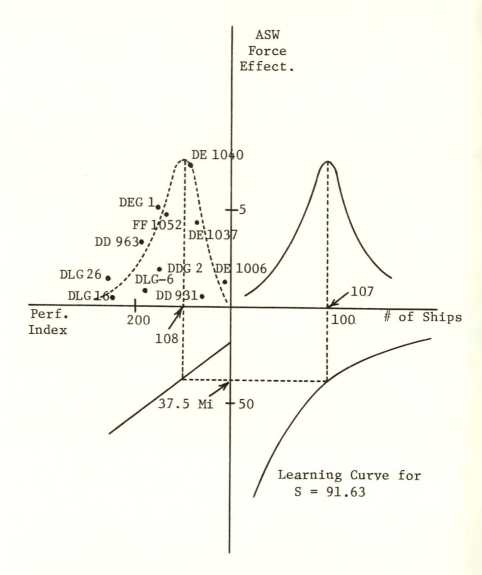

FIGURE 7

Design to Cost Model for ASW Warfare

Source: Rodrigues (1978).

for relatively lethality. Calculation of gun and
missile effectiveness showed that modern ships are
competitive with each other but that the older DD 931
with large gun armament is quite superior! Unfortunately, this shows the weakness of including the
"curtain of steel" model in our calculations. As
a final step the ASW and AAW effectiveness measures
were scaled, combined as a product and plotted again
as shown in Figure 8. This completed the analysis
of the complex model of force effectiveness.

Next Rodrigues evaluated the design of the
FFG-7 class as compared with Admiral Price's graph.
He computed the ASW effectiveness of the FFG-7 as
108 and the combined ASW with AAW and surface warfare effectiveness at about 160. If designed only
for ASW, the FFG-7 is very near optimal as shown in
Figure 9. In the combined ASW and AAW the FFG-7
also does very well. The question of sensitivity
to the total budget is addressed in Figure 10, which
shows very little change from Figure 9 in the determination of the optimal design.

A sensitivity analysis on the unit effectiveness, cost per unit and learning curves is shown as
Figure 11. Unfortunately, the usual variations in
these parameters would produce considerable deviation from optimal choice of the performance for the
FFG-7. This may be a much larger problem than we

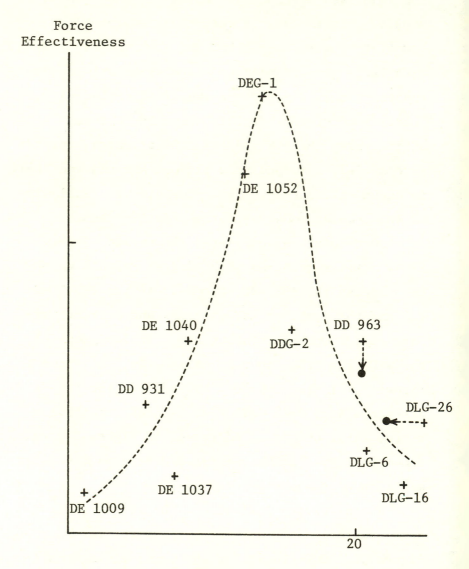

FIGURE 8

Combined ASW, AA and Surface Effectiveness
vs. Perf. Index

Source: Rodrigues (1978).

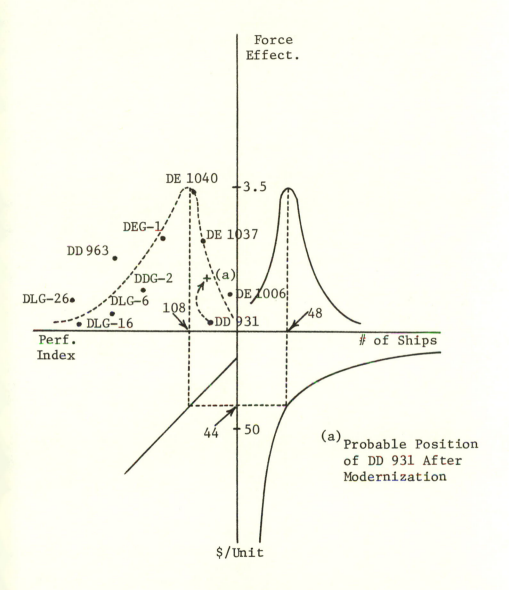

FIGURE 9

Combined Design-to-Cost Model

Source: Rodrigues (1978)

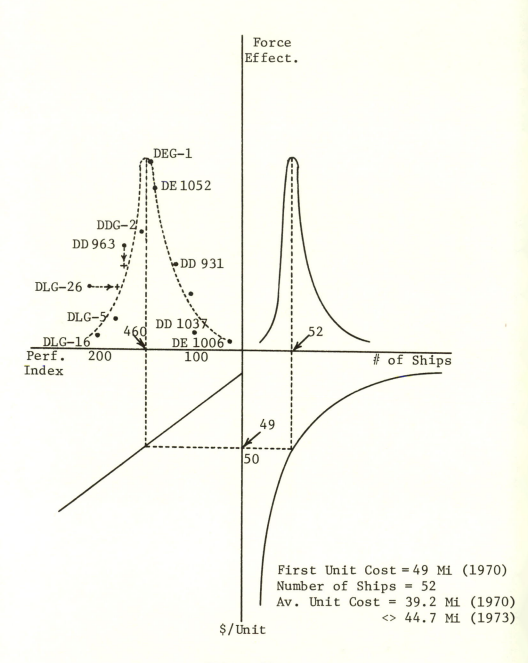

FIGURE 10

Combined Model for ASW, AA,
and Surface for Budget = $2 Bi

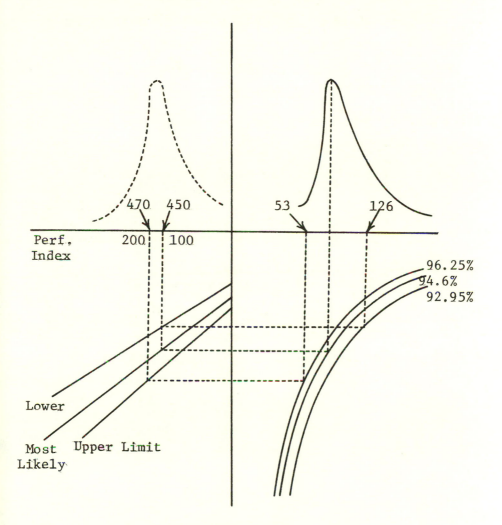

FIGURE 11

Uncertainty on the Combined
Design-to-Cost Model for a Budget of $3 Bi

imagined. Cost growth for example, if applied against a fixed budget, can totally destroy the optimality of the design.

REFERENCES

Rodrigues, J. A. T. C. (1978). "The FFG-7 Frigate: An Application of the Design-to-Cost Concept," unpublished MS Thesis, Naval Postgraduate School.

Sovereign, M. G. (1975). "A Conceptual Model for Setting Design-to-Cost Goals," Proceedings of the 36th MORS Symposium, Quantico, Va., pp. 202-14.

Washburn, A. (1976). "Gross Measures of Surface to Surface Naval Firepower," Naval Postgraduate School.

Wilson, R. (1972). "The Escort Ship Cost Model (ESCOMO)," Center for Naval Analyses, Alexandria, Va.

6

MILITARY PROCUREMENT IN FRANCE:
REGULATION AND INCENTIVE CONTRACTS*
Jean-Pierre Ponssard

1. Introduction

Since the end of the Second World War, the military
procurement policy in the U.S. has been the object of
many tentative reforms. Among these, the choice of the
appropriate contracting modes (cost plus, fixed price,
design to cost, total package deal and so on) has attracted the attention of a few economists, in particular

---

*This work has been partially supported by research
contracts from the Defense Department and the Ministry
of Industry.

An earlier version of this paper was presented at
the Earie Meeting in September 1979, Cergy Pontoise
and at the Markets and Hierarchies Colloquium in Jan-
uary 1980, London.

since the extensive study of Scherer (1964).[1] However,
it seems quite difficult to assess the influence of
the academic work in this area on the real decision
making processes. For instance, according to Fox,[2]
in spite of his quite sceptical conclusions, multi-
clause incentive contracts were never so much used
than after the publication of Scherer's book. In fact,
it seems that the system has the capacity to reject
many economically oriented reforms. To some extent,
except that the academic work is most nonexistent, a
similar story can be told in France.

The objective of this paper is to provide some
understanding for the minor impacts of such a reform.
It concerns the use of the so-called incentive contract:
over the last ten years as part of the French military
procurement policy. To provide such an understanding
the idea is to construct what could be called a qualitative model of the functioning of the procurement
policy which in some rational way encompasses its main
structuring characteristics. This approach is based
on several levels of considerations including technical
institutional and cultural features and not merely
economic ones.

---

[1] Scherer (1964).

[2] Fox (1974).

This model draws specifically on the work of
Goldberg and Williamson on regulation.[3] In particular, it appeared quite fruitful to take as a unit
of analysis the transactions that take place between
the Defense Department and its industrial contractors
on a given program.

The data on which this research is based has
been indirectly collected over a three year period
through a number of specific studies for the Defense
Department. These studies included economic surveys
of ongoing programs, interviews with both administrative and industrial professional on the procurement
policy, elaboration of documents for management semi-
nars on the negotiation of contracts. That is to
say, the theoretical hypotheses were not drawn in
advance but result from an a posteriori attempt to
rationalize the detailed information collected on the
way (for a comprehensive description the reader is
referred to Charvet and Ponssard).[4] (The present paper
is part of a research project initiated in 1977. I
am particularly indebted to B. Charvet and P. Levine
for their contributions to this project.) As such,
this methodology is representative of the research
direction that has been developed by the Centre de

_____

[3]Goldberg (1976); Williamson (1975).

[4]Charvet and Ponssard (1978).

Recherche en Gestion in the recent years. One characteristic of this direction is its reliance on detaile clinical studies made in collaboration with the adminis tration or the industry.[5]

2. The Regulatory Framework of Military Procurement
    in France

2.1. The Main Structuring Characteristics of the
     Transactions

The unit of analysis that shall be used is the notion of program. A program consists in a number of stages including research, development, production, maintenance. It concerns a system which presumably can be associated with the achievement of some strategic goal. As such it gives rise to "transactions" between the Defense Department and its contractors. These transactions, to some extent, are regulated by a number of contracts. Typically a program may be associated with half a dozen contracts or more. (Wheth or not the good unit of analysis is the program is debatable. In my opinion, the contract as such is too narrow as will appear in the subsequent discussion. However, some issues may be directly handled in terms of the more macro "militaro-industrial complex.")

---

[5] Berry, Moisdon and Riveline (1978).

Examples of programs are given in Appendix 1.

To characterize the framework in which the transactions on a program take place, four assumptions
will be made.

Assumption 1: Length of transaction. The life
span of a program generally extends over ten years.
In terms of technological development a program follows a go and stop procedure: at the beginning one
tries to look ahead as much as possible and then,
after the development, the specifications are more or
less frozen to allow standardized use over several
years. This means that at the beginning there is
considerable uncertainty both in the demand as in
the production functions. This uncertainty is an
inherent ingredient of the very notion of program.
Another consequence of the notion of program is the
fact that important financial considerations are associated with each program since it may represent
work for so many years.

Assumption 2: Mode of rivalry. The competition that takes place over programs may in some sense
be qualified as Schumpeterian. In France, it is competition by all means (economic, technical, political,
and so on) to acquire a monopoly position for the completion of the program and its possible extensions.
Since parallel R&D is exceptional and parallel production never takes place, the transactions on a given

program are more or less characteristic of bilateral
monopoly but this period may be preceded by intensive
competition possibly for programs in quite different
areas. It is clear that formal competitive bidding is
either excluded or may be used only as a cover up
procedure for the very reasons that it is impossible
at the early stages to state simple criteria on which
the selection should be made for the whole program.

Assumption 3: Contracting framework. Although
a program is usually associated with a number of formal contracts it may be more appropriate to describe
the contracting framework under which the transactions
are done as encompassing two levels: a general constitution that determines the overall relationship
and guidelines to adopt to changing circumstances,
and a specific contractual document that governs the
technical and financial short term considerations.
This short term legal document is a reference but,
especially at the beginning stages of a program, it
is rather the rule than the exception to introduce
modifications on technical specifications, time delivery, quantity, prices and so on. A written document which is not updated is outdated. It probably
means that something is going wrong.

Assumption 4: Organizational structure. The
Defense Department is a large organization and it is
appropriate to distinguish among its internal units

to understand the way the procurement policy is carried out. The procurement of military programs requires that a number of functions be undertaken. It
includes: initiation of programs and budget approval,
definition of technical and economic specifications,
selection of contractors, negotiation of formal documents, follow-up of program both technically and economically, reception of equipment, cost auditing of
contractors, payments, control of procedures....

These functions are scattered among many entities
that are more or less antagonistic rather than hier-
archically linked to each other. The antagonistic
feature may be partially attributed to different re-
cruitment channels so characteristic of the French
Administration in general. For our purpose it is convenient to distinguish between three main groups:
the users who handle the initiation and budget approval
of programs, the engineers who have the technical and
procurement responsibilities and as such include technical services, purchasing offices and cost auditing
offices, and the controllers who exercise an a priori
control on legal documents and general procedures.
The latter also provide general information on the
"constitution" through general rules for determining
profit margins, uses of revision indices for prices,
accounting procedures for cost auditing and so on.

A special note should be made about the purchasing offices. They are part of the engineer group but among the three subgroups we distinguished, they are the ones with the lower status and though they may be calle "negotiators" quite often they may be more appropriatel described as the persons who write up the legal short term documents using data provided by the other service (controllers, technical services and cost auditing offices).

2.2. The Broad Lines of the Resulting Price Policy

As already mentioned, a program consists of many contracts. Traditionally one makes a distinction be- tween cost plus and fixed price contracts. With a cost plus contract an estimated cost is given but pay- ment is based on the accounted a posteriori cost and either a percentage or fixed margin is added. With a fixed price, payment is based on the a priori evalua- tion of the cost and the addition of a percentage mar- gin. Ordinarily, the price policy on a program goes as follows: (i) at the R&D stages either cost plus, in case of large financial expenses, or fixed price, in case of minor expenses (in the latter case, the price is determined as much from the available budget as from the estimated cost); (ii) at some stage of development, a unit production cost is estimated by the contractor; (iii) the first production contracts

are cost plus including the estimated cost as a ceiling, a cost auditing is required after stabilization
of production; (iv) the last production contracts are
fixed price using the results of the cost auditing.

There is, of course, some variance on the price
policy including the use of incentive contracts. This
shall be precisely discussed in the following section.
However, it is certainly true that the preceding description is representative of the broad lines of the price
policy. The distinction between cost plus and fixed
price should not be overemphasized for two reasons
related to the contractual framework described earlier.
One reason has to do with the usual updating of short
term documents, this updating includes directly or in
a disguised fashion price adjustments so that a fixed
price contract in some circumstances may turn out to
give rise to payment based on the a posteriori accounting cost except that the administrative arrangement is
more complicated. The other reason comes from the way
fixed price contracts are negotiated in the first place.
The price is decomposed into a number of direct and
indirect parts which are usually determined through
cost auditing results from the earlier stages either
on the specific program or from the general past data
of the contractor (such as overhead costs). Moreover
there are a number of rules for margins as well as so
many percent for internal research in electronics and

so many in aeronautics and so on. Altogether a fixed
price is just as much based on accounting costs as a
cost plus, the only difference being that for the
former the data comes from the past whereas for the
latter it will be gathered in the future. It seems
quite exceptional that a purchasing officer writes up
a fixed price entrant whenever a large financial amount
is at stake and he has no past certified data provided
by a cost auditing office. Exception requires that
price competition played some role, which we described
as quite rare, or that he has some data on a recent
similar program, which is also rare.

Altogether the constitution that governs the overall relationship on a program may be qualified as cost
plus oriented whatever form the short term contracting
mode may be used.

3. The Use of Incentive Contracts: Empirical Results
    and Interpretation

3.1. Background Information
    a) Contracting modes. Let P and C denote pri
and cost respectively then, a fixed price contract may
be written as

$$P = P_0$$

and a cost plus contract as

$$P = C(1 + r_0)$$

in which r_0 denotes unit profit margin. A fixed price may be arrived at from a cost estimate C_0 and a unit margin r_0 that is $P = C_0(1 + r_0)$. In a cost plus contract a cost estimate may also be mentioned but is not contractual.

The economic rationale for choosing between these two modes of contracts is usually stated as follows:[6] the real cost is uncertain and the risk attitudes of the two parties (administration and contractor) are different giving rise to a risk sharing argument in favor of cost plus mode. But the contractor keeps some decision variables after the contract is signed and so there is a moral hazard argument that calls for the inclusion in the contract of an incentive for the contractor to control its cost. The dilemma between these two arguments gives rise to the incentive contract, a combination of fixed price and cost plus, written as:

$$P = (1-\beta)C_0(1 + r_0) + \beta C(1 + r_0)$$

$$= C_0(1 + r_0) + \beta(1 + r_0)(C - C_0)$$

---

[6] Weizmann (1978).

Varying β from 0 to 1, one gets contracts that smoothly vary from fixed price to cost plus (see Figure 1).

Historical perspectives show that cost plus contracts have also been introduced because of moral considerations. Military procurement uses tax payer money and the administration is particularly concerned with profit margin. This is reinforced by the fact that, ethically, military equipment is different from any other goods: making money in such a market is a moral attitude that is badly resented by the public opinion as well as by the people directly involved. Cost plus contracts have the advantage of making explicit the ex post profit margin. Of course, they may practically give rise to "reasonable" margins and excessive costs and also excessive profit through subcontractors, tax loopholes, etc. The doubling or tripling of initial cost estimates for military programs seem to have been the rule rather than the exception in the fifties. This fact engendered a reinforcement of the legal obligations for military contractors in terms of cost allocation for ex post contro the introduction of ceiling prices and of profit margin determined in absolute terms rather than in percentage (i.e., $P = C + \Delta$) as well as uses of fixed price whenever possible. However, the idea of moral profit margi

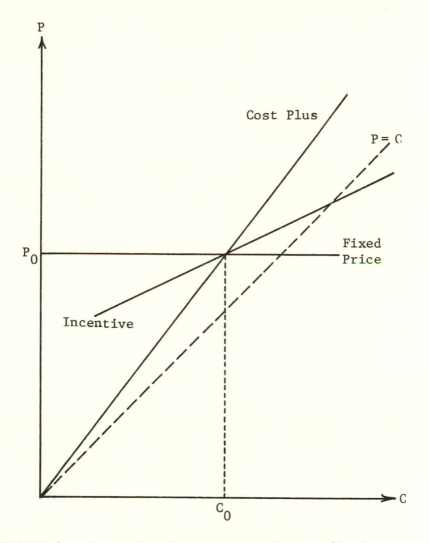

FIGURE 1.   Incentive Contracts as Intermediaries
            between Cost Plus and Fixed Price

remains deeply rooted in spite of the fact that a
guide issued in 1969[7] encourages the purchasing officers to determine the "economic" margin depending
on risk, ability to reduce cost, value added, etc.
Practically, margins may vary from 5% for a cost plus
contract to 9% for a fixed price contract. They remain largely determined by conventional attitude.
They were officially introduced in 1969[8] as more economically rational than cost plus contract with ceiling
prices.

b)   General attitudes held within the Defense
Department.   In fact, incentive contracts have been
used in the Defense Department since the early fifties.
But, whereas their use in the U.S. seems to have been
very intensive, achieving a peak in 1970 (according
to Fox),[9] in France they have remained quite marginal.
There are no statistical or economic reports on the
contracting modes used by the Defense Department and
no internal office is in charge of defining specific
policies.   The outcome is that practices may vary
from one purchasing office to the other.   There seems
to be little attention to the development of cumulative

---

[7] Circulaire d'Octobre 1969.

[8] Circulaire de Février 1969.

[9] Fox (1974).

data on current practices, most of the people we met
for this study reported that it was the first time
that they ever used an incentive contract. Heads of
purchasing offices that were concerned with procurement practices and incentive contracts in particular
within their own service, would often explain that new
guidelines are needed, that the 1969 text is outdated,
that they had their own ideas on what the role of an
incentive contract should be but that they had no
practical example where it had been applied. It is
interesting to report the general attitudes towards
what incentive contracts should be. They fall into
three categories.

(i) "Traditional additude." This attitude emphasizes the uncertainty of a military program at the
development stage and the unreasonableness of defining
a contractual target cost for unit production. There,
it already appears as a success to be able to impose
a ceiling price and any attempt to go further is seen
as potentially dangerous because the contractor would
propose high targets thus giving rise to excessive profits. Moreover, it is claimed that competition on the
international market, such as aeronautics, is a strong
enough incentive to provide efficiency. Under these
conditions, incentive contracts appear of little practical use.

(ii) "Economic attitude." This attitude is based
on the economic rationale for the introduction of incentive contracts. It is believed that contracting
modes may have an impact on the ex post cost and so
it criticizes cost plus contracts. But it also recognizes the difficulty of negotiating a "reasonable"
target cost admitting that everything is in the setting
of a "though target."

(iii) "Unconventional attitude." This attitude
is called unconventional because "paradoxically" it
claims that incentive contracts should be used only
when the purchasing office has data on unit production cost and uncertainty is low. The idea is that
one can make a difference between a real effort to
control cost and bad forecasting only if an objective
reference target cost can be determined. Since this
is usually impossible at the beginning of a program
the administration should develop a strategy that
brings information at the early stages and then introduces incentives for cost reduction for the remaining
stages.

3.2. Empirical Results and Interpretation

Ten case studies of incentive contracts have been
carried out. These are presented in detail in Appendix 2. The data collected in 1977 has been partially

updated but some case studies are still incomplete
because the underlying programs are still going on
and liquidation has not taken place yet. Nevertheless,
there are a number of points that emerge.

a) It appears that incentive contracts may be
used at any stage of the program while from an economic point of view one would expect to observe most
of them at the development and early production stages
where the uncertainty is the highest. In fact, they
seem to be used in a variety of circumstances to avoid
a deadlock in a negotiation either between users and
engineers (to reinforce credibility of contractor's
proposal), between purchasing officers and controllers
(to avoid critics for accepting fixed prices without
certified data), between purchasing officers and contractors (on the appropriate fair margin on a contract).
Occasionally the economic rationale is present (stimulate contractor's efficiency by moving away from cost
plus to the direction of fixed price) but this is
certainly not the main reason irrespectively of whether
it works or not.

b) As far as the precise incentive formula is
concerned, it may be characterized as three main underlying types with local variations. The three types
are as follows (see Figure 2).

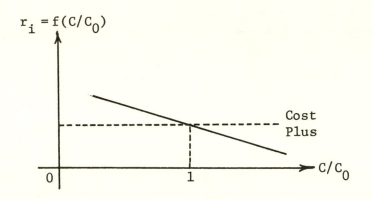

Type 1:   Incentive contract as refinement of cost plus

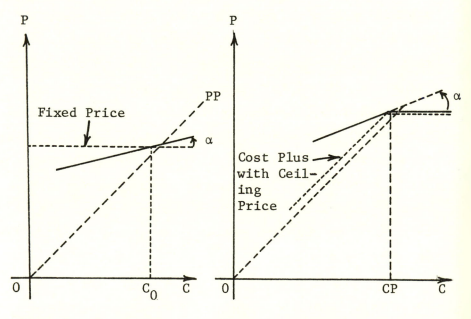

Type 2: Incentive contract as refinement of fixed price

Type 3: Incentive contract as refinement of cost plus with ceiling price

FIGURE 2

Type 1: $P = C(1 + r_0) + (1 - \beta)(1 + r_0)(C_0 - C)$.

In this case the term $(1 - \beta)(1 + r_0)(C_0 - C)$ may be interpreted as an incentive margin whereas r_0 is the usual margin for cost plus contract. Then, given current attitudes towards profit margin, the term $(1 - \beta)(1 + r_0)(C_0 - C)$ will be rewritten in terms of a percentage margin, noted r_i , as a function of C/C_0 : $r_i = f(C/C_0)$. Altogether $r_0 + r_i$ will not exceed 8 to 10% whatever the underlying uncertainty (compare case studies 1 and 2).

Type 2: $P = C_0(1 + r_0) + \beta(1 + r_0)(C - C_0)$.

This formula looks like a fixed price contract with a sharing term. Then r_0 may be like 8%, the usual fixed price margin. However, if the sharing coefficient, $\alpha = \beta(1 + r_0)$, is .5 and $C = .8C_0$, then the a posteriori margin might go up to 20% (see case studies 3 to 7).

Type 3: $P = PP + \beta(1 + r_0)(C - CP)$.

In this formula, PP is considered as a ceiling price and CP as a ceiling cost. This formula is par- ticularly easy to use whenever the purchasing office has a reference point coming from a preceding contract (see case studies 8, 9, and 10).

In the last two cases, maximal percentage margin
considerations might be reintroduced with the dilemma
that if a 10% unit is used this severely hinged the
range on which the incentive formula is operating.
These observations show that in spite of the fact
that theoretically an incentive contract may be considered simply as an intermediary between fixed price
and cost plus (all three types are mathematically
equivalent) and selected according to economic considerations, the formulation as extensions of current
practices is far more determining of the final shape
(comparison of cases 1 and 2 on one hand, and cases
5 and 6 on the other hand, reveals such striking simi-
larities without common economic basis: cf. Appendix
2). Moreover, moral attitudes towards profit margin
play a significant role in a more or less explicit
way depending on the precise formulation which is used.
The difficulty in handling margin economically may
come from the following question which is not faced
by the administration: what is the a priori appropriate range for the margin on an incentive contract so
that it is acceptable a posteriori. This question is
never faced either for cost plus contract (only a
posteriori arguments) or for fixed prices contract
(only a priori arguments).

     c) In the vast majority of the case studies

(9 out of 10) the target cost is the contractor's
proposal. Moreover, as already emphasized, it is
quite often readjusted under different pressures such
as technical modifications asked or accepted by the
technical services. It is difficult to assess whether
the target cost and the proposals are influenced by
the contracting mode, and the purchasing officers are
certainly aware that such might be the case. Then
one may consider tactical games in which the purchasing officers try to introduce an incentive contract
only by surprise, whereas the contractor expects fixed
price, keeping the proposal as a ceiling cost. The
contractors of course refuse such tricks, if they can.
This kind of game is significant of the difficulty
that the purchasing officers have to handle a price
negotiation without certified data. Indeed, a good
classification of contract should distinguish not on
the underlying uncertainty but on the existence or
not of asymmetrical information at the negotiation
stage. Then, one may paradoxically interpret the de-
served preference of purchasing officers for incentive
contract given their own risk aversion to face excessive margins and the contractors' preference for fixed
price given that as far as they are concerned the uncertainty is small.

    d) The fact that contractors often expressed
preferences for fixed price contracts deserves special

attention. In one case (number 1), an incentive contract was substituted to a long practice of cost plus
partly for internal reasons to the Defense Department
(reinforce contractor's credibility). Nevertheless,
given the exceptionally large financial amount of this
contract, it certainly gave rise to more efficiency
within this contractor. But the managers who said
that they had introduced new internal control procedures (which lead to some protest from the workers,
used to operate with cost plus contracts), also said
that they were happy with the change towards incentive
contracts because "with a cost plus contract any guy
from the administration may come and give advice on
anything; now we simply ask him whether he takes the
responsibility to have the target cost changed, most
of the time he can't; we feel more in charge." In
this case, the incentive contract seems to have introduced a degree of centralization within the administration favorable to the contractor. At any rate a
proper modelization should certainly consider that
both the administration and the contractor keep decision variables after the contract negotiation.
This case appears quite exceptional in terms of the
available data and ordinarily whether or not the contract mode would introduce specific changes within
the contractor is obscure. Quite often one has the
feeling that the contractor does not really care and

only considers this as an administrative problem that
will only complicate liquidation. The fact that an
incentive contract usually implies a cost auditing
means that it may take four to nine years before complete liquidation of the contract. This long time
delay is a severe practical limitation.

However, our interpretation of the contractors'
general attitude, without discounting these specific
arguments, relies on the constitution assumption.
To the contractor, the important feature is that the
overall relationship with the administration is cost
plus oriented. Then it is of minor importance to argue
on the form of the short term contracts.

4.   Concluding Remarks: A Long Term Institutional
    Perspective

The major question addressed in this paper concerns the limited impact of an economically oriented
reform, the so-called incentive contracts, on the
overall procurement policy of the French military administration. The idea that is developed relies on
a qualitative model based on four major assumptions
that structure this procurement policy. These are:
length of the transaction, mode of competition, contracting framework, organizational structure. Then,
it is shown that the empirical results collected on

incentive contracts may be easily interpreted in this
model. At the same time, this model provides an explanation for their minor impact on the procurement policy.
To summarize, one may say that the incentive contract
literature focuses on the short term contracting problem and fails to encompass the other major structuring
characteristics of the transactions. To develop a
more useful formalization of incentive contract one
should at least integrate bounded rationality in con-
junction with uncertainty, asymmetrical information at
the negotiation stage as well as strategic variables
available to both parties after contract negotiation.
The development of such a formal model may be helpful
not so much in terms of theorems on efficiency but
in the necessary conceptualization that is required on
the way. In this respect Holmstrom's work, though on
a different context, seems to go in that same direction.[10]

There are a number of other points that can be
discussed in relation with this paper. They are concerned with the general subject of regulation. It
has been our intention to provide some detailed empirical data on the precise meaning of regulation. In
view of the results one may argue that the word regulation is too general and some qualification should

---

[10]Holmstrom (1979).

be made. We use this word to mean the institutional
framework between a public administration and an industrial sector which is close to vertical integration.
In this sense it certainly is different from the usual
U.S. meaning associated with the operation of regulatory agencies controlling public utilities.

Following Williamson, one may then compare different institutional frameworks in terms of their comparative efficiency.[11] His normative conclusions
would then be to recommend either market or hierarchical
structure depending on the characteristics of the specific transactions under study. With respect to this
argumentation and in view of this precise case of
military procurement, one should certainly conclude
that vertical integration is the best mode. In fact,
in France, some of the military contractors are indeed
nationalized firms but some are not. Recently the
Government did acquire stock holdings in Dassault, a
major private military contractor in aeronautics. However, the issue of nationalized versus private firms
appears mainly as a political issue and not as an
economic one. Now whether or not strong behavioral
differences on the procurement policy are induced but
the legal status of the contractor remains to be proved.
On the other hand, one may distinguish antagonistic

---

[11]Williamson (1979).

forces in favor of deregulation. While, at some time,
the regulatory framework appeared quite satisfactory
for the contractors it may become a constraint in their
future development. Two main reasons support this
view: the fact that military technology may no longer
be so advanced relative to civil technology so that
the frontiers become loose, second the increased need
of French firms to define their strategy at the international level. Things as simple as accounting methods
presently defined exclusively to cope with regulation
may prove unable to adapt to this change in the environment. Such a move is presently taking place in the
regulatory framework that used to characterize the relationship between the Telecommunication Department
and its industrial contractors. There is appears more
as a major strategic move that as the result of a
transaction specific analysis.

     In conclusion, we may say that while the analytic
framework provided by Williamson appeared as a good
starting point to understand the procurement policy
of the French Defense Department, it seems difficult
to follow his normative implications. The comparative
study of institutional frameworks, as shown by Chandler
in his historical comparison of railways in the U.S. and
France, requires political, sociological as well as
economic insights that can be best developed in a long
term perspective.[12] In this respect it would appear

quite difficult to state that in our model one assumption comes first and implies the others. As for efficiency assessment, as shown by Chandler for the railways, it may vary from one historical period to the other. Altogether the overall procurement policy appears more as a by-product of an historical context than as the result of a rational economic process.

APPENDIX 1: Examples of Ongoing Programs (data collected in 1977 and partially updated)

Program A (ground missles)

This program is to substitute a former ground missile system developed between 1960 and 1964, operational between 1970 and 1980.

The first studies begin in 1970 under research contracts within the contractor that produces the former system. In 1973 a five year development contract of 1,500 MF (1 MF = 10^6 French Francs) is attributed to the contractor, the new system is scheduled to be operational between 1980 and 1990.

The main negotiation takes place in 1973. There is only one contractor that is considered for this program. The discussion is on the opportunity of the program, performance of the contractor on the previous

---

[12] Chandler (1979).

program on costs, time delivery, etc.

The development contract is updated every year
in terms of technical specifications and costs. It
includes a multiple clause incentive contract (case
study number 1) and a cost auditing.

Program B (vehicles)

This program concerns a new system. In 1969 three
contractors are attributed to parallel research contracts. In 1971 two contractors only are attributed to
a development contract, one of the three being disre-
garded for technical reasons. In 1974, it is time to
select the contractor that will be attributed to the
2,000 MF program (production cost only). The discussion is on time delivery and technical advance since
the two prototypes are judged comparable in terms of
cost. One prototype is almost operational but not so
advanced, the other requires more work but is more
promising. The first one is selected and a three
year incentive contract (case study numbers 5 and 6)
is issued in 1975 to deliver 585 units (out of an
estimated total of 4,000). In 1977, the contract is
revised because of a budget squeeze (from 585 to 455
units), because of the appearance of an export contract
(400 units). Altogether unit cost is increased by
5%. Technical modifications are also introduced and
price adjustments are made accordingly. Furthermore

a one year extension of the 1975 contract is introduced.
The end of program is scheduled for 1990. In 1978
another three year contract is made (to cover production up to 1983). The price will depend on a cost
auditing that will take place in 1979, it is basically
a cost plus with a ceiling.

Program C (telecommunication equipment)

This program is to substitute for a former system
developed in the fifties by contractor F. The idea
of a new program emerges in 1967 and paper studies are
begun. In 1969, six contractors including F are con-
sulted. In 1971 a formal bidding procedure is organized and contractor F is selected. It satisfies technical specifications and proposes the lowest price.
There are only two other proposals and they are considered as technically unsatisfactory. Detailed
analysis shows that contractor F has maintained close
contract with the Defense Department during the years
1969-1970 and partially contributed to the technical
specifications. In 1971, it already is at the prototype stage. The first units are delivered in 1978,
three years late as scheduled in 1971. They are covered
by a fixed price contract. Altogether program cost
is about 200 MF. A cost auditing will take place in
1979 to determine further price arrangements. The
program has gone under considerable modifications under

two types of pressure: first the rate of technical
change in electronics is quite fast during that period,
second, the mission of the system has been enlarged.
In 1975 an attempt is made by an outside contractor to
offset the monopoly position of contractor F. This
seems possible because of non-military contracts for
similar systems and of a technological breakthrough
in one component of the system. Competition is harsh
in the non-military sector but nothing happens in the
Defense Department until 1979 when one considers a
program reduction. In the meantime an export agreement is negotiated between the two "competitors";
its domestic counterpart, if any, remains unknown
(for more detailed analysis on this program see
Ponssard).[13]

Appendix 2:   Incentive Contracts (data collected in
              1977 and partially updated)

The case studies are presented by means of a table
summarizing the available relevant information. It
is organized from development stages to late production stages. The exact formula that was used in each
case may be read from the respective curves that follow
the table presentation. In the tables, the formulae

---

[13]Ponssard (1981).

No.	Program	The Incentive Contract (I.C.)	Observations
1	· missiles · development contract for the period 1973–1973 with a multiple I.C. (cost, time, others), $C_0 = 1{,}500$ MF · C_0 proposed by contractor expected a cost-plus contract, it comes from a cost estimate plus an amount to cover uncertainty ($\simeq 15\%$ of C_0)	· type 1 · range: (.8, 2.5) · $r_0 + r_1$: (8.5%, −1.5%) · renegotiation of C_0 every year $\pm 2\%$. · 1 out of 3 prototype systems is cancelled because of general budget squeeze in 1975, reducing C_0 by $\simeq 25\%$ · in 1979, the purchasing office estimates that $C \simeq .75$, technical modifications increased C_0 by $\simeq 15\%$ to be liquidated in 1980	· this is example A, the I.C. comes from the difficulty of obtaining concensus for program continuation within the DOD · the contractor that usually had cost plus contracts introduced new management tools on this occasion, reputation is at stake, happy that DOD people not putting their nose everywhere to make modifications and impose sub-contractors · partial cost auditing results obtained in 1979 are used to negotiate a fixed price production contract, this is seen as a major advantage of the I.C. on the R&D contract · a disagreement on correct inflation index to be used may result in global renegotiation of I.C. (purchasing office states that there is a contract flaw and that $C \simeq .92$, general inflation in industrial prices is $\simeq 15\%$ per year during this period)
2	· binoculars · development contract, 1970 · $C_0 = 1.4$ MF · production was cancelled · C_0 proposed by contractor expecting a fixed price	· type 1 · range: (.8, 1.5) · $r_0 + r_1$: (8%, 0%) · C_0 : +30% · outcome 1974: $C = 1.10$; $m = 5.5\%$	· the purchasing office wants to try an I.C. on this contract (low stakes, high uncertainty) · the contractor appears mainly interested by the production stage that will not come

No.	Program	The Incentive Contract (I.C.)	Observations
3	•radars •development contract 1974 including I.C. on unit production cost •C_0 proposed by contractor as point estimate of 84 MF for 6 units with a 20% range.	•type 2 •range: (.8, 1.2) •$r_0 = 7\%$, $\alpha = .7$ •outcome 1980	•the purchasing office wants to avoid that the estimate moves up and imposes a ceiling with an I.C. •many technical modifications decided by engineers without modification of C_0. headquarters are expecting a budget cut reducing number of units to be produced. •contractor says "we have to start all over again because of so many changes"
4	•transmission •development contract 1975 including I.C. on unit production cost •C_0 proposed by contractor as point estimate, doubled from initial estimate, the purchasing office obtains a reduction of 20% using data from other country but agrees on maximal m	•type 2 •range: (.7, 1.3) •$r_0 = 12.50\%$, $\alpha = .7$ •outcome 1978: the I.C. becomes fixed price $P = 1.15C_0$ for 1/3 of total production	•the purchasing office wants to avoid any further climbing of cost estimate •the change from I.C. to fixed price is unclear. A cost auditing on first production contract will be used for remaining contracts

No.	Program	The Incentive Contract (I.C.)	Observations
5	•vehicles •I.C. concerns the 53 MF contract for industrialization, production of 4,000 units for a total cost of 2,000 MF on 10 years will follow •C_0 proposed by contractor expected fixed price •two competitors •export potential market	•type 2 •range: (.8, 1.2) •r_0 = 7.25%, α = .4 •outcome 1980	•this is example B •the purchasing office wants to try an I.C. and thinks it will be easier to pass the controller's office that way (inexistence of certified data) there are two joint contractors •contractors are surprised by I.C. given competition context. They claim that they optimize total program cost thus not influenced by I.C. on industrialization contract only
6	•vehicles (5 continued) •the I.C. concerns the first 3 year production contract C_0 = 273 MF for the period 1975-1978	•type 2 •range: (.8, 1.2) •r_0 = 7.25%, α = .4 •C_0 + 5% •outcome 1980	•the purchasing office that negotiates this contract is different from the one that negotiates the industrialization contract •the I.C. is suggested by contractors to avoid cost plus with ceiling price since fixed price is judged unacceptable by purchasing office (risk of excessive profit). The same I.C. as for industrialization contract is used but slightly lower

No.	Program	The Incentive Contract (I.C.)	Observations
7	•cranes •the I.C. is on first production contract, 1970 •$C_0 = 33$ MF C_0 proposed by contractor expecting a fixed price	•type 2 •range: (.9, 1.08) •$r_0 = 6\%$, $\alpha = .67$ •C_0 : +2% •outcome 1977: $C = 1.02$; $m = 5.07\%$	•the I.C. comes from an argument on the fair margin to be used 6% or 8%
8	•computers •the I.C. concerns the first production contract, 1970 •$C_0 = 77$ MC C_0 is proposed by contractor expecting fixed price	•the I.C. is left open to be determined ex post in view of results •outcome 1976: $C = .85$, $m = 11.4\%$	•the purchasing office feels the price is too high but the contractor insists on fixed prices •the contractor says that the contracting mode was not known in the production department of the firm
9	•turbines •the I.C. concerns the second production contract, 1968 •$C_0 = 12.3$ MF C_0 is proposed by contractor expecting fixed price	•type 3 •$\alpha = .67$ •outcome 1977: $C = .92$, $m = 10.67\%$	•the contractor proposed a higher price than for the first contract. It is taken as a ceiling and an I.C. is introduced
10	•transmitting system •the I.C. concerns the fifth production contract 1971-73 •$C_0 = 125$ MF	•type 3 •$\alpha = .54$	•the I.C. comes from an argument on the right experience curve to be used •labor unit time declined resulting in significant savings for next contracts. On the other hand overhead cost increased for current contract leaving contract almost unchanged

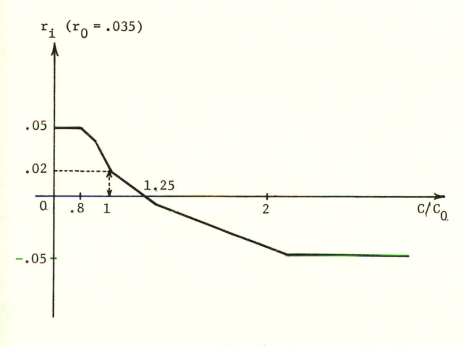

Case 1

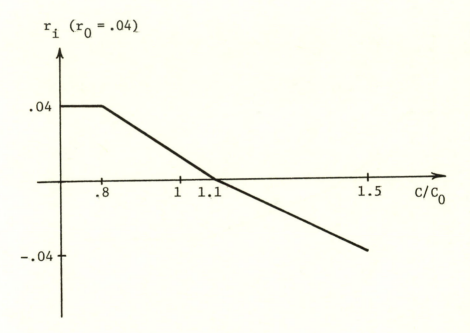

Case 2

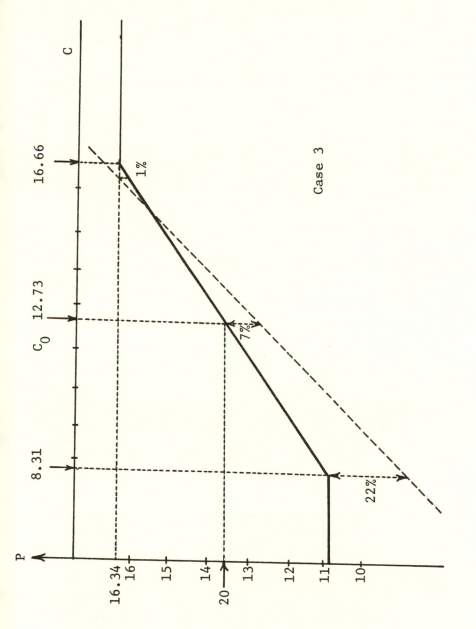

Case 3

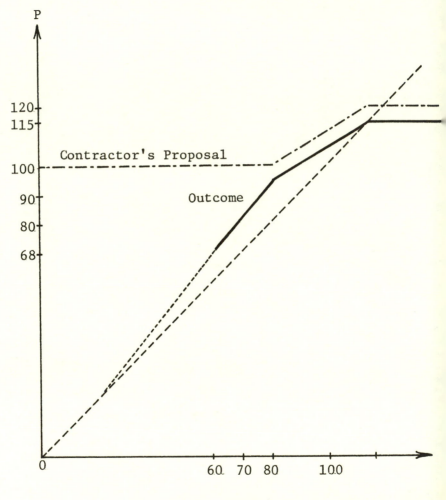

Case 4

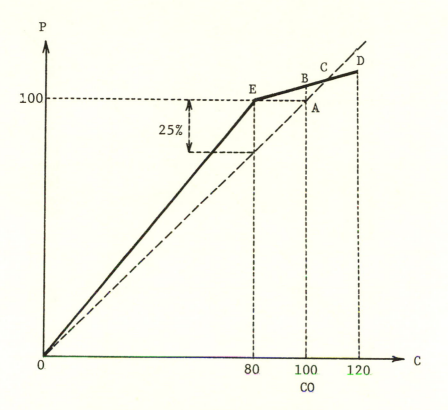

Case 5: Two Joint Contractors

	Contractor X		Contractor Y	
	PR	PV	PR	PV
A	100	100	100	100
B	100	107.25	100	107.10
C	107.86	107.86	107.6	107.6
D	120	112.716	120	112.716
E	80	99.25	80	99.10

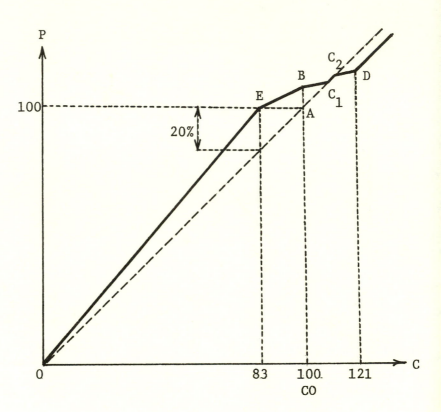

Case 6: Two Joint Contractors

	Contractor X		Contractor Y	
	PR	PV	PR	PV
A	100	100	100	100
B	99.4	107.25	99.147	107
C_1	107.25	107.25	107	107
C_2	107.92	107.92	107.92	107.92
D	83.75416	100.50499	83.55893	100.27072
E	121.12	113.2	121.12	113.2

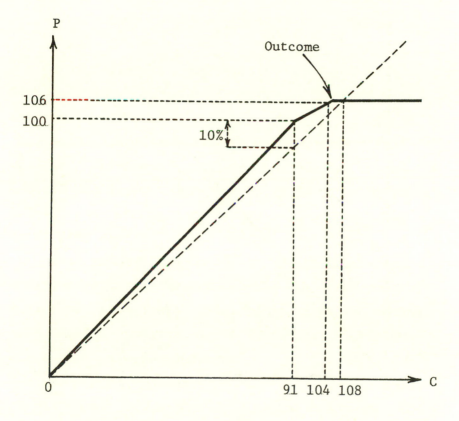

Case 7

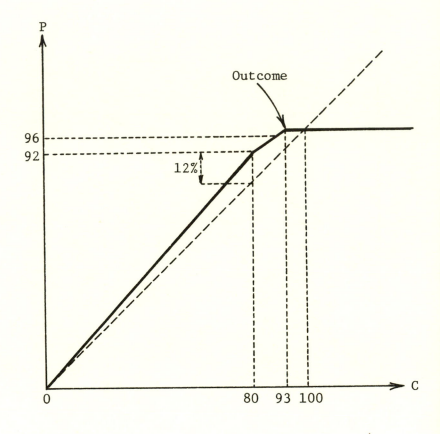

Case 8

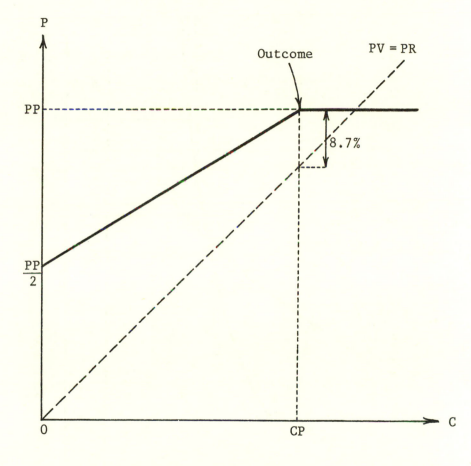

Case 9

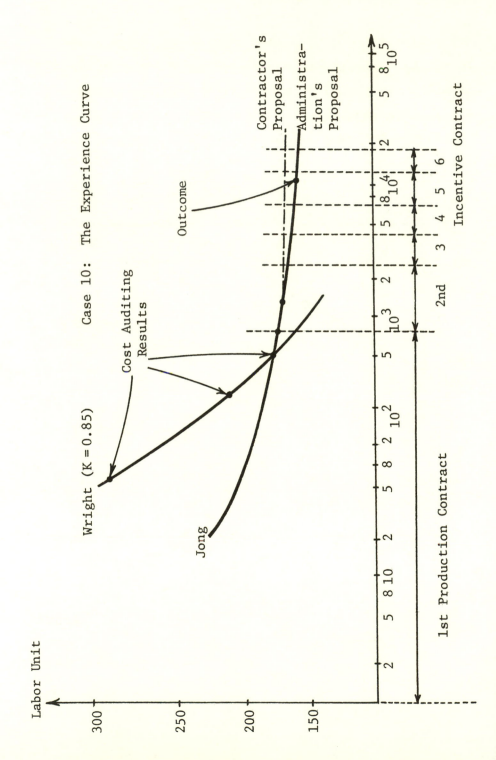

Case 10: The Experience Curve

are condensed according to the three types described
in Section 3.2, the range of application is specified,
outside this range the contract is practically immaterial since negotiation would probably take place
though not contractually stated. For incentive contracts of type 1, the maximal variation of
$r_0 + (1-\alpha)(C_0 - C)$ is given in the percentage of C ;
for type 2 the values of r_0 (%) and α are given;
for type 3, only α is given. If the target cost
has been renegotiated for whatever reasons, it is mentioned, it usually corresponds to an increase. Finally,
the financial outcomes, whenever know, are stated.
It turns out that it takes from 4 to 9 years for an
incentive contract to be liquidated. This is due to
the fact that production takes 2 to 4 years, then cost
auditing takes another year and only then the contract
can be liquidated. An incentive contract is rarely
liquidated by the persons who initiated it especially
within the administration. This does not encourage
cumulative experience.

REFERENCES

Berry, M., J. C. Moisdon, and C. Riveline (1978).
     "Qu'est-ce que la recherche en gestion?" Informatique
     et Gestion, pp. 108-109.

Chandler, A. D. (1979). "The Railroads--A Cross-Cultural
     Comparison, Colloque CNRS-MIT, Paris, February.

Charvet, B. and J. P. Ponssard (1978). "Réflexions sur l'utilisation et l'efficacité des clauses d'intéressement dans les marchés industriels du Ministère de la Defense," Ecole Polytechnique, R.M.

Fox, J. R. (1974). Arming America: How the U.S. Buys Weapons, Cambridge: Harvard University Press.

Goldberg, V. P. (1976). "Regulation and Administrated Contracts," The Bell Journal of Economics, Vol. 7, No. 2.

Holmstrom, B. (1979). "Equilibrium Long-Term Labor Contracts," Swedish School of Economics and Business Administration, ISBN-951-955-076-9.

Ponssard, J. P. (1981). "Marchés publics et innovation: concurrence ou régulation?" Revue Economique, Vol. 1.

Scherer, F. M. (1964). The Weapons Acquisition Process: Economic Incentives, Boston: Division of Research, Harvard Graduate School of Business Administration.

Weizmann, M. (1978). "Efficient Incentive Contracts," Communication au Seminaire du CEPREMAP.

Williamson, O. E. (1967). "The Economics of Defense Contracting: Incentives and Performance," in R. N. McKean, ed., Defense Economics. New York: Columbia University Press.

Williamson, O. E. (1975). Market and Hierarchies, Analysis and Antitrust Implications. New York: Macmillan.

Williamson, O. E. (1979). "Transaction-Cost Economics: The Governance of Contractual Relations," Communication au Colloque Markets and Hierarchies, London.

Administrative Documents

Circulaire No. 2485 du 4 Mars 1969 relative aux clauses
de caractère incitatif dans les marchés publics.

Circulaire du Premier Ministre à MM. les Ministres et
Secrétaires d'Etat et guide pour la négociation des
prix et des marges dans les marchés de gré à gré,
dates du 10 Octobre 1969.

Circulaire du 14 Septembre 1972 du Ministre de l'Economie
et des Finances, relative aux conditions de détermi-
nation des prix de certains marchés publics.

N A

7

ON COST ANALYSES FOR ENGINEERED CONSTRUCTION
Robert M. Stark

Comparisons of a priori cost estimates with a posteriori payments is about as pervasive as it is instinctive. In virtually every project of engineered construction there are any number of circumstances that intervene between the time preconstruction estimates are made and the time after construction when payments are made. These can include design changes; construction alternatives; an unstable monetary system; and environmental, labor, or managerial changes. These circumstances (always seemingly unique to each project) distort such "before" and "after" cost comparisons. Still, many seek insights and conclusions from cost comparisons. One feels that

somehow an experienced "eye" can compensate for the
disparities attributable to the intervening changes.
Of course, there is some merit to such feelings and,
besides, the data may be the best available. However, there is a temptation to overlook the fact that
the history of science is cluttered with examples of
contradictory conclusions which were supported by
the same experimental observations.

Imagine an idealized project of engineered construction for which there are no change orders, design
changes, and so on—only the customary uncertainties
of relevant "before" and "after" costs. These circumstances are about as favorable as can be hoped for
as a basis for making conclusions from "before" and
"after" comparisons. Yet, an analytic result (to
be developed shortly) contains the shocking implication that even under these idealized conditions, a
basis to support such cost comparisons is fundamentally inadequate. We will demonstrate that for a
simple (but fairly general) analytic formulation of

an engineering design these a priori and a posteriori
costs can be regarded as unit samples from populations having different probability distributions.

Samples from a population and its probability
distribution may be compared meaningly. However,
small samples from different populations pose an added
impediment to reaching conclusions from cost comparisons. This tends to explain why experienced engineers
often express a grudging respect for the complexities
and nuances of estimating beforehand costs and assess-
ing proper payments afterwards. The perennial quest
for alternatives and modifications in contracting modes
and practices are an implicit consequence.

The remainder of this chapter describes the basis
for the above analytic assertions.

GEOMETRIC PROGRAMMING

Geometric programming is a mathematical means
for solving constrained and unconstrained nonlinear
optimization problems. It is popular among engineers because of the aptness of its format for problems of interest to them and the design oriented
insights it provides.[1]

[1] Beightler and Phillips (1976); Stark and Nicholls
(1972); Zener (1971).

Imagine that the costs of each of the (major) design components are expressed in terms of cost parameters and design variables. For example, the predesign cost of a simple structure, a dam, say, is expressed as a function of its height (the design variable). The relevant costs are the construction cost (an increasing function of dam height) and over-topping costs (a decreasing function of height). The sum of these is the total cost to be minimized by an appropriate choice of dam height (subject to constraints).[2] For another example, imagine a fixed tonnage that is to be transported periodically by a (to be designed) fleet of ships. At one design extreme, a single gigantic ship can be used or, at the other extreme, a number of small ships. Smaller ships can be propelled at higher speeds, but they cost more. Larger ships move at lower speeds but entail lower building costs.[3] The design of this fleet and the structural design are only two over-simplified examples of engineering problems that have been formulated as geometric programs.

For ease of discussion, we represent the sum of the costs of the design components (and any

---

[2] Beightler and Phillips (1976); Stark and Nicholls (1972).

[3] Folkers (1973).

constraints) by the symbol

$$P(\underset{\sim}{c};\underset{\sim}{x})$$

where $\underset{\sim}{c}$ signifies the various cost coefficients
and $\underset{\sim}{x}$ the various design variables (dam height,
ship speed, etc.) whose values are to be determined
such that $P(\underset{\sim}{c};\underset{\sim}{x})$ is minimized. Specifically, the
symbol $P(\underset{\sim}{c};\underset{\sim}{x})$ is the _primal_ problem of geometric
programming described by eqs. (1) and (2) of the
Appendix.

It is a mathematical fact that to a proper
primal geometric program there corresponds a _dual_
geometric program denoted symbolically by

$$D(\underset{\sim}{c};\underset{\sim}{w})$$

where $\underset{\sim}{c}$, as above, signifies the various cost
coefficients, and $\underset{\sim}{w}$ are "weights." In part, at
least, these $\underset{\sim}{w}$ are positive fractions of unity
representing the proportion of the total resources
(costs) to be allocated to the various components
that compose the design. Again, $D(\underset{\sim}{c};\underset{\sim}{w})$ is a symbol for eqs. (3), (4), and (5) in the Appendix.
Examination of those equations indicates that the
algebraic structure of the dual is a product of
exponentiated cost coefficients and weights. In
particular, there is no explicit dependence upon

the design variables (x) .

A basic theorem of geometric programming asserts that at optimality (denoted by an asterisk) the minimum value of the primal equals the maximum value of the dual.[4]

$$\min P(c;x) = P^*(c;\ x^*) = D^*(c;\ w^*) = \max D(c;w)$$

The basic special case, for which eqs. (4) and (5) uniquely determine the "weights" (w^*) independent of the cost coefficients (c) , is called a zero-degree geometric program. In view of the ubiquitousness of zero-degree programs, the precision of the mathematical results available for them, and for ease of discussion, the results to be described apply to that special case.[5] Mathematical extensions to higher degree geometric programs appear in Ellner and Stark.[6]

SUMMARY...

To support the introductory assertions concerning a priori and a posteriori sums, a class of non-

---

[4] Beightler and Phillips (1976); Stark and Nicholls (1972).

[5] Stark (1977).

[6] Ellner and Stark (1980).

linear optimization formats, known as geometric programs, were described as being especially suited for
engineering design problems. The primal problem is
one of minimizing a polynomial-like function of cost
coefficients and design variables (x's) . Typically,
costs are not known with precision until the job is
complete. This implies that values of the design variables must be chosen before costs are known in order
for the work to proceed. Of course, since the choice
of design variables depends upon the costs, this
further implies that an a priori optimal design choice
based upon cost estimates is improbable. Finally,
having chosen the design value, the (x's) , the
primal function (that is, the total cost estimate)
can be regarded as a linear function of the component
costs. Application of the well known central limit
theorem points toward the assertion that a priori
cost estimates can be regarded as samples from a normal tending probability distribution.[7]

...AND CONCLUSION

Now, the dual problem corresponding to the primal
problem also represents the total cost since at optimality the primal and dual have the same value. The

---

[7]Stark (1977); Stark and Mayer (1979).

dual function depends upon the cost coefficients
(c's , as in the primal), and the weights (w's) .
In the zero-degree case at hand, the mathematical
structure of the dual function is as an exponentiated
product of cost coefficients and weights. Recall,
that the primal problem required a choice of design
variable values (x's) in order for the design to
proceed. This is not so for dual problems. That
accounts for the colorful descriptions as "here and
now" and "wait and see" problems, respectively. After
the design has been executed, and the costs determined,
the "weights" (being actual proportions of the total
cost) are known and the dual evaluated. However,
these a posteriori costs can be regarded as samples
from a lognormal tending probability distribution.
This follows since the lognormal probability distribution has similar limiting properties for exponentiated products of random variables as the normal
distribution does for sums.[8] The references cited
provide more rigorous mathematical support for interested readers. A feature of the project cost assertions is that they fortunately tend to improve with
increasing design complexity. This follows since
increased design complexity is represented by increased

---

[8]Ellner and Stark (1980); Stark (1977); Stark and
Mayer (1979).

numbers of cost coefficients in both primal and dual
functions. The precision of both probabilistic limit
theorems cited improve with increased numbers of random coefficients.

APPENDIX

A geometric program can be written as

$$\min Z_0(\tilde{X}) = \sum_{j=1}^{m_0} c_{0j} \prod_{k=1}^{n} X_k^{a_{0jk}} \tag{1}$$

subject to

$$Z_i(\tilde{X}) = \sum_{j=1}^{m_i} c_{ij} \prod_{k=1}^{n} X_k^{a_{ijk}} , \quad i = 1, 2, \ldots, \ell \tag{2}$$

where the X_k are design decision variables, the
c_{ij} are positive-valued cost coefficients, and the
exponents a_{ijk} are arbitrary real numbers. In an
engineering-design context, the component costs,
$c_{0j} \prod_k X_k^{a_{0jk}}$, sum to the total project cost. Thus,
$Z_0(\tilde{X})$ is an objective function to be minimized subject to a number of technological, feasibility,
and/or economic constraints, $Z_i(\tilde{X})$. Equations (1)
and (2) are called the <u>primal geometric program</u>.

Corresponding to every primal geometric program there is a dual geometric program given by

$$\max \ D(\tilde{w}) = \prod_{i=1}^{\ell} \ \prod_{j=1}^{m_i} \left[\frac{c_{ij} \lambda_i}{w_{ij}} \right]^{w_{ij}} \tag{3}$$

where

$$\lambda_i = \prod_{j=1}^{m_i} w_{ij} \ , \quad i = 0, \ \dots, \ \ell$$

and the w_{ij} are "optimal" weights which satisfy the following linear equations

$$\prod_{i=1}^{\ell} \ \sum_{j=1}^{m_i} a_{ijk} w_{ij} = 0 \ , \quad i = 1, \ \dots, \ n \tag{4}$$

and

$$\sum_{j=1}^{m_0} w_{0j} = 1 \tag{5}$$

A unique attribute of the geometric programming dual is that the minimum value of the primal problem, $z_0^*(\tilde{X})$, is equal to the maximum value of the dual, $D^*(\tilde{w})$.

Notice that the constraints of the dual problem

involve n+1 equations in m $(=\sum_i m_i)$ unknowns.
The difference between the number of unknowns and
number of equations is the <u>degree</u> <u>of</u> <u>difficulty</u> of
the geometric program. In general, the larger the
degree of difficulty, the more difficult it is to
solve the dual program.

   This chapter deals with the zero degree of difficulty case. A distinctive feature of its dual
constraints is that they uniquely determine the "optimal" weights independent of the values of c_{ij} .
That is, the minimum project cost in the engineering
design sense is

$$Z_0^*(\tilde{X}) = D^*(\tilde{w}) = A(\tilde{w}) \prod_i \prod_j c_{ij}^{w_{ij}} \tag{6}$$

where $A(\tilde{w})$ is a function of the w_{ij}'s which are
uniquely determined by eqs. (4) and (5)

REFERENCES

Beightler, C. S. and D. T. Phillips (1976). <u>Applied</u>
  <u>Geometric Programming</u>. New York: John Wiley &
  Sons.

Ellner, P. and R. M. Stark (1980). "On the Distribution of the Optimal Value for a Class of Stochastic Geometric Programs," <u>Naval Research and</u>
  <u>Logistics Quarterly</u>, Vol. 27, pp. 549-71.

Folkers, J. S. (1973). "Ship Operation and Design,"
    in M. Avriel, D. J. Wilde and N. Rijkhart (eds.),
    Optimization and Design. Englewood Cliffs, N.J.:
    Prentice Hall, Inc.

Stark, R. M. (1977). "On Zero Degree Stochastic Geo-
    metric Programs," Journal of Optimization Theory
    and Application, Vol. 23.

Stark, R. M. and R. H. Mayer, Jr. (1979). "A Limit
    Distribution for Pre-Design Parametric Costing,"
    Proc. Specialty Conference, Amer. Soc. Civil En-
    gineers, New York.

R. M. Stark and R. L. Nicholls (1972). Mathematical
    Foundations for Design-Civil Engineering Systems.
    New York: McGraw-Hill.

Zener, C. (1971). Engineering Design by Geometric
    Programming. New York: John Wiley & Sons.

BIOGRAPHICAL SKETCHES

DeMayo, Peter

Captain, U.S. Navy, Executive Director for Contracts, Naval Air Systems Command. Responsible for acquisition of naval aircraft, engines and missile systems. Formerly technical advisor for shipbuilding claims, to the Assistant Secretary of the Navy.

Engelbrecht-Wiggans, Richard

Assistant Professor of Industrial Engineering, Department of Mechanical and Industrial Engineering, University of Illinois at Urbana-Champaign. Research interests: non-cooperative game theory and its applications to the design of market mechanisms such as auctions, contracts and procurement. Author of papers on the theory of auctions and competitive bidding, computer simulation event synchronization, network design and multi-attribute utility.

Graham, David R.

Chief of the Policy Analysis Division, Office of Economic Analysis, Civil Aeronautics Board. Formerly a study director and analyst for the Center for Naval Analysis. Principal research interests: government regulation of business, and government contracting and procurement.

559

Hammon, Colin P.

> Economist at the University of Washington Applied
> Physics Laboratory. A career naval officer (Cap-
> tain, Aviator), he commanded an aviation squadron
> and served on the staff of the Secretary of the
> Navy. He served as an instructor of Operations
> Analysis at the Naval Academy, Professor of Man-
> agement Science and Economics at the War College,
> and economic analyst at the Center for Naval
> Analyses. Research interests: shipbuilding and
> airframe cost and productivity analyses, ocean
> transportation economics, and bidding behavior
> as applied to military contracting and Outer
> Continental Shelf oil and gas leasing.

Harris, Milton

> Professor of Finance and Managerial Economics,
> J. L. Kellogg Graduate School of Management,
> Northwestern University. Formerly Associate
> Professor of Economics, Graduate School of In-
> dustrial Administration, Carnegie-Mellon Univer-
> sity. Research interests: economics of infor-
> mation and uncertainty, incentive contracts,
> auctions, dynamic analysis. Author of articles
> on optimal incentive contracts, resource alloca-
> tion under asymmetric information, optimal pric-
> ing schemes and auction design, and other topics.

Holt, Charles A., Jr.

> Assistant Professor of Economics, University of
> Minnesota. He is currently conducting research
> on auctions, oligopoly theory, and decision theory
> He received a Ph.D. from Carnegie-Mellon Univer-
> sity, and his dissertation "Bidding for Contracts"
> is published in Bayesian Analysis in Economic
> Theory and Time Series Analysis, the 1977 Savage

Dissertation Award Theses, A. Zellner and J. B. Kadane, editors (North-Holland, 1980).

Lohrenz, John

Senior Resource Analyst with Gulf Oil Exploration and Production Company. Formerly with the Conservation Division of the U.S. Geological Survey responsible for the development of Federal mineral revenue and production data bases.

Maskin, Eric

Associate Professor of Economics at Massachusetts Institute of Technology. He has written a series of articles on decentralized planning mechanisms with dispersed information and has worked on social choice theory and the theory of contracts.

Milgrom Paul R.

Associate Professor of Managerial Economics and Decision Sciences at the J. L. Kellogg Graduate School of Management, Northwestern University. Author or coauthor of five other articles and one book on auction theory and of several other articles on the theory and application of game models involving incomplete information. Fellow of the Society of Actuaries and consultant to numerous insurance companies.

Monash, Curt A.

Analyst, Paine Webber Mitchell Hutchins. Formerly Research Associate, Kennedy School of Government, Harvard University. Author of papers on game theory.

Myerson, Roger B.

> Professor of Managerial Economics and Decision
> Sciences at Northwestern University. Research
> interests: game theory and mathematical econo-
> mics especially the theory of cooperative games
> under uncertainty.

Ponssard, Jean-Pierre

> Professor in Economics and Management Science,
> Ecole Polytechnique, Paris, France. Research
> interests: government procurement, structuring
> of contractual elations, strategic planning,
> game theory and related topics. He is the author
> of Competitive Strategies (North-Holland, 1981)
> and of articles in Management Science and Inter-
> national Journal of Game Theory.

Ramsey, James B.

> Chairman of the Department and Professor of Eco-
> nomics at New York University. His areas of
> specialization are in statistics, econometrics,
> and microeconomics. Professor Ramsey is affili-
> ated with the American Economic Association, the
> Econometric Society, the American Statistical
> Society, the Institute of Mathematical Statistics
> and the Mont Pelerin Society. His most recent
> publications are APL-STAT A Do it Yourself Guide
> to Computational Statistics written with G. Mus-
> grave, published by Lifetime Learning Publications,
> The Economics of Exploration for Energy Resources,
> published by JAI Press in 1981, and The Oil Muddle
> Control vs. Competition, published by Ethics and
> Public Policy Center in 1981.

Riley, John G.

> Professor of Economics at UCLA. His published
> research covers a wide range of areas in econo-
> mic theory, including urban economics, interna-
> tional trade, intertemporal fairness, market
> signalling and auction design. Currently he is
> continuing an examination of market institutions
> which arise because of informational asymmetries.
> Auction and related sorting mechanisms are a
> primary focus of this study.

Rothkopf, Michael H.

> Senior Research Scientist, Analysis Research
> Group, Xerox Palo Alto Center. He has spent
> seventeen years at Shell and Xerox doing research
> and development in management science methods.
> He was Supervisor of Economics and Statistics
> in Shell Development Company's Applied Mathema-
> tics Department and Division Head for Economic
> Models and Planning Techniques in Shell Interna-
> tional Petroleum Company. He has written and
> coauthored over 30 papers dealing with a wide
> variety of management science topics including
> eight on competitive bidding.

Samuelson, William F.

> Assistant Professor of Economics, Boston Univer-
> sity Graduate School of Management. Research
> interests: decision and game theory, bargaining
> and competitive bidding. Author of articles on
> auctions, fair division, and competitive bidding.

Sherman, Roger

> Professor of Economics and Executive Director of
> the Thomas Jefferson Center, University of Vir-
> ginia. Author of Oligopoly: An Empirical Approach

(1972), The Economics of Industry (1974), and Antitrust Policies and Issues (1978), plus articles on industrial organization and regulation.

Shubik, Martin

Seymour H. Knox Professor of Mathematical Institution Economics at Yale University. He received his B.A. and M.S. degrees in Mathematics in 1947, and M.A. in Political Economy in 1949 from the University of Toronto, Ontario, Canada and Ph.D. degree in Economics from Princeton University in 1953. Dr. Shubik is fellow of the Econometric Society and the World Academy of Arts and Sciences. He is author of numerous books and articles, primarily in strategic analysis.

Smith, Charles H.

Operations Research Analyst with the U.S. Army Procurement Research Office at Fort Lee, Virginia. He obtained an M.B.A. from the College of William and Mary and a Ph.D. in mathematics from the University of Maryland. His recent research has focused on quantitative issues in systems acquisition. Previously he was with the U.S. Army Training Support Center and the Naval Research Laboratory.

Smith, Vernon L.

Professor of Economics at the University of Arizona, with previous positions at Purdue University, Brown and The University of Massachusetts. Formerly a Fellow, Center for Advanced Study in the Behavorial Sciences and Sherman Fairchild Distinguished Fellow, Cal Tech. Author of numerous books and articles on microeconomic theory,

bidding and auctioning, corporate financial
theory, economics of natural resources, and
experimental economics.

Sovereign, Michael G.

Professor of Operations Research and Administrative Sciences at the Naval Postgraduate
School in Monterey, California. Formerly Director of Special Projects, Office of the Assistant Secretary of Defense (Comptroller).

Stark, Robert M.

Professor of Mathematical Sciences and Civil
Engineering and Chairman of the Operations Research Program at the University of Delaware.
His research interests relate to quantitative
problems of engineering management. Additional
information appears in Who's Who and in American
Men of Science.

Varley, Thomas C.

Director, Operations Research Program Office
of Naval Research responsible for developing
basic and applied research program in all phases
of management science and operational analysis.
Has published in various journals including
Management Science, Naval Research Logistics
Quarterly, and Defense Management Journal.

Waller, Ray A.

Deputy Division Leader, Analysis and Assessment
Division, Los Alamos National Laboratory. Form-
erly a Group Leader and Staff Member in the Los
Alamos Statistics Group. He was also a member

of the Statistics Department, Kansas State University. He is the author of Statistics: An Introduction to Numerical Reasoning (1979) and co-author of Bayesian Reliability Analysis (1982).

Weber, Robert J.

Member of the managerial economics faculty at the J. L. Kellogg Graduate School of Management, Northwestern University; he previously taught in the Yale School of Management. He is an editor of the International Journal of Game Theory. His current research and consulting interests include auction design and competitive bidding, and games with incomplete information.

Williams, Arlington W.

Assistant Professor of Economics at Indiana University at Bloomington. Research interests: microeconomic theory, experimental economics, design and analysis of computerized trading environments.

Wilson, Robert

McBean Professor of Decision Sciences, Graduate School of Business, Stanford University. Research interests: strategic behavior, role of information in economic phenomena, incentives.